MAKING
THE
FOREVER
WAR

COLUMBUS STATE
UNIVERSITY

HALLOCK ENDOWMENT FOR MILITARY HISTORY

A VOLUME IN THE SERIES

Culture and Politics in the Cold War and Beyond

EDITED BY

Edwin A. Martini and Scott Laderman

MAKING THE FOREVER WAR

Marilyn B. Young
on the Culture and Politics
of American Militarism

**Edited by
Mark Philip Bradley and
Mary L. Dudziak**

Afterword by Andrew Bacevich

University of Massachusetts Press
AMHERST AND BOSTON

Copyright © 2021 by University of Massachusetts Press
All rights reserved
Printed in the United States of America

ISBN 978-1-62534-568-4 (paper); 569-1 (hardcover)

Designed by Sally Nichols
Set in Minion Pro
Printed and bound Books International, Inc.

Cover design by Frank Gutbrod
Cover photo by JO1 Gawlowicz, *U.S. Navy, Destroyed Iraqi T55-A main battle take lies abandoned beside a road at the edge of an oil field following Operation Desert Storm,* 1991.

Library of Congress Cataloging-in-Publication Data

Names: Young, Marilyn Blatt, author. | Bradley, Mark, 1961– editor. | Dudziak, Mary L., 1956– editor. | Bacevich, Andrew J., writer of afterword.
Title: Making the forever war : Marilyn Young on the culture and politics of American militarism / edited by Mark Philip Bradley and Mary L. Dudziak ; afterword by Andrew Bacevich.
Other titles: Marilyn Young on the culture and politics of American militarism
Description: Amherst : University of Massachusetts Press, [2021] | Series: Culture and politics in the Cold War and beyond | Includes bibliographical references and index.
Identifiers: LCCN 2020053347 (print) | LCCN 2020053348 (ebook) | ISBN 9781625345684 (paper) | ISBN 9781625345691 (hardcover) | ISBN 9781613768235 (ebook)
Subjects: LCSH: United States—History, Military—20th century. | United States—History, Military—21st century. | United States—Military policy. | Militarism—United States. | Cold War—Influence. | Vietnam War, 1961–1975—United States. | Korean War, 1950–1953—United States. | War and society—United States.
Classification: LCC E181 .Y683 2021 (print) | LCC E181 (ebook) | DDC 355.00973—dc23
LC record available at https://lccn.loc.gov/2020053347
LC ebook record available at https://lccn.loc.gov/2020053348

British Library Cataloguing-in-Publication Data
A catalog record for this book is available from the British Library.

Excerpt from "Body Count" in chapter 5 first published as track 4 on Body Count, *Body Count,* Sire Records, 1992. Reprinted by permission.

Excerpt from Richard Rovere in chapter 10 first published in "Letter from Washington," *New Yorker,* August 5, 1950, 48. Reprinted by permission of Condé Nast.

Excerpts "The Hearth" and "Shrapnel" from *Collected Poems* by C. K. Williams. Copyright © 2006 by C. K. Williams. Reprinted by permission of Farrar, Straus and Giroux.

TO THE STUDENTS OF MARILYN BLATT YOUNG

*The royalties from this book will be donated to the
Marilyn B. Young Memorial Fund at New York University,
which promotes scholarship and dialogue on
U.S. foreign relations, American wars and militarism,
antiwar activism, and decolonization.*

Marilyn B. Young. Photograph by Sara Krulwich (2016)

"Our continuous task must be to make war visible, vivid, an inescapable part of the country's self-consciousness, as inescapable a subject of study as it is a reality."

—Marilyn B. Young

CONTENTS

MAKING
THE
FOREVER
WAR

INTRODUCTION

Mark Philip Bradley and
Mary L. Dudziak

"There seem to be only two kinds of war the U.S. can fight: World War II or Vietnam," Marilyn B. Young wrote in 2005. World War II fit neatly into the American self-image, remembered as a triumphant battle against evil in the world. New conflicts have been framed in World War II imagery: 9/11 was Pearl Harbor, Iraqi leader Saddam Hussein was Hitler. The U.S. war in Vietnam jarred this self-conception, she observed, as the effort to continually reimagine the world in the image of World War II was compromised by a nagging question: "Is this another Vietnam?" Aversion to a repeat of Vietnam was not merely the prospect of defeat. It was "the daily experience of an apparently endless war."[1]

Young's historical scholarship speaks to urgent twenty-first century questions: Why does U.S. war never end? What are the origins of ongoing military conflict? How have U.S. leaders justified their decisions? Why does the American public support this, and how could opposition be so fractured? What are the consequences for countries and peoples on the receiving end of U.S. military force? Through her teaching, writing, and public speaking, Young argued that a core driver of the forever war is the repeated failure to learn lessons of the past.

Marilyn Young (1937–2017) remains the preeminent historian of war's place in modern American history. Best known as the author of the seminal 1992 *The Vietnam Wars: 1945–1990*,[2] Young's trenchant and often deeply critical historical work on U.S. wars and empire over the forty years of her distinguished career found a wide and admiring audience. Her writings moved across the twentieth and early twenty-first centuries, making forceful interventions on the origins of the American empire in East Asia, the relationship between Cold War and the global processes of decolonization, and the larger meanings of the U.S. wars in Korea, Vietnam, Afghanistan, and Iraq. Young's work remains startlingly relevant today.

This collection makes Young's writings on war accessible to a new generation, bringing historical insight to some of the most pressing problems of our day. If her prescient contributions are more important than ever, some of her writings are hard to access. *Making the Forever War* brings together the most important of Young's essays for the first time. It includes unpublished essays archived with her papers at New York University that have just recently been opened to researchers, along with a curated selection of previously published works. The collection closes with an afterword by Andrew Bacevich, a longtime collaborator with Young, who urges readers to honor her memory by refusing "to sanitize and falsify war."

In what was perhaps her final published essay, Young wrote that "armed with drones and Special Forces, an American president can fight wars more or less on his own, in countries of his own choosing. American wars do not end but continue—quietly, behind the back of the public which funds them."[3] Marilyn Young's writings illuminate and sharply criticize how this came about and why it continues. They also fundamentally shift our understandings of the place of America in the world, and suggest how an honest reckoning with the past can change the way we approach the present and the future.

Throughout her career Young played a leading role in the making of a critical history of U.S. foreign policy. A reassessment of American wars in Asia was, for her, the necessary starting point of that critique. "The people who bitch about Vietnam bitch about it because we intervened in what they say is a civil war," President Richard M. Nixon told his national security advisor Henry Kissinger and White House chief of staff Bob Haldeman in an April 1971 Oval Office meeting. "Now some of those same bastards want us to intervene in Bangladesh."[4] Although we don't believe Young and Nixon ever met one another in person, Young was, to use Nixonian parlance, one of those bastards who bitched. About Nixon policy toward Vietnam and Bangladesh, to be sure, but also more broadly about practices of American war and the all too frequent silence by historians and public intellectuals about their corrosive effects on American state and society.

As a professor in the Residential College at the University of Michigan and later in the History Department at NYU, Young's scholarly interests took her from the war of 1898 and U.S. participation in the Chinese Boxer Rebellion in her first book, *The Rhetoric of Empire: American China Policy, 1895–1901*,[5] to Vietnam in her celebrated *The Vietnam Wars*. These works along with a series of landmark essays on the Chinese civil war, the Korean War, and the memory of the Vietnam war contributed to a fundamental reconceptualization of the Cold War and American empire in the twentieth century. At the same time they would form the intellectual scaffolding of her late career turn to interrogating ongoing war in the twenty-first century.

Young's inclination to push against received Cold War understandings of the world around her came at a very young age. Indeed, her childhood growing up in Brooklyn put her at the center of American leftist politics. Sixteen years old in 1953, Young watched as more than ten thousand mourners gathered for the funeral of Julius and Ethel Rosenberg, executed after their conviction for serving as atomic spies for the Soviet Union in what remains one of the most celebrated and contested cases of espionage during the Cold War. She did so from the fire escape of her family's East Flatbush apartment, until her father told her to "get back inside" because the "FBI is taking pictures."[6] The Red Scare came to her high school when the principal and two teachers were brought before a United States Senate subcommittee for circulating a statement that denounced free enterprise.

As an undergraduate at Vassar College in the mid-1950s, Young (then Marilyn Blatt) was a member of the editorial board of the college newspaper, where she took up issues such as civil rights and women's rights. She also began to write about foreign policy, voicing strong support for the United Nations as "the only hope of bringing any kind of peace to a world torn with ideological differences." Young's career-long willingness to speak truth to power emerges in the pages of the *Vassar Miscellany*, too. Commenting on a 1955 speech by the California Republican senator and minority leader William Knowland, a hard-line anticommunist who blamed President Truman for "losing" China to Mao, she wrote, "It is incredibly naïve of Mr. Knowland to ignore the fact that we are living in a world community."[7]

Young's doctoral study at Harvard University, where she received her Ph.D. in history in 1963, produced *The Rhetoric of Empire* (1968). In its interpretative posture the book is one critical node in an emergent New Left interpretation of the perils of U.S. engagement in the world. University of Wisconsin historian William Appleman Williams's 1959 *Tragedy of American Diplomacy*[8] was the opening salvo in what became an increasingly contentious scholarly and popular debate throughout the 1960s over the mainsprings of American diplomacy in the wake of the growing failures of American Cold War policies. Young, along with scholars like Walter LaFeber, Thomas McCormick, and Lloyd Gardner,[9] agreed with Williams that the history of American foreign relations was best understood as a history of empire "through which the preponderant strength" of the United States "would enter and dominate all underdeveloped areas of the world."[10] In *Rhetoric of Empire*, Young fleshed out the ways in which early twentieth-century American policy in China implicitly offered critical genealogies for the assertion of American hegemonic power in the region after 1945.

Young continued to play a central role in the development of New Left historiography and its efforts to reassess American culpability in the Cold War. Scholarly accounts of the origins of the Cold War written before the 1960s generally ascribed primary responsibility to the Soviet Union. In this then prevailing view it was only after repeated provocations by the Soviets that the United States was drawn into the conflict, and even then reluctantly.[11] The insistence in much of the New Left scholarship, including Young's, that the United States was to blame offered a powerful revisionist challenge to these more traditional and admiring accounts of American diplomacy.[12]

But Young's concern with the use of "cold war" to characterize world order after 1945 went deeper. "The wars America fought or supported after 1946 were not cold," she wrote in an unpublished essay. Their "incalculable . . . death and destruction is somehow rendered marginal" in the framing of hot wars as cold. A further problem, she argued, with the "meliorating" term "cold war" is that "it tends to cast policies pursued in that period as if they were discontinuous with the past."[13] For Young, cold war was not a sharp rupture but rather another episode in the long American practice of what she would later term forever wars.[14] These critical perspectives also shaped Young's activism in and outside of the academy. In 1968 she helped found the Committee of Concerned Asian Scholars, a group that presented a radical critique of the culpability of area studies and the academy in what its members saw as the recklessness of official American policy in Vietnam and elsewhere in Asia. Through her opposition to the Vietnam war and later the wars in Afghanistan and Iraq, Young made vital contributions to broader social movements in the United States with rich and enduring traditions of anti-imperialist and antiwar politics.

Young's engagement with second-wave feminism also shaped her nuanced understanding of American society and the wider world. Former colleagues at Michigan in the 1970s recall that Young oversaw the first consciousness-raising sessions there. She later founded the Women's Studies Department at NYU. Young's visits to Maoist China in the early 1970s and the friendships with Chinese women she made there shaped her view, articulated most forcefully in the influential volume *Promissory Notes*[15] that she co-edited on women in socialist societies, that patriarchy was as fully present in socialism as it was in late capitalism.

Young's synoptic history of America's thirty-year involvement in Vietnam in her 1992 *The Vietnam Wars* marked the culmination of her three-decade engagement with American war and empire in Asia. It also reflected what Young said were the ways in which Vietnam "changed the shape of my moral world."[16] Still widely read and frequently assigned in undergraduate classrooms, *The Vietnam Wars* offered a scathing indictment of U.S. Cold War failures in Vietnam. Young argues Vietnam was an entirely unnecessary war waged by American politicians and generals who were blind to on-the-ground political realities and the power of nationalism in a decolonizing world. At the same time she was also insistent on the ways in which the war, including sustained American bombing campaigns that in tonnage exceeded World War II–era bombing of Germany and Japan, devastated states and peoples in Vietnam, Laos, and Cambodia.

For Young, a key element of the politics of war was culture, especially how war was remembered. She received an early lesson on the fractured nature of war remembrance from her uncle, who served in World War II. As a child, Young was curious about the war, and she pestered her uncle, asking him what the war was like. He finally responded, snapping at her: "The bombardier's head rolled around the cabin all the way back to base. Now don't you ever ask me that again!"[17] It was an early example of what would become an important theme in her writing: the disconnect between the public memory of war and the soldier's raw experience.

Throughout Young's lifetime, U.S. armed conflict persisted, but fewer American children would have uncles to ask about war. The military draft ended after the U.S. war in Vietnam, and over time military service became concentrated in particular families and communities. Although conflict was geographically distant, the "shadow of war," as Michael Sherry has written, militarized American culture, so that "war and national security became consuming anxieties and provided the memories, models, and metaphors that shaped broad areas of national life."[18] Meanwhile, after World War II, global conflict fueled global U.S. military expansion and provided a logic for U.S. intervention in Asia, Latin America, the Middle East, and elsewhere. The eventual break-up of the Soviet Union did not reset the worldwide projection of U.S. military power. Instead, over a decade before terrorists brought down the World Trade Center buildings on September 11, 2001, U.S. empire was rebranded as a fight against rogue regimes and terrorism, and the U.S. launched what Andrew Bacevich has called "America's war for the greater Middle East."[19] After 9/11, the shadow of war at home hardened through the proliferation of physical security barriers and legal restrictions on immigration, and the public acquiesced in government mass surveillance, touted as protection against another catastrophic attack. Technologies of war, especially armed drones, enabled the United States to use force remotely, so that even soldiers deploying lethal force were protected from bodily harm.

War was both ever present and physically absent for most Americans. This was not a contradiction, Young explained. Limited impacts at home, and a focus on U.S. soldiers without attention to war's devastation and futility, enabled its persistence. The way the culture of American war enabled the forever war became a central theme in Young's work.

Young wrote a torrent of articles and essays beginning in the early 2000s that focused on the wars of the post-9/11 era in the Middle East and beyond. During this period, she was a founder of Historians Against the War in the wake of the Bush administration's 2003 war in Iraq. She helped oversee the group's efforts to foster campus teach-ins across the country by coediting *The New American Empire: A 21st Century Teach-In on U.S Foreign Policy*.[20] She ran a vibrant Cold War Seminar as codirector of the Center for the United States and the Cold War at the NYU's Tamiment Library. In 2011 she served as the elected president of the Society for Historians of American Foreign Relations. Her presidential address, which serves as the closing essay of this volume, explored the meanings of American war across the history of the United States.

Part 1 of this collection draws together some of Young's most enduring essays on America's twentieth-century wars in Asia and the role of empire. It opens with "The Age of Global Power," in which Young argues that prevailing notions of the United States as exceptional, as powerful, and as passive have fundamentally obscured the real exercise of American power in the world. Historians, she claims, need to begin to write a history of America and the world that is mindful of the simultaneous reality of American dominance and its dominant self-absorption over the last century. This essay is followed by works by Young on the Korean and Vietnam wars, and the ways in which American policy toward them presaged elements of the forever wars in the early twenty-first century.

In "Hard Sell: The Korean War," Young examines public doubts about the war in Korea and its acquiescence to the Truman administration's prosecution of war on the peninsula, arguing the Korean case demonstrated to future administrations that American wars could in fact be waged without public enthusiasm and understanding. "U.S. Opposition to War in Korea and Vietnam," a previously unpublished work, addresses why there was so little organized dissent in the United States during the Korean War as compared with Vietnam. She contends that opposition to the war in Korea was just as strong but was stymied by anticommunist repression. Instead of active opposition, there was passive acquiescence and, ultimately, electoral vengeance. "The Same Struggle for Liberty" explores official American framings of war in Korea and Vietnam to bring to the surface what Young calls a persisting American dilemma, "how to acquire . . . an empire without naming it, or better, in the name of the right of self-determination for all peoples." Finally, "Counting the Bodies in Vietnam" considers the ways in which the pressing desire of the United States to locate and return American bodies and the virtual disinterest in the bodies of Vietnamese soldiers and civilians reveals whose bodies really "count" in American wars.

Part 2 of this collection brings together her most significant writings on unlimited war and the perils of forgetting. Importantly, she does not date the forever war from the aftermath of the September 11, 2001, terrorist attacks. Instead, the longer history of limited war gives rise to permanent war. This is in part because limited wars "cannot end in unconditional surrender and total victory. . . . They do not so much end as stop, until the next one begins." Ongoing war is enabled by the isolation of American civilians from its violence. They lacked an intimacy with war's carnage, and could not "imagine being bombed, rather than bombing."[21] She illustrates the importance of culture, including novels and films, and the way the memory of war is crucial to war politics. The construction of memory does not happen only after the fact, but during the war itself.

In "The Big Sleep," Young argues that soldiers have had to confront a tension between their own experience of war and what Americans at home imagined it to be. Soldiers could not bring home what war actually felt like. It was not just that they sought to protect family members from what they knew—like the screams of drowning comrades during a river-crossing accident. Their memories would jar home front ideas of war as victorious. Some soldiers could only reintegrate at home by reimagining their own experience so that it lined up with expectations. Policy was then informed by this revision of memory, so that this "big sleep" enabled the next war.

As the twentieth century progressed, technology changed the experience of killing. Devastating aerial bombing in the U.S. wars in Korea and Vietnam made war seem abstract to American leaders, Young argues in "Bombing Civilians: From the Twentieth to the Twenty-First Centuries." With their faith that bombing would send a message of strength, limited war became total war short of the use of nuclear weapons. She follows the trajectory of American air power to the use of drones in Pakistan.

In "Permanent War," Young shows the way the memory of Vietnam continued to haunt American war makers. This led President George H. W. Bush and other presidents and military leaders to do their best to frame wars so that they could be understood as heroic, like World War II, and not like Vietnam. The second Gulf War was "Cold War redux," Young argues, a permanent war against terrorism instead of against communism.

When the United States attacked Iraq in 2003, Young reflected on the "puerile arrogance" of the George W. Bush administration's idea of "pre-emptive war." Engaged in nothing less than a "plot against history," and enabled by the press, they had falsely convinced many Americans that Iraq was allied with the al Qaeda terrorists behind the 9/11 attacks.[22] Five years later, she reflected on the way Vietnam still served as the starting point for American war policy. In the form of a top ten list, "U.S. in Asia, U.S. in Iraq: Lessons Not Learned . . ." discusses the lessons America presidents have learned from Vietnam—among them controlling the press and historical narratives, upping the ante when the going gets tough, and the need for heroes—but she also argues that a central lesson has been lost on policy makers: the need for accountability for the criminality of American practices of war.

Young's ideas about the way unlearned lessons and failures of memory enable ongoing war come together in her reflection: "'I was thinking, as I often do these days, of war': The United States in the Twenty-First Century." Over time, war's persistence has been enabled by its increasing invisibility. The role of historians, she urges, is "to speak and write so that a time of war not be mistaken for peacetime."

Throughout her storied career, Young combined no-nonsense critical bite with enormous warmth and generosity. Here her lifelong love of opera may best illustrate how she managed the potentially conflicting elements through which she most frequently engaged in the world: politics and friendship. Italian opera was her favorite, and she especially liked Verdi's *Don Carlo*. Perhaps this is not so surprising. At stake are the lives and liberty of the people of Flanders at the time of the Spanish Inquisition, and Don Carlo, the independent-minded son of the Spanish king, is there to ensure they get their freedom. But what Young liked best in the opera is the celebrated and rousing duet between Don Carlo and his dear friend Rodrigo as they pledge that "their souls be infused with love, will and hope" in the fight for liberty. "That," Young turned to one of us at a performance of *Don Carlo* at the Metropolitan Opera House in New York City and said, "is what it is all about." Critique of American empire and war are central to the enduring relevance of Young's work. But so too is the spirit by which she made her claims and the ends to which she hoped they would be put. Just as she argued as a young editorial writer for the *Vassar Miscellany*, there is no sustainable path before us other than a just peace. Young helped us see how, amidst darkness and ideological division, there is also love and hope.

NOTES

1. Marilyn B. Young, "Permanent War," *positions: asia critique* 13, no. 1 (Spring 2005): 178.
2. Marilyn B. Young, *The Vietnam Wars: 1945–1990* (New York: HarperCollins, 1991).
3. Marilyn B. Young, "How the United States Ends Wars," in *Not Even Past: How the United States Ends Wars*, ed. David Fitzgerald, David Ryan, and John M. Thompson (New York: Berghahn Books, 2020), 252.
4. Richard Nixon, Henry Kissinger, and H. R. Haldeman, April 12, 1971, 10:24–10:33 a.m., Oval Office, Conversation No. 477–1, White House Tapes, Nixon Presidential Materials, National Archives; our thanks to Erez Manela for drawing this conversation to our attention.
5. Marilyn B. Young, *The Rhetoric of Empire: America China Policy, 1895–1901* (Cambridge, Mass.: Harvard University Press, 1968)
6. "Marilyn Young, Historian Who Challenged U.S Foreign Policy, Dies at 79," *New York Times*, March 9, 2017.
7. "Knowland and the UN," *Vassar Miscellany*, 39, no. 17 (March 1955): 2.
8. William Appleman Williams, *The Tragedy of American Diplomacy* (New York: W.W. Norton & Co., 1972). The first edition of this classic work was published in 1959.
9. Walter LaFeber, *The New Empire: An Interpretation of American Expansionism, 1860–1898* (Ithaca, N.Y.: Cornell University Press, 1963); Thomas J. McCormick, *China Market: America's Quest to Informal Empire, 1893–1901* (Chicago: Ivan R. Dee, 1967); and Lloyd C. Gardner, *Economic Aspects of New Deal Diplomacy* (Madison: University of Wisconsin Press, 1964).
10. Williams, *The Tragedy of American Diplomacy*, 45.
11. See, for instance, Herbert Feis, *Roosevelt-Churchill-Stalin: The War They Waged and the Peace They Sought* (Princeton, N.J.: Princeton University Press, 1957).
12. Among the leading New Left accounts of the Cold War, see Gar Alperovitz, *Atomic Diplomacy: Hiroshima and Potsdam* (New York: Vintage, 1965); Gabriel Kolko, *The Politics of War: The World and United States Foreign Policy, 1943–1945* (New York: Pantheon Books, 1972); Lloyd C. Gardner, *Architects of Illusion; Men and Idea in American Foreign Policy, 1941–49* (Chicago: Quadrangle Books, 1970); and Walter LaFeber, *America, Russia, and the Cold War, 1945–1966* (New York: Wiley, 1967).
13. Marilyn Young, "The Changing Cold War in Asia, 1949–1989," unpublished, undated essay, Cold War in Asia folder, box 2, Marilyn Young Papers, Tamiment Library and Robert F. Wagner Labor Archives, Elmer Holmes Bobst Library, New York University.
14. Marilyn Young's first engagement in her writing with the term "forever war" may have been a 1998 essay in which she compared the conception of ongoing war in Joe Haldeman's 1998 novel *The Forever War* with George Lucas's 1977 film *Star Wars*. She argued that Lucas and Haldeman captured the twin poles of the American cultural understanding of war. Lucas portrayed sharp divisions

between good and evil, but Young thought Haldeman's 1200-year slog through never-ending conflict was a more accurate fit. Marilyn B. Young, "The Forever War," *Itinerario* 22 (1998): 79–80.

15. *Promissory Notes: Women and the Transition to Socialism*, ed. Sonia Kruks, Rayna Rapp, and Marilyn B. Young (New York: Monthly Review Press, 1989).

16. Marilyn Young, unpublished essay, circa 1971, box 2, Vietnam Articles (Mine) folder, Marilyn Young Papers, Tamiment Library, New York University.

17. Marilyn Young's recollection, as told to Mary L. Dudziak.

18. Michael S. Sherry, *In the Shadow of War: The United States since the 1930s* (New Haven, Conn.: Yale University Press, 1995), xi..

19. Andrew J. Bacevich, *America's War for the Greater Middle East: A Military History* (New York: Random House, 2016).

20. *The New American Empire: A 21st Century Teach-in on U.S. Foreign Policy*, ed. Marilyn B. Young and Lloyd Gardner (New York: New Press, 2005). On Historians Against the War, see Jim O'Brien, "Historical Notes on Historians Against the War," *Historians for Peace and Democracy*, https://www.historiansforpeace.org/our-history/.

21. Marilyn B. Young, "Limited War, Unltd," unpublished lecture, pp. 1–2, emailed from Young to Dudziak, April 2009. Young delivered this lecture at the Kluge Center, Library of Congress, on July 8, 2009, https://www.loc.gov/item/webcast-4683/.

22. Marilyn B. Young, "Ground Zero: Enduring War," in *September 11 in History: A Watershed Moment?*, ed. Mary L. Dudziak (Durham, N.C.: Duke University Press, 2003), 28.

PART I

MAKING
AMERICAN WARS

1

THE AGE OF GLOBAL POWER

The interesting task of this volume is to develop a way of thinking about and writing the history of the United States that avoids the customary practice of American historians, especially in the post–World War II period, of transforming the commonsense notion of different national histories into a conviction that the United States is unique. "Of the controlling themes in contemporary United States history writing," Daniel Rogers observes in a recent essay, "none were pressed more urgently upon professional historians by the surrounding culture than a desire not merely for difference but for a particularity beyond all other nations' particularities: a yearning for proof of its own uniqueness so deep that it tied every other nation's history in fetters."[1] Other nations might be enchained by universal laws of history, but the United States was the Ptolemaic center of the world, around which they all revolved. Oddly, this conviction was accompanied by another, equally firm one: that the U.S. effort to "create some order out of the chaos of the world," as Dean Acheson put it, was simply a response to the "Soviet menace."[2] The United States was thus at once powerful and passive. The flurry of postwar plans, doctrines, interventions, alliances, and wars was a reaction to external aggression (flexibly understood to include "internal subversion").

The combination of the three—America as exceptional, powerful, and passive—has yielded policies and interpretations that are intellectually tautological and politically solipsistic. The United States has not been an aggressor, because, by definition, it does not commit aggression. The hostility of others to the United States cannot, again by definition, be a

First published in *Rethinking American History in a Global Age*, ed. Tom Bender (Berkeley: University of California Press, 2002), 274–94. Copyright © 2002 by the Regents of the University of California. Published by the University of California Press.

response to American actions, because the United States does not invite hostility but only reacts to it. What the United States claims it intends, rather than what it does, should persuade any fair-minded observer of the righteousness of its policies.

There is a double Archimedean dilemma involved in the effort to think about U.S. history outside of its own terms. Where can the historian stand in order to lever the history of the United States off its assumed centrality? Policy makers and, in large measure, the American public live deeply inside an exceptionalist ideology that has retroactively shaped the material world the historians interpret. Most analyses begin with the injunction that it is necessary to understand and convey to readers the worldview of the policy makers before engaging in an analysis of the choices they have made. "You must remember what it was like in the 1940s [or 1950s, or 1960s]," historians of U.S. foreign policy chide those among them who seem to be treating the United States too critically. The result is often a rendering of U.S. history that reproduces U.S. ideology. But the second part of the dilemma may be the more difficult. It arises from the fact that for the past fifty years, the United States has been the most powerful country in the world. Europe, Asia, Latin America, and Africa might serve as reasonable ground on which to rest one's lever, were it not that, since at least 1945, each of these continents, one way and another, has had little choice but to engage the centrality of American power.

Obviously, I do not mean that the United States totally dominated all aspects of the daily lives of the world's population, nor that it always and everywhere imposed its will. People around the world have found reasons enough of their own to engage in civil and other wars, with the result that the United States has sometimes had to conclude that domination over half a country was better than none. But in its impact on global culture, economics, military hardware, and international diplomacy, no other power or coalition of powers comes close to the United States. This is especially the case since the collapse of the Soviet Union, but I would argue it has been true for much longer. To write the history of the United States in the world from outside its claims to a limitless horizon means to take the country as simply one nation among others. This is true and also not true. So the problem is not only how to think about the United States without reinstating its own centered sense of itself but how to do this without ignoring the success it has had in achieving, in Melvyn Leffler's words, a "preponderance of power," a centralizing power, in the world.

Another way to describe the problem is in terms of the inability of many Americans to envision other countries *as* countries in their own right. Thus the United States is able to operate without awareness of the way in which even minor exercises of U.S. power affect the lives of others, sometimes without even remembering that anything happened at all. Fundamentally, other countries simply do not have much purchase on the American imagination. Here is an example: the result of an American-engineered overthrow of the government of Cheddi Jagan in Guyana in 1963 reduced that country to a state of unprecedented poverty and corruption. America's man in Guyana, Forbes Burnham, ruled the country through "force and fraud," accumulating over $2 billion in foreign debt, the equivalent of five times its GDP; interest payments consumed 80 percent of Guyana's revenue and 50 percent of its foreign earnings. Thirty years later, in 1992, after the country's first free elections in the three decades, Cheddi Jagan was returned to office, and shortly thereafter President Clinton nominated one of the architects of the Kennedy administration's plot to overthrow Jagan as ambassador to Georgetown. The nomination was withdrawn when the Guyanese protested, and, in a move toward damage control that only drew more attention, U.S. government records of Kennedy's policy toward Guyana, which were scheduled to be released, instead were sealed. Apparently, neither Clinton nor any of his senior advisers remembered the plot; if they did, the nomination was a deliberate insult, but this seems less likely than that they simply forgot. "Maybe President Clinton doesn't know our history," Cheddi Jagan remarked, "but the people who advise him should at least know their own history."[3] John Lewis Gaddis, the preeminent historian of American foreign relations, does know U.S. history and includes the incident in his recent book on the Cold War, but he is no more interested than Clinton in the history of Guyana. "Bill Clinton," he writes, "had been a precocious teenager . . . and could not have been expected to know. But the fact that none of his senior advisers remembered the crisis . . . suggests how much has changed since the days when Americans saw dominoes lined up, ready for toppling, all over the 'third world.'" Guyana makes its appearance in Gaddis's book solely as an example of the shift in Washington's perceptions since the United States won the Cold War.[4] For the historian, as for Washington, Guyana does not really exist.

H. W. Brands's history of the Cold War, *The Devil We Knew*, begins by locating America in an international context. The United States is neither a city on a hill nor, as in some versions of revisionist history, an evil empire; rather, the Cold War was "simply the management of national interests in a world of competing powers." Yet as a metaphor that launched military Keynesianism, erased domestic divisions of class and race in the service of a homogeneous anticommunist cause, and turned complex issues into simple choices, the Cold War had the power to create a hermetic virtual reality of Manichean divisions and savage "limited" wars. Brands understands the self-intoxicating nature of Cold War ideology: "Americans recognized the utter peril that arming the world on an unprecedented scale was placing them in. They felt the economic burden of maintaining the most powerful and expensive military establishment in human history. Recognizing the peril and feeling the burden, they naturally came to believe that it was all necessary." Although Brands seems to want to normalize U.S. history, he cannot concede that, apart from its power, it was a nation like any other. Americans, he writes, "have from the beginning of their national existence demonstrated an incurable desire to make the world a better place."

Had he written that Americans "have from the beginning of their national existence believed themselves to have demonstrated, or were told they had demonstrated, an incurable desire to make the world a better place," the reader might have looked forward to an analysis of this curious phenomenon. But Brands says something different: "In 1945, nearly all Americans and probably a majority of interested foreigners had looked on the United States as a beacon shining the way to a better future for humanity, one in which ideals mattered more than tanks. During the next forty years, American leaders succeeded in convincing many Americans and all but a few foreigners that the United States could be counted on to act pretty much as great powers always have." This "incurable desire to make the world a better place" also defines the United States for Loren Baritz: America, he writes, "must be for freedom, for dignity, for genuine democracy, or it is not America." Baritz concludes that "it was not America in Vietnam." Who was it then?[5] The problem may be that the United States was itself in Vietnam and that the belief in America as a shining beacon was the spark that lit and kept burning the fire of the Cold War.

Diplomatic historians are aware of the irony of writing about U.S. engagement with other nations as if it were a monologue. We are instructed to learn other languages, to use foreign archives, to write not just bilaterally but multilaterally. But to do this without at the same time addressing the consistency with which other countries have remained insubstantial to U.S. policy makers and their public distorts the record beyond the redress of polyglottal achievement. As the United States made war against Korea, for example, Dean Acheson insisted that the war wasn't a "Korean war on either side" but rather "the global strategy of global purpose on both sides."[6] Countries were counters in a zero-sum game, reversing Kant's categorical imperative. Not only were these countries not taken as ends, they mattered only insofar as they figured in America's calculation of its own economic or political interest. When China was "lost," Korea became important for entirely extrinsic reasons. It was not, Senator Henry Cabot Lodge pointed out, "much good, but it's ours."[7] Or, for an example closer to the present, we can contemplate Secretary of State Madeleine Albright's acknowledgment to an interviewer asking about the deaths of an estimated half a million Iraqi children due to American-imposed sanctions that it was a "hard choice," but "we think the price is worth it."[8]

American power is thus compounded by a conviction that the world at large is isomorphic with its own needs and ambitions, or should be. In November 1965, Secretary of Defense Robert McNamara warned President Johnson that the Chinese were attempting to construct a coalition in Asia. If they succeeded, McNamara was certain the president would agree, this would constitute a "straightforward security threat." But there was another more important thought that the secretary wished to share with Johnson: "namely, that we have our view of the way the U.S. should be moving and of the need for the majority of the rest of the world to be moving in the same direction if we are to achieve our national objectives." "Our ends cannot be achieved," McNamara went on, "and our leadership role cannot be played if some powerful and virulent nation—whether Germany, Japan, Russia or China—is allowed to organize their part of the world according to a philosophy contrary to our own."[9] It would take no great effort to accumulate a collection of Favorite American Imperial Quotes: Henry Kissinger, who did not see "why we need stand by and watch [Chile] go communist due to the irresponsibility of its own government"; John J. McCloy on the right of the United States "to have our cake and eat it too," operating independently in South America while retaining the right to "intervene promptly in Europe"; Acheson's promise to "help people who believe the way we do, to continue to live the way they want to live."[10] The combination of nationalism and universalism these statements reflect may characterize all imperial states, but the point I want to stress is that during much of this century the United States has had the power to act on the basis of its imperial self-image. This makes it difficult for the historian attempting to decenter the history of U.S. foreign relations, not to speak of the people on whom its power is visited.

The work of John Lewis Gaddis is an example of how the past fifty years look if one takes America at its own word. Unlike earlier mainstream historians, Gaddis does not hesitate to name America imperial. However, he believes that the American empire, in contrast to others, was built without either "imperial consciousness or design." The long-standing tradition of the United States was anti-imperial, at least outside the Western hemisphere, despite "departures" like the Spanish-American War. After World War II, empire was, like greatness on Malvolio, thrust upon the United States by Europeans who found Stalin's approach to imperial management unattractive and so invited a protective American overlordship. On the whole, the American empire has been a good one, perhaps even—as the Founding Fathers themselves intended—an empire for liberty. "The Americans," Gaddis concludes, "constructed a new kind of empire—a democratic empire—for the simple reason that they were, by habit and history, democratic in their politics."[11] Gaddis has recently rediscovered the role of ideology in Soviet policy. He now argues that the Cold War was visited upon a reluctant American-led free world by the romantic, paranoid, revolutionary visions of Josef Stalin. The United States, by contrast, operated outside of ideology.[12]

Gaddis does address various U.S. policy excesses. He labels the U.S. intervention in Guatemala in 1954, for example, a "massive overreaction to a minor irritant." On the impact of that overreaction, which led to a civil war lasting four decades in which some two hundred thousand people died at the hands of the U.S.-supported right-wing government, Gaddis has only a brief comment, which releases the United States from any responsibility for the consequences of its actions. "[The intervention] did little to alter the course of events inside Guatemala," he writes, "where Arbenz's regime had made so many enemies among the landowners and the military that it probably would not have lasted long in any event."[13] Since the intervention "probably" did not alter the miserable course of Guatemalan history, any consideration of that history need not detain us nor enter into an understanding of Cold War American history.[14] It is certainly possible that the Arbenz regime would have fallen without U.S. encouragement; it is, however, certain that it *was* overturned with considerable U.S. help, with such consequences as we know.

Gaddis offers his assertion that the United States lacked "imperial consciousness" as an empirical description of the American way of empire. A brief but comprehensive review of twentieth-century U.S. foreign policy by Walter LaFeber reaches a different conclusion. U.S. policy, LaFeber argues, demanded a world "safe and assessable for the American economic system." Rather than a commitment to a "democratic empire," he finds, policies "shaped by the desire to create democratic systems in foreign lands formed the exception rather than the rule . . . When explicitly pro-democratic policies were advanced, the cost involved was usually perceived to be slight. When the cost promised to be high the push stopped."[15] But no one in the Kennedy administration questioned Cheddi Jagan's legitimacy. He had been elected three times before Kennedy ordered his overthrow; but, as "some sort of Marxist," Arthur Schlesinger Jr. pointed out, the question was "whether he was recoverable for democracy." He displayed "deep pro-communist emotion" and the United States could not afford a "quasi-communist regime on the mainland of Latin America."[16]

Gaddis's "democratic empire" is obviously more gratifying to Americans than the one described by LaFeber; it is what politicians tell the country about itself, what high school teachers teach, what students believe. And it lies at the heart of the difficulty involved in any effort to rewrite the national story. For a conviction that an American empire, as opposed to those established by other nations, is democratic, that American interests are consonant with the last, best hopes of all mankind, occludes both the fact of U.S. power and the effect of its exercise. The syllogism is simple: all nations deserve freedom and democracy, the United States embodies both, and its policies, despite some excesses, seek to bestow them on others. Such an ambition, in the absence of military and economic power, would be impossible; but the ambition renders the power itself innocent, harmless, essentially invisible to itself.

I want now to discuss the disparity between the impact of U.S. power on the world and the soft impact of the world on the United States at the point where the impact is hardest and therefore possibly clearest: when international relations turn violent, in moments of armed U.S. intervention.

One likely place to start an exploration of the remarkable power of the nationalist narrative to cushion and mute that impact is the Spanish-American war. Indeed, calling it the Spanish-American war made Cuba, where it took place, and its long struggle for independence, invisible. As Louis A. Pérez Jr. has pointed out, "It is not simply that the historiography has failed to represent the presence of Cubans as relevant to outcomes; it has not even noticed their absence."[17]

Lasting a mere 100 days, with only 379 combat dead and 1,600 wounded on the U.S. side, and an astonishing yield of new possessions (from the Caribbean to Southeast Asia), the war of 1898 was the first limited war in American history. Recent analyses by literary critics and cultural historians have stressed two aspects of the conflict: the way it served to unify the nation and the role it played in reestablishing structures of racial and gender hierarchy in a period of increasing instability. Amy Kaplan understands the war as a "nostalgic recuperation of the heroism of an earlier generation and . . . a purgative final battle, healing the wounds and divisiveness of internecine war while completing the goals of national reunification."[18] Gail Bederman, among others, concentrates on the linking of manliness, race, and imperialism by politicians like Theodore Roosevelt.[19] And Anders Stephanson, in his meditation on the concept of Manifest Destiny, writes of the "all-pervasive" concept of race and the way in which the new racial laws enacted by state legislatures in the 1890s against blacks "found a logical connection to the need to keep subject aliens abroad in their proper place."[20]

Such efforts to recast standard American historical accounts by rejecting a focus on the state or on state-to-state relations, however, run the danger of being themselves as reflexive as the histories they mean to displace. Writing from a Caribbean perspective, the historian Ada Ferrar observes that in these analyses, the areas that came under U.S. rule are present "only as sites where American anxieties and desires unfold."[21]

In a recent essay, Pérez carefully disassembles the ideology that governed U.S.-Cuban relations from 1898 to 1959. He analyzes first the "debt of gratitude" Americans believed Cubans had incurred for their liberation from Spain and then the necessity Cubans have felt to contest the American representation of the war of 1898. "The revolution of 1959," he writes, "canceled the debt."[22] On the Cuban side, perhaps, but current U.S. policy toward Cuba derives, at least in part, from a persistent U.S. conviction of

Cuban "ingratitude." The difference between Cuban and American representations of 1898 is that the United States has the power to harm those who insist on their own.

The war against Spain, understood as a crusade for Cuban liberation, did not raise many questions about American national identity. But the general public found it more difficult to assimilate the brutality of the campaign against Filipino insurgents than it did the easy victory over Spain. The United States sent 126,500 soldiers to the Philippines, of whom 4,234 died. Michael Hunt has calculated that this was "perhaps the highest ratio for any U.S. war." Not surprisingly, Filipinos suffered greater losses: 20,000 war dead and possibly as many as one-tenth of the population dead as a result of famine and disease between 1899 and 1903.[23] Despite efforts at military censorship, press reports of U.S. atrocities appeared early and plagued the military throughout the war. Journalists and politicians who had fully supported the war against Spain as the fulfillment of an American emancipatory mission turned sharply against the administration when it became clear that the annexation of the Philippines could be achieved only by force of arms. By 1901, reports of the widespread rape and murder of Filipino noncombatants and the systematic torture and summary execution of prisoners of war forced a congressional investigation of army tactics. Chaired by a reluctant Henry Cabot Lodge and stacked with war-friendly witnesses, the investigation ran parallel with two courts-martial revealing shocking details of the ongoing war of extermination against the insurgents on the island of Samar.

Even the jingo press seemed embarrassed. At Balangiga, in October 1901, Brigadier General Jacob Smith, who had learned how to fight "savages" at Wounded Knee, had ordered his troops to kill every Filipino male over the age of ten and turn Samar into a "howling wilderness." Smith was not the only military figure to draw on the experience of the Plains wars. "The country won't be pacified," one returning soldier told the press, "until the niggers are killed off like the Indians."[24] The war was doubly domesticated; and, as with Indians and rebellious African Americans, the real victims were the soldiers, not the Filipinos. What were the soldiers to do, one editorial pointed out, "try moral persuasion on the infuriated bolomen who were massacring our soldiers daily?" Within months, Smith had been forgiven by the mainstream press; the anti-imperialists were being accused of treason, and editorial writers deplored those who had maligned our "brave soldiers" in their fight against "the savages and cannibals over there."[25]

The *New York Times* set out the dilemma: "A choice of cruelties is the best that has been offered in the Philippines. It is not so certain that we at home can afford to shudder at the 'water cure' unless we disdain the whole job. The army has obeyed orders. It was sent to subdue the Filipinos. Having the devil to fight, it has sometimes used fire."[26]

Theodore Roosevelt shrank from neither fire nor water. The water cure (in which prisoners were persuaded to talk by force-feeding them water and then pounding on their swollen stomachs), he reassured a friend, was just "an old Filipino method of mild torture. Nobody was seriously damaged, whereas the Filipinos had inflicted incredible tortures on our people."[27] Many Americans took refuge in such rationalizations and were relieved when Roosevelt announced victory on July 4, 1902, although fighting would continue for many years thereafter. On Roosevelt's orders, Secretary of War Elihu Root congratulated the army for having fought a "humane war" against a "treacherous foe." Root praised the army for having abided by the rules of war in a situation where it was "impossible to distinguish friend from foe." In a peroration resonant with familiar colonial tropes (peaceful natives intimidated into opposing the colonial power), Root concluded: "Utilizing the lessons of the Indian wars, [the army] has relentlessly followed the guerrilla bands to their fastness in the mountains and jungles and crushed them. . . . It has added honor to the flag which it defended."[28]

In retrospect, the rapidity with which disturbing accounts of American military behavior in the Philippines were erased is a little surprising. Efforts by the anti-imperialist press to gather and publish antiwar sentiments from returning soldiers had mixed results. Although a majority of officers and men criticized the war, they were unanimously opposed to withdrawal short of total victory. Even those against annexation insisted that the United States had first to beat the Filipinos "into submission." The historian Stuart Creighton Miller found the sentiments of Corporal Moses Smith typical: "Now I don't believe that there is a soldier or American but believes the Filipinos must be whipped thoroughly. After that we can give them their independence under an American protectorate."[29] Returning veterans, when they spoke in public at all, defended army tactics as necessary in a guerrilla war. The only sustained protest by veterans was over their loss of benefits, since the conflict in the Philippines was classified as an insurrection rather than a war. Efforts to draft these aging veterans into the movement against the war in Vietnam consistently stumbled over their imperturbable patriotism.[30]

Miller, contemplating the difference between the response to the Vietnam and the Philippine wars, has argued that the popularity of imperialist expansion at the turn of the century defused any lasting opposition to the means by which empire was acquired. Indeed, many anti-imperialists shared both the imperialists' patriotism and their racism. Some anti-imperialists saw a U.S. empire as a deviation from the righteous path of the Founding Fathers, but imperialists argued that it was expansion that really fulfilled the original vision.

Those who sent the U.S. Army to the Philippines, the men who fought there, and most of the historians who have written about it since were also protected from disturbing memories of the actual conduct of the war by their conviction that American intentions had been good. Even Miller, while setting out the horrors of the war, concludes that in the Philippines, as later in Vietnam, Americans were motivated "in part by good intentions to elevate or aid the victims, and not simply to conquer and exploit them."[31] Henry Adams expressed a similar sentiment, though with some irony:

I turn green in bed at midnight if I think of the horrors of a year's warfare in the Philippines; . . . we must slaughter a million or two foolish Malays in order to give them the comforts of flannel petticoats and electric railways. . . . We all dread and abominate the war, but cannot escape it. We must protect Manila and the foreign interests, which, in trying to protect the natives from Spain, we were as obliged to assume responsibility for.[32]

William Vaughn Moody's poem "On a Soldier Fallen in the Philippines" is less confident. Laurels and flags will have to be heaped on the dead soldier so that he will "doubt not nor misgive," the reasons for his death. For the dead soldier must be protected from recognizing what was the case: the terrible possibility that his "bullet's scream went wide of its island mark" and struck instead "the heart of his darling land where she stumbled and sinned in the dark."[33] This sympathetic silence reassured the public that the purposes for which it had sanctioned a war were not vitiated by its brutalities.

A good illustration of how a shield of righteousness could protect even dissident Americans against loss of their Ptolemaic certainties is John Dos Passos's novel *1919*, which savagely indicts the society that produced the industrialists, militarists, and politicians Dos Passos deemed responsible, not just for World War I, but for the imperialist Spanish-American War that had preceded it. Peopled by both fictional and historical characters, *1919* fuses the two realms in a culminating vision of the burial of the Unknown Soldier, a figure who, by definition, has no history. The author denies him even a meaningful annihilation: he died simply because "the shell had his number on it." John Doe dies messily as well as meaninglessly: the "blood ran into the ground, the brains oozed out of the cracked skull and were licked up by the trenchrats, the belly swelled and raised a generation of bluebottle flies." Once dead, the Unknown Soldier is taken home in a flag-draped coffin to "God's country," where he suffers an ironic and multiple commemoration: medals of all nations are pinned to "where his chest ought to have been" and everyone brings flowers. "Woodrow Wilson brought a bouquet of poppies."[34] The relentless list of medals, the hypocrisy of diplomats, generals, admirals and politicians, the ghoulish concluding image of Wilson with a bouquet of poppies crescendo to a furious rejection of war.

Yet the ferocity of *1919*'s conclusion is also patriotic in its assumption that genuine honor could have been gathered, as well as a meaningful death. For Dos Passos never loosens his embrace of the idea of America, which he enshrines in a vision of its common people. Richard Poirier has observed that most American writers critical of the United States "are rather madly in love" with the country. "There is perhaps no other literature quite so patriotic because none is so damning of the failure of the country to live up to its dreams and expectations."[35]

Mobilization for war has never been easy or automatic, as both Woodrow Wilson and Franklin Delano Roosevelt discovered, although once launched, the memory of prior resistance yielded to a stronger need to make supportable what had seemed in prospect and briefly in retrospect, insupportable. In this respect, America is not exceptional, of course. The literature of World War I, in Europe as well as in the United States, snatched the attractions of war from even the most realistic representations of its irrationality, inhumanity, and sheer craziness. World War II recruits joined up to fight inspired by blurred, self-serving memories of

World War I veterans and the contradictory messages of postwar literature and cinema. British and American soldiers who fought in World War II, Paul Fussell has written, "couldn't help noticing the extra dimension of drama added to their experiences by their memories of the films about the Great War." Thus, the parapets of the no-man's-land of World War I appear, geographically most out of place, in Norman Mailer's *The Naked and the Dead*.[36] Subsequently, virtually every American who spoke or wrote of his experience in Vietnam did so in the language of the World War II movie imagery he brought with him to Saigon.

But construing World War II as an American crusade, a process that began during the war and has continued to the present day, does speak to American exceptionalism. Most Americans imagine their country to have won the war more or less on its own. Few know anything at all about the role played by the Soviet Union. Just how strenuous an effort was involved in the creation of America's self-image is evident in the work of the most popular U.S. World War II correspondent, Ernie Pyle. In his daily columns (published in three volumes during the war itself), James Tobin writes, Pyle constructed a "mythical hero, the long-suffering G. I. who triumphed over death through dogged perseverance" and by his unquestioning commitment to the Four Freedoms. The myth gave readers "the sense that they were seeing a hard-bitten portrait of war as it really was, yet also a sense that life was affirmed and went on in the midst of death."[37] Many correspondents contributed to this myth, which Hollywood then standardized. In a 1958 collection of his war journalism, John Steinbeck insisted that everything he reported had really happened. The reporters weren't liars; it is "in the things not mentioned that the untruth lies." They were not reported only in part because of military censorship. Mostly it was because "there was this huge and gassy thing called the War Effort." Judgments about what should be omitted were largely a matter for the correspondent himself to decide, and he carried "the rule book in his head and even invented restrictions for himself in the interest of the War Effort." The rules were simple: first, cowardice did not exist in the U.S. Army and "of all the brave men the private in the infantry was the bravest and the noblest." This was necessary because given the danger and the stupidity of what was asked of them, privates had to "be reassured that these things . . . were actually necessary and wise, and that he was a hero for doing them." Second, there were no "cruel or ambitious or ignorant commanders"; third, none of the five million young men in the military had any interest whatsoever in sex. It wasn't just that reporters went along with the War Effort, Steinbeck remembered, it was that "we abetted it. Gradually it became a part of all of us that the truth about anything was automatically secret and that to trifle with it was to interfere with the War Effort." Central to self-censorship was the correspondents' sense of responsibility to their readers at home. "The general feeling was that unless the home front was carefully protected from the whole account of what war was like, it might panic."[38]

At a certain point, Pyle came dangerously close to forgetting the rules, and rather than risk that, he left the Italian campaign before it was over, explaining to his readers that he had been "too close to the war for too long. . . . I had come to despise and be revolted by war clear out of any logical proportion. I couldn't find the Four Freedoms among the dead men." He feared that his disgust and war weariness would lead him to "begin writing unconscious distortions and unwarranted pessimisms," that he was unable any longer to see "the little things that you at home want to know about the soldiers." In his strained effort to explain himself, Pyle almost reported a war he knew he shouldn't report, revealing what the public had no wish to read about and military authorities would certainly have censored. Between the lines, the dead bury the cause for which they were supposed to have died, the cause Americans at home continued to see as justification for their deaths. Rather than write this suppressed and dangerous story, Pyle decided to stop reporting altogether, until he was able to write as he knew he should.[39]

Two years later, in an unpublished column found on his body after his death, Pyle explained why the news of victory in Europe left him feeling not elated but only relieved. All he finally remembered of the war, he wrote, were "dead men by mass production . . . in one country after another—month after month and year after year. Dead men in winter. Dead men in summer. Dead men in such familiar promiscuity that they become monotonous. Dead men in such monstrous infinity that you come almost to hate them."[40]

Because correspondents made every effort to follow the rules, to keep their revulsion within "logical proportions," the real war in Europe and the Pacific went largely unreported, known only to the men who fought it. Peace came with a final atrocity, the nuclear bombing of Hiroshima and Nagasaki. When the troops came home, it was to a hero's welcome and a home front moved by its own sense of self-sacrifice, justice, and power. Paul Fussell and Gerald Linderman, among many other accounts of World War II, make it clear that troops in the field fought in order to survive and for one another.[41] But these veterans of World War II, like their predecessors, surrendered their war to the one civilians told them they had fought.

The consciousness of America's destructive power, illuminated by the atomic bombs with which the war ended, was obscured by the fear the mobilization of the population for the Cold War engendered. Almost immediately the United States assumed the familiar stance in which it was more threatened than threatening.[42] The Cold War enshrined World War II as the "good war," a sacred icon of national virtue, even as World War II served to explain and justify the Cold War. America was at the center of them both: then, the pursuit of world justice; now, the focus of the Soviet threat. Russian communists replaced German Nazis; Red China replaced fascist Japan. Every effort was made to convince Americans that the Cold War was a real war, and when public faith in the need for tripling the defense budget wavered, the news that the North Koreans had crossed the thirty-eighth parallel invigorated it.

The absence of domestic consciousness of U.S. actions abroad is apparent in the ignorance of the great majority of Americans that the United States had been actively intervening in Korea from 1945 to the outbreak of war.[43] North Korean actions seemed gratuitous, inexplicable except as a preemptive move on the part of the Soviet Union against the United States. So powerful was the rhetoric of the Cold War and its Manichean division that the antiwar movement of the 1960s initially criticized the Vietnam war because it seemed to lack the morality and logic of the Korean conflict. Yet for five years, the U.S. government had helped the government of Syngman Rhee suppress a popular left-wing nationalist movement; armed and trained the South Korean army and police forces; arranged for a U.N.-supervised election establishing a separate government in the south; and turned a blind eye to South Korean violations of the thirty-eighth parallel.

Despite brutal tactics, high casualties, and public doubt about war aims, or possibly because of them, the public seems largely to have screened out the war.[44] Its savagery was, on occasion, however, reported in considerable detail.[45] And at least one senator, Edwin Johnson of Colorado, insisted that the United States had unwisely intervened in a civil war and should seek an immediate cease-fire. The "only tangible result" of the war, Senator Johnson insisted, had been the "indescribable misery which has been heaped upon the Korean people."[46] Public approval, which had been high in June 1950, reversed itself after Chinese entry into the war in January 1951: 66 percent of Americans polled were in favor of withdrawal, and 49 percent now thought the intervention should never have taken place.[47] But the impression of those fighting the war was that it had simply been forgotten. "It would be easier to take if people back home were helping," Harry Brubaker complains in James A. Michener's 1953 novella, *The Bridges at Toko-Ri*. "But in Denver nobody even knew there was a war except my wife." "If any war that our country ever engaged in could have been called a forgotten war," General Matthew Ridgway complained bitterly, "this was it."[48]

Certainly, that has been true until very recently. Samuel Hynes Jr., the author of a recent book entitled *Soldier's Tale: Bearing Witness to Modern War*, says, quite simply, "I have nothing to say . . . about the war in Korea, a war that came and went without glory, and left no mark on American imaginations—though nearly as many Americans died there as in Vietnam."[49] Given the literary legacy of the Vietnam war, W. D. Ehrhart, a poet and Vietnam veteran, decided that Korea must have left some traces, and a determined search eventually uncovered a small body of work, most of it written long after the war was over. "The Vietnam war," Ehrhart wrote in an introduction to an anthology of six poets, "seems to have been a catalyst for most of these poets, releasing pent-up feelings that had perhaps been held in check by the personal and cultural stoicism bequeathed to them by their generational older brothers."[50] When he asked the poets themselves why Korea had been passed by so lightly, several answered in terms of the war's "lack [of] nobility," of it having been a "nonwar," "futile," "bloody, a dirty uncompromising conflict with few positive images." These factors called upon to explain the silence surrounding Korea, however, are the same as those generally adduced to explain the volubility of Vietnam veterans.

The Korean War did occasion some soul-searching in its aftermath, but it was focused almost entirely on the behavior of American prisoners of war while in Chinese captivity. Had they collaborated with the enemy? To what degree? Why did so many die, so few try to escape? What had happened to the young manhood of America? Some rather odd answers were offered. Betty Friedan, in her influential book *The Feminine Mystique*, thought the prisoners were "models of a new kind of American"— "apathetic, dependent, infantile, purposeless," the children of women "who lived within the limits of the feminine mystique."[51]

The focus on the individual failure of prisoners discouraged questions as to whether their behavior was connected to the particular war they were asked to fight. It was a war, the novelist William Styron wrote, in 1963, in which the "issues were fuzzy and ambiguous, if not fraudulent, a war that could not possibly be 'won,' a senseless conflict so unpopular that even the most sanguinary politician or war lover shrank from inciting people to a patriotic zeal, a war without slogans or ballads or heroes."[52]

For a time, it seemed that, with the Vietnam-American War, the American national story, whose plot casts the United States as defensive in a treacherous world, had at last come to an end. Everyone knows how the Vietnam war hastened the unraveling of America's sacred history, already under way as a result of the Civil Rights movement. And yet even this war has not entirely escaped the force field of American solipsism. At the conclusion of Oliver Stone's movie *Platoon* the hero muses that the United States had not fought the enemy but itself in Vietnam. Most of the movies about the war, except those that fantasize a surrogate victory, such as the Rambo series, offer a similar analysis. The moviemakers would seem to agree with Richard Nixon: only Americans can defeat America. With the exception of the occasional female victim who stands metaphorically for Vietnam as a whole, film versions of the war, like many of the memoirs and histories, lack Vietnamese. Most accounts of the war begin with the statement that it was the most divisive war in U.S. history, save only the Civil War. But the Vietnam-American War was a civil war in Vietnam, not in the United States.

A recent experiment in writing the history of the Vietnam-American War from both the U.S. and the Vietnamese sides was intended to break the bell jar. Its failure finally to do so is as interesting as its limited success. Over a period of four years, a group of American historians and officials met with their Vietnamese counterparts. Robert S. McNamara was the moving force. Convinced the war was the result of "mutual misperception, misunderstanding, and misjudgment by leaders in Washington and Hanoi," McNamara was anxious both to explain the United States to the Vietnamese and to get them to admit their responsibility. "*If each side had known the truth about the other's reality, might the outcome have been less tragic?*" he asks with italicized intensity.[53] Responsibility for the tragedy of the Vietnam war, McNamara argues, was shared; the blood guilt of 3.8 million Vietnamese and 58,000 Americans must be mutually carried. Vietnam's failure lay in its inability to understand, and disarm, the

American Cold War "mind-set." The United States was not, the Americans repeatedly insisted, an imperialist country; it did not want to dominate Vietnam; it had gone to the aid of a threatened ally. But the American Cold War mind-set that McNamara patiently explained to the Vietnamese sounds impervious to outside reasoning. Why could not the Vietnamese, during the Geneva Convention or earlier, have explained to the Americans that they were not tools of the Russians and the Chinese, one American official demanded. But we did, the Vietnamese responded, and you would not listen. But, the same official persisted, what was it "that made you think [in the 1950s] that the United States was your enemy? Was it propaganda from the Soviets and the Chinese? Was it Dulles?"[54]

The Vietnamese reminded the Americans of their aid to the French during the first Indochina war, and the Americans responded that, after all, French requests for American intervention at the time of Dien Bien Phu had been rejected, and, in any case, aid to France had had to do with the situation in Europe, not Vietnam. As Colonel Herbert Schandler put it,

> [T]he United States was taking a *world* view of all these issues. The Iron Curtain was falling all across Europe. This was shocking. We had fought a bloody war in Europe, and had won, only to have half of Europe reconquered by a totalitarian system. . . . Communism, we felt, had to be stopped. The Iron Curtain then fell in Asia in 1954 with the armistice in Korea and with the Geneva Accords. . . . Sometimes it looked to us [as though] we were on the losing side of history.

And Chester Cooper, who attended the Geneva Convention as a representative of the CIA, explained that the United States had not been Vietnam's enemy at the time and that Vietnamese policy decisions based on fear of U.S. intervention had been misguided:

> Yes, of course, eventually we became enemies. . . . But I am telling you as authoritatively [sic], as a member of the U.S. government at the time we are talking about, and as one who dealt every day with these issues, that you were wrong in your assessment *then*, in the mid-1950s. Wrong, wrong, wrong! We had made no such decision to intervene. But because you *assumed* that we were hostile, and were seeking to destroy you, then you did things, you made statements, that appeared to us to confirm the views of people like John Foster Dulles that *you* were our mortal enemy.

Luu Doan Huynh conceded that perhaps America had not been ready to intervene at that precise moment in time. "But really," he went on,

> your bullets are killers of our people. We see that this is America's gift to Vietnam—allowing the French to kill our people. This is the most convincing evidence we have of America's loyalties. . . . So how can we conclude you are not our enemy? . . . we understand all your arguments about U.S. interests and the French and so on. We believe Mr. Chester Cooper when he says that he did not consider Vietnam an enemy. But please try to understand me when I say: *Blood speaks with a terrible voice!*[55]

There was a similar exchange over the Diem regime. Cooper thought "it's fair to say we wished [Diem] well" but denied that there had been a U.S. military presence in Vietnam at that time. The Vietnamese refrained from correcting him but pointed out that Diem's security forces had been trained in the United States. "Now Mr. Chester Cooper says that the orders to kill our people in 1955 did not come from Washington. Okay. But how could we know this? He was your guy, and he was killing our people. You see, blood again—blood speaks loudly when you are the one who is bleeding."[56]

The conclusions McNamara drew from these discussions with the Vietnamese stress mutuality of misperception. "Hanoi," he writes,

> in effect projected onto the United States a kind of colonial mode of operation not significantly different from the French. . . . However, unlike the French, the Americans were ambivalent about their global role and were not colonialists in the way that the French could be characterized. Had Hanoi understood this—had it achieved a more empathetic understanding of American fears and motivations—it could have appealed to a strong set of American motives emphasizing self-determination and anti-colonialism. But Hanoi did *not* understand this.[57]

Of the disparity of power between the two countries, of the difference between bullets and "statements," McNamara has nothing to say. Nor do any of the participants reflect on the fact that had America not lost the war, had Vietnam been divided as was Korea, the discussion itself would never have taken place. It is intolerable to McNamara to assume responsibility for the Vietnam war. The fault lies not only in "missed opportunities for peace" on both sides but with the Vietnamese failure to understand that the United States, as an aspect of its essential character, is for self-determination—appearances to the contrary notwithstanding. America's overwhelming power vis-à-vis Vietnam disappears in this formulation, and the abiding conviction of American dedication to universal values remains, untouched by history.

In the forlorn last days of America's occupation of Saigon, an American reporter pressed a reluctant diplomat for the "lessons of the war." "They will be whatever makes us think well of ourselves," he replied, "so that our sleep will be untroubled."[58] In seeking to ensure the national repose, the United States is hardly unique. To help their countrymen sleep better, historians and politicians have often transformed past unpleasantness into something palatable, and calls to rethink national history are more often calls for nationalist revival than self-criticism. It is especially important that the history of foreign wars, which might pose a serious challenge to somnolence, be domesticated, so that neither the country's self-image nor its capacity to make war in the future is too severely damaged. Anders Stephanson has argued that the history of the country has until recently moved between two poles in its relation to the rest of the world: the first "was to unfold into an exemplary state *separate* from the corrupt and fallen world, letting others emulate as best they can." The second approach, usually identified with Woodrow Wilson, "was to push the world along by means of regenerative *intervention*."[59]

In both modes, the central, indeed the singular, referent is American. The self-aggrandizement of the truly powerful, the fact of U.S. power combined with the solipsism of the majority of America's inhabitants, has shaped the history of the past fifty years and more. Efforts to internationalize America's history, to diversify and multiply its culture, need to keep in mind the reality of American hegemony and its dominant, self-absorbed culture. Of course, that hegemony is continuously challenged, both at home and abroad; of course, the United States is not exceptional, only exceptionally powerful. Decentering America in one's head is a good thing. But it does not of itself create a world free of its overwhelming military and economic power, and it is crucial to remember the difference or the effort to decenter American history will run the danger of obscuring what it means to illuminate.

NOTES

1. Daniel T. Rogers, "Exceptionalism," in *Imagined Histories: American Historians Interpret the Past*, ed. Anthony Molho and Gordon S. Wood (Princeton, N.J.: Princeton University Press, 1998), 21.
2. Quoted in the obituary of Dean Acheson, *Time Magazine*, October 25, 1971, 20. I am grateful to Lloyd Gardner for the reference.
3. Tim Weiner, *New York Times*, October 30, 1994, 10.
4. John Lewis Gaddis, *We Now Know: Rethinking Cold War History* (New York: Clarendon Press, 1997), 186.
5. H. W. Brands, *The Devil We Knew: Americans and the Cold War* (New York: Oxford University Press, 1993), 225, 228; Loren Baritz, *Backfire: A History of How American Culture Led Us into Vietnam and Made Us Fight the Way We Did* (New York: William Morrow & Co., 1985), 341.
6. Bruce Cumings, *The Origins of the Korean War*, vol. 2, *The Roaring of the Cataract, 1947–1959* (Princeton, N.J.: Princeton University Press, 1990), 628.
7. Quoted in Lloyd Gardner, "Do We Learn from History?" (unpublished manuscript), 7.
8. Quoted in Noam Chomsky, "Crisis in the Balkans," *Z Magazine*, May 1999, 43.
9. Quoted in Lloyd Gardner, "From the American Archives," *Diplomatic History* 22, no. 2 (Spring 1998): 335.
10. Kissinger quoted in Thomas J. McCormick, *America's Half-Century: United States Foreign Policy in the Cold War* (Baltimore: Johns Hopkins University Press, 1989), 186; McCloy quoted in Gabriel Kalka, *The Politics of War: The World and U.S. Foreign Policy, 1943–1945* (New York: Pantheon, 1968), 470–71; Acheson quoted in William Appleman Williams, *America Confronts a Revolutionary World, 1776–1976* (New York: Morrow, 1976), 171–72; Kissinger is quoted in John Prados, *Presidents' Secret Wars: CIA and Pentagon Covert Operations since World War II* (New York: Ivan R. Dee, 1986), 317.
11. Gaddis, *We Now Know*, 39, 289, acknowledges that this beneficent empire held sway primarily in Europe and Japan. About Latin America, the Middle East, and Southeast Asia, he is more circumspect, even agnostic. In these areas, invitations were periodically extended and withdrawn to both the United States and its imperial rival the Soviet Union. "Whether the Russians or the Americans responded more brutally—or more humanely—it is difficult to say: as always the 'third world' defies easy generalizations." Gaddis, *We Now Know*, 286.
12. See Melvyn Leffler, "The Cold War: What Do 'We Now Know'?" *American Historical Review* 104, no. 2 (April 1999): 501–24.
13. Gaddis, *We Now Know*, 178.
14. Gaddis, *We Now Know*, 178.
15. Walter LaFeber, "The Tension between Democracy and Capitalism during the American Century," *Diplomatic History* 23, no. 2 (Spring 1999): 284.
16. Arthur M. Schlesinger Jr., *A Thousand Days: John F. Kennedy in the White House* (Boston: Mariner Books, 1965), 774, 778. The British, still the colonial power at the time, urged Kennedy to support Jagan, declaring that his rival

Forbes Burnham, was an "opportunist, racist and demagogue intent only on personal power." But Kennedy had been deeply disturbed after a conversation in which Jagan expressed admiration for Paul Sweezy and the *Monthly Review*. "I have the feeling," Kennedy told Schlesinger, "that in a couple of years he will find ways to suspend constitutional provisions and will cut his opposition off at the knees." To avert this disaster, Kennedy leaned on the British to suspend the constitution and delay independence until Jagan was safely out of the way (778, 776, 777).

17. Louis A. Perez Jr., *The War of 1898: The United States and Cuba in History and Historiography* (Chapel Hill: University of North Carolina Press, 1998), 109. See esp. ch. 4.

18. Amy Kaplan, "Black and Blue on San Juan Hill," in *Cultures of United States Imperialism*, ed. Amy Kaplan and Donald E. Pease (Durham, N.C.: Duke University Press Books, 1993), 219.

19. Gail Bederman, *Manliness and Civilization: A Cultural History of Gender and Race in the United States, 1880–1917* (Chicago: University of Chicago Press, 1995), chap. 5, passim.

20. Anders Stephanson, *Manifest Destiny: American Expansion and the Empire of Right* (New York: Hill and Wang, 1995), 90.

21. Ada Ferrer, *Insurgent Cuba: Race, Nation, and Revolution, 1868–1898* (Chapel Hill: University of North Carolina Press, 1999), Introduction.

22. Louis A. Perez Jr., "Incurring a Debt of Gratitude: 1898 and the Moral Sources of United States Hegemony in Cuba," *American Historical Review* 104, no. 2 (April 1999): 398.

23. Michael J. Hunt, "East Asia in Henry Luce's 'American Century,'" *Diplomatic History* 23, no. 2 (Spring 1999): 324.

24. Stuart Creighton Miller, *"Benevolent" Assimilation: The American Conquest of the Philippines, 1899–1903* (New Haven, Conn.: Yale University Press, 1982), 219, 220, 222; "The American Soldier and the Conquest of the Philippines," in *Reappraising an Empire: New Perspectives on Philippine-American History*, ed. Peter W. Stanley (Cambridge, Mass.: Harvard University Asia Center, 1984), 20. The Filipinos would not be the last insurgents to find themselves redefined as American Indians. Soldiers in both the Korean and the Vietnam wars referred to the country outside their bases as Indian country. In one much-praised Korean War novel, Thomas Anderson's *Your Own Beloved Sons . . .* (New York: Random House, 1956), for example, a sergeant standing guard invokes older, equally heroic moments: he has the feeling of "being watched by *something* out in front of his position. . . . Perhaps, a hundred years before, another man much like him had stood thus, watching the night over the American continent while behind his back, in the center of the circle of closely parked wagons, his woman and children, and the women and children of other men, slept together on the ground thus encircled and captured from the unknown." Anderson, *Your Own Beloved Sons*, 8.

25. Miller, *"Benevolent" Assimilation*, 246.

26. Miller, *"Benevolent" Assimilation*, 247.

27. Miller, *"Benevolent" Assimilation*, 235.

28. Miller, *"Benevolent" Assimilation*, 254.

29. Miller, "American Soldier and the Conquest of the Philippines," 19.

30. But in 1971 a veteran of the Samar campaign felt moved to tell the press that the massacre at My Lai was hardly unique: his own mission had involved a fishing village. "We snuck through the grass as high as a man's head until both platoons had flanked them. We opened fire and killed all but one. They were unarmed." Quoted in Miller, *"Benevolent" Assimilation*, 267. For views of veterans on Vietnam, see 272–73.

31. Miller, *"Benevolent" Assimilation*, 269.

32. Quoted in Marilyn B. Young, *The Rhetoric of Empire: American China Policy 1895–1901* (Cambridge, Mass.: Harvard University Press, 1968), 270.

33. Quoted, in Miller, *"Benevolent" Assimilation*, 275–76.

34. John Dos Passos, *1919* (New York: Mariner Books, 1969), 466–67.

35. Richard Poirier, *Norman Mailer* (New York: Viking Adult, 1972), 27.

36. Paul Fussell, *The Great War and Modern Memory* (New York: Oxford University Press, 1977), 221, 320; Norman Mailer, *The Naked and the Dead* (New York: Rinehart & Company, 1948).

37. James Tobin, *Ernie Pyle's War: America's Eyewitness to World War II* (New York: Free Press, 1997), 143.

38. John Steinbeck, *Once There Was a War* (New York: Penguin Books Ltd., 1958), xi, xii, xiii, xvii.

39. *Ernie's War: The Best of Ernie Pyle's World War II Dispatches*, ed. David Nichols (New York: Random House, 1986), 166, 167.

40. *Ernie's War*, 419.

41. See Paul Fussell, *Wartime: Understanding and Behavior in the Second World War* (New York: Oxford University Press, 1989); and Gerald Linderman, *The World within War: America's Combat Experience in World War II* (New York: Harvard University Press, 1997).

42. Tom Engelhardt, *The End of Victory Culture: Cold War America and the Disillusioning of a Generation* (New York: University of Massachusetts Press, 1995).

43. Walter Sullivan, reporting for the *New York Times* from December 1949 to April 1950, was an exception. His predecessor, Richard Johnston, arrived in Korea on board the ship carrying Lt. Gen. John Hodge, and he shared Hodge's perspective and identified with Hodge's mission.

44. Arne Axelsson attributes this attitude to public distaste for limited war: "The widespread disenchantment with the strategy used in Korea was expressed as a refusal to consider this war relevant to America and Americans." Arne Axelsson, *Restrained Response: American Novels of the Cold War and Korea, 1945–1962* (Westport, Conn.: Greenwood Press, 1990), 62.

45. See, e.g., John Osborne, "The Ugly War," *Time*, August 21, 1950, 20–22.

46. *Congressional Record*, May 17, 1951, 5424.

47. Rosemary Foot, *The Wrong War: American Policy and the Dimensions of the Korean Conflict, 1950–1953* (Ithaca, N.Y.: Cornell University Press, 1985), 107.

48. James A. Michener, *The Bridges at Toko-Ri* (New York: Dial Press, 1953), 35.

Ridgway is quoted in Axelsson, *Restrained Response*, 62. This was also the theme of most of the forty novels Axelsson surveys.

49. Samuel J. Hynes Jr., *Soldier's Tale: Bearing Witness to Modern War* (New York: Penguin Books, 1997), xiii.

50. W. D. Ehrhart, "Soldier-Poets of the Korean War," *War, Literature and the Arts* 9, no. 2 (Fall/Winter 1997): 8. Much of the publication on Korea, as well as two TV documentaries about it, are explicitly the product of the Vietnam war. Callum McDonald's book title is a succinct expression of this: *Korea: The War before Vietnam* (New York: Free Press, 1986).

51. Betty Friedan, *The Feminine Mystique* (New York: W. W. Norton & Company, 1963), 275.

52. William Styron, "The Long March," in *This Quiet Dust and Other Writings* (New York: Random House, 1993), 334.

53. Robert S. McNamara, *Argument without End* (New York: PublicAffairs, 1999), 6.

54. McNamara, *Argument without End*, 83–84.

55. McNamara, *Argument without End*, 82, 85, 87.

56. McNamara, *Argument without End*, 94.

57. McNamara, *Argument without End*, 379.

58. Quoted in Ward Just, "The American Blues," in *The Other Side of Heaven: Postwar Fiction by Vietnamese and American Writers*, ed. Wayne Karlin, Le Minh Khue, and Truong Vu (New York: Curbstone Press, 1995), 7.

59. Stephanson, *Manifest Destiny*, xii (emphasis in original).

2

HARD SELL: THE KOREAN WAR

An old antiwar poster asked, "What if they gave a war and nobody came?" To paraphrase that poster, what if they tried to sell a war and nobody bought? Judging by the past, the answer is that they'd have it anyhow. It's not that people won't support wars, even shoddy ones, as the experience of the United States in the years 1975–91 indicates, provided the wars are very short and there are few American casualties.[1] With enough time and rising casualty figures, people begin to ask more probing questions: Is this war really necessary? What have these deaths achieved?[2] The common assumption among many politicians, pundits, and historians is that if only the president could bring the people to understand the necessity of the war into which he has led them, the complaining would stop and everyone would support the government.

In the case of the war in Korea, Steven Casey has stressed the degree to which President Harry Truman was constrained in his marketing of that conflict, America's first post-1945 war. If Truman went too far, he risked inciting a public call for immediate preventive war against the Soviet Union or, later in the war, against China. Casey suggests that Truman's enforced moderation made it impossible for his administration to mobilize public opinion behind his policies.[3] The corollary would seem to be that, had Truman been free to mobilize opinion fully, the public might have supported the war, maybe even with enthusiasm. I have two possibly contrary propositions: first, that the lack of public enthusiasm for the Korean War may not have been due to poor presidential marketing,

First published in *Selling War in a Media Age: The Presidency and Public Opinion in the American Century*, ed. Kenneth Osgood and Andrew K. Frank (Gainesville: University Press of Florida, 2010), 113–39. Reprinted with permission of the University Press of Florida. This essay has been lightly edited to minimize overlap with other works in this volume.

but rather that people had serious doubts about the value of the war they were being asked to fight or, indeed, about the value of fighting any war at all. The second proposition is that while any administration would prefer public enthusiasm and understanding, wars can be prosecuted without either. Public acquiescence in the deaths suffered and inflicted in Korea represented an achievement for the government and one that would serve future administrations.

Others have explored the ways various presidents have marketed wars, both hot and cold, to an often reluctant public.[4] This essay takes up the other side of the marketing process and examines how the public responded to the selling of a war. Rather than focus on presidential salesmanship, it addresses issues of public acceptance and resistance, as reflected in the press, movies, literature, and opinion polls.[5] These sources reveal that the Korean War was a hard sell from the outset—even in the age of McCarthy, the public responded with ambivalence to "Mr. Truman's War" on the Korean peninsula.

A CONFUSING WAR

The Korean War was not only hard to sell during the three years in which it was fought; it has been a hard sell ever since. It is remembered as having been forgotten: a product that failed to move, a war that wasn't new and improved, a Ford Pinto of a war. Sometimes those who write powerfully and movingly about other wars simply refuse to discuss this one. Thus in his book *The Soldiers' Tale: Bearing Witness to Modern War*, Samuel Hynes wrote, "I have nothing to say about the war in Korea, a war that came and went without glory, and left no mark on American imaginations—though nearly as many Americans died there as in Vietnam."[6]

Over 2 million Americans served in Korea; 33,686 Americans and between 2 and 3 million Koreans died in it; 103,284 Americans and uncounted Koreans were wounded—all in the space of three years. The war was reported daily in the press and weekly in national newsmagazines. It produced stark photographs that filled the pages of *Life* and disturbing reflections on the nature of modern warfare by frontline correspondents who observed it close up.[7] It was televised, featured on the radio, and dramatized on movie screens within months of its beginning. Major fighting—such as the retreat south before the onslaught of Chinese troops in the winter of 1950—produced giant headlines. Young men everywhere had reason to fear being drafted. Still, the Korean War seemed to be swallowed up even as it unfolded. The real sales job the government did was this: it managed to wage an immensely bloody war with a conscript army as if the war weren't quite happening. Or rather, it fought with the sullen acquiescence of a public whose one recourse to change, given the prevailing political atmosphere, was electoral—a recourse the public took with alacrity in 1952.

Although in the first few months of the conflict in Korea, every poll indicated initial public support for Truman's intervention, there were many signs that the public was less than enthused and more than a little confused about the war. Members of Congress grumbled that it would never have been necessary if Truman had done right by Chiang Kai-shek, and when ground troops were ordered to the peninsula on June 30, some voices were raised about the constitutionality of it all. No one greeted news of the war with pleasure. Veterans of WWII were bitter about being recalled to the military after so brief a respite. William Styron, a reserve officer in the Marine Corps, recalled that for veterans like himself, "who had shed their uniforms only five years before—in the blissful notion that the unspeakable orgy of war was only a memory and safely behind—the experience of putting on that uniform again and facing anew the ritualistic death dance had an effect that can only be described as traumatic."[8] Styron was not alone. Hanson Baldwin, military analyst for the *New York Times*, reported on a growing "mutiny" among reserve air force officers who refused flight duty in Korea in protest against what they felt to be the disruption of their settled lives so soon after their demobilization.[9]

At first, the Korean War fit more or less comfortably into a WWII template. Even the way the war began was reminiscent—or at least the way the beginning was reported. North Korean tanks did not drive or rumble but surged and swept across the thirty-eighth parallel to fall upon an unsuspecting South Korea in images that melded Nazi Blitzkrieg with Japanese perfidy in Pearl Harbor. To be sure, it was all happening in a country most people could neither visualize nor locate. But thick arrows moving relentlessly across clearly defined borders were familiar markers on the geography of the American imagination.

One difficult issue in the first month of war was how to name what was occurring. It could not be a war—no congressional declaration had been given or requested. Newspapers described what U.S. troops were doing as a "police action." But, Richard Rovere observed, "this describes their role, not the country's." Or, as a character in the 1951 film *Fixed Bayonets* put it, "If this is a police action, where are the cops?"[10]

Without a name to identify it, congressmen feared it would be impossible to tell when whatever it was ended. There was "no word or phrase in the vocabulary of foreign relations to describe our present role in Korea." But it could not be called a war. Second only to speedy mobilization to meet the Korean commitment was the necessity to "avoid giving the world, in particular the Soviet Union, the impression that we consider general war inevitable."[11] Whatever the Russians thought, according to a Gallup poll in late June, fully 57 percent of the public believed World War III had begun.[12]

There was considerable confusion, too, about who the enemy was.[13] The country was given to understand that the Russians were behind the North Korean move, which led some impatient people to demand a nuclear attack on Moscow. Others prepared for a long, drawn-out war of resistance. Buster Campbell, president of the Northwest Ski Association and ski coach at the University of Washington, announced the organization of five thousand skiers as "a potential mountain guerrilla force in case of invasion by an enemy." The unit was trained to guard mountain passes, hydroelectric projects, domestic water supplies, power lines, and communications as well as "to carry on guerrilla warfare." Campbell and his fellow veterans of the Tenth Mountain Division were determined, he told the *New York Times*, to have "something concrete to do in the event of war."[14]

There were a few public protests against the war, and they were put down by the police. In late July 1950, the New York Labor Conference for Peace sought permission to hold a peace rally in Union Square Park but were refused. The Supreme Court of the State of New York upheld the ban, declaring that a rally would seriously disrupt traffic. Judge Eugene L. Brisach thought that "the right of public assembly is a paramount one," but that the rally would "provoke incidents." On August 3, a crowd, estimated by the sponsors as fifteen thousand strong, gathered in defiance of the ban. They were met by one thousand police. The *Times* reported that the police "used restraint," but demonstrators who refused to disperse were "severely beaten," and mounted police "rode onto crowded sidewalks." In the end, fourteen people were arrested.[15]

The merchants, businessmen, lawyers, farmers, and housewives of Webster City, Iowa, did not organize peace rallies and were certainly not "Reds." They supported a negotiated peace, and thought there was no "real quarrel" between the United States and China, but that Russia had prompted Chinese intervention. Most had supported Truman's initial intervention, but by December 1950 the overwhelming majority thought it was a mistake. A spokesman for a group of farmers told the *U.S. News & World Report* that it was "foolish to fight little fires until Russia is ready to launch an all-out attack." They were not pacifist, however. If war was necessary, it should be decisive.[16]

The note consistently struck in newspaper interviews with random citizens echoed the voice of Webster, Iowa: a longing for peace, an assumption that peace was the normal state of things. That longing for peace occasionally was translated into a desire for the sort of war people had imagined WWII to have been: a total war to be followed, *this* time, by total peace. A letter to Truman from Mrs. Steve Evans of Forbus, Texas, expressed both views. She had five sons serving in the military, and at least three were in Korea. One son was missing, and she worried that he was a prisoner of war. Evans warned that if Truman used atomic weapons, there would be "a civil war here" in the United States, for "mothers and fathers won't sit back and let their sons be killed when it could have been prevented." The Bomb should be dropped on Russia, but not until after the boys were home. "Please help our boys first and dear God, send my darlings back to me," she implored, "and *give us peace once more.*" Mrs. Jane Culbertson of St. Louis, Missouri, whose husband was a prisoner of war, urged Truman to sign a cease-fire as soon as possible: "We, the little people, did not send our boys to Korea—it is time the men responsible bring them back."[17]

There were also protests from soldiers on active service. A young lieutenant accosted the reporter Marguerite Higgins: "As his lips trembled with exhaustion and anger, he said, 'Are you correspondents telling the people back home the truth? Are you telling them that out of one platoon of twenty men, we have three left? Are you telling them that we have nothing to fight with, and that it is an utterly useless war?'" The journalist Mike Royko remembers thinking, "What is this? I didn't know anyone who was in Korea who understood what the hell we were doing there. . . . We were over there fighting the Chinese, you know? Christ, I'd been raised to think the Chinese were among the world's most heroic people and our great friends. . . . I was still mad at the Japs."[18]

In the spring of 1951, a Marine Corps lieutenant, worried his letter might not reach the president, took the precaution of sending a copy to his local newspaper, the Fort Wayne *News-Sentinel*. Lieutenant Gale C. Buuck wanted the following questions answered: "How many YEARS are you going to let American manpower, materials, and money drain into this Korean sewer? How many more of my men must die on account of your stubborn refusal to pull out of Korea? . . . None of us know why we are here and none of *us* can understand why we stay. Never have American men fought in a more useless war. . . . Surely, someone back home ought to wake up Congress or somebody and get us out of here." Buuck's plea received a great deal of local publicity. The *News-Sentinel* ran the letter and endorsed its views in an editorial: "You have asked the same questions, Lieutenant, which we and many of our readers have been asking 'Shall we pull out of Korea?' If the Commander-in-Chief had been able to justify sending you to Korea in the first place, he might find answering this one much easier. But having no clearly defined purpose, Mr. Truman has no clearly defined answer." Of course, Truman had defined the purpose of the war: to repel aggression. The problem was that the war continued, requiring renewed and slightly different statements of purpose: to liberate the north; to give prisoners of war freedom of choice. By the spring of 1951, none were satisfied nor satisfying. The Chinese reproduced Buuck's letter as a propaganda leaflet, with a safe-conduct pass on the reverse side.[19]

Individual congressmen occasionally called for peace and were red-baited. Edwin Johnson, Democratic senator from Colorado, introduced a cease-fire resolution in the Senate in May 1951. His constituents supported him, but he was largely ignored by the press. The resolution received a single paragraph in the *New York Times* featuring *Pravda's* support for it. The right wing of the Republican Party attacked Johnson, but he insisted that all his resolution did was "turn Korea back to the Koreans. . . . If we wait for an unconditional surrender before we start developing peace terms, we better start preparing for a hundred years' war."[20]

As for Republican opposition to the war, it was incoherent, veering between impassioned calls for total withdrawal and a vast expansion of the war. The Republicans' awareness of deep public disaffection was apparent in the 1952 presidential campaign.[21] When putting Taft's name in nomination at the 1952 Republican Convention, Senator Everett Dirksen's address was a powerful, if opportunistic, call for peace, calling Korea "an undeclared, unconstitutional one-man war."[22]

AN AMBIVALENT WAR IN HOLLYWOOD

The film industry was ready from the first to help the government explain why it had to send the boys to Korea. The industry's reaction to the outbreak of war was a rush on the registration of possible titles. On June 28, the Title Registration Bureau of the Motion Picture Association announced it had received five titles hand delivered by various producers: *Korea, South Korea, Crisis in Korea, Formosa*, and, rather ominously, *Indochina. Film Daily* boasted of the film industry's instant response to the call to battle: "For the third time in a generation, the awesome shadow of Mars shot full across the American industry . . . and, as twice before . . . the industry fell into line and asked for its marching orders from the government."[23]

Francis S. Harmon, who had chaired the coordinating committee between Hollywood and various government agencies during WWII, returned to act as liaison.[24] Any request for military assistance in the making of a movie had to come before the Motion Picture Production Office. If, in the view of the Motion Picture Section of the relevant service, the script did not make a contribution to the "national Defense and the Public good," no cooperation would be forthcoming. Scripts were rewritten to gain the military's approval and the free hardware that went with it.[25]

The war in Korea was the unspoken background to educational films on preparing for atomic warfare and military service. In the tradition of Frank Capra's *Why We Fight*, the Movietone News Division of 20th Century Fox released a thirty-minute war promotional called *Why Korea?* which won the 1950 Academy Award in the best short documentary category.[26] In a brief review, *Variety* explained that it was designed to "clear up possible doubts as to the wisdom or necessity of sending troops to such a remote and seemingly unimportant area" and thought it would be "enlightening to those who have been in the dark as to 'Why Korea?'"[27] The first task of the documentary was to remove any lingering sense that the Soviet Union had played a major role in WWII, and it did so initially by listing the casualties in WWII, starting with the British and ending with the Norwegians, without mentioning the Soviet Union.

This was followed by a capsule history of the background to the Korean War in the form of a recitation of pre-WWII aggression and appeasement, including the Soviet attack on Finland. When the Soviet Union itself was attacked, "we thought the Russians had learned a lesson and we came to their aid." Reversing the military history of WWII, the narrator continues: "Without our help, the Russians would surely have lost." That established, the rest of the film lists Soviet violations, from free elections in Korea and Eastern Europe, to disorder in France ("Frenchmen fighting Frenchmen under directions from Moscow"), Italy, Colombia, Greece, China, Iran, Great Britain, and even New York, where communist leaders, who would have been liquidated in Russia, were given a fair and open trial. In a declaration of globalization avant la lettre, the film concludes: "There are no longer any geographic boundaries. Blood shed in Korea today is the same as if blood were shed in Rome, Paris, London, New York, Washington, Chicago, or San Francisco. . . . What we are defending is not geographic borders, but a way of life."[28] Nevertheless, the secretary of the Independent Theater Owners of Ohio asked the membership to delay showing *Why Korea?* until the government agreed to sponsor a second feature, *Why We Should Get out of Korea.*[29]

Film Daily and 20th Century Fox pledged themselves to the war effort (in the light of the House Un-American Activities Committee's ongoing attack on Hollywood, this was hardly surprising), yet the films actually produced during the war did not march to battle with any great clarity. On the whole, Hollywood preferred the certainties of the war recently and decisively won to a "police action," whose origins and ends were both uncertain. But WWII functioned, implicitly, to sanctify the new war. Reviewers spelled it out. In November 1950, *American Guerrilla in the Philippines*, starring Tyrone Power, opened in theaters across the country. "Now that Americans are again battling in another Far Eastern land," the *New York Times* reviewer observed, "where the nature of warfare is erratic in the face of a grim, deceptive foe, there is a fitful contemporary graphicness" about the film. The reviewer went on to characterize the similarities: "The many scenes . . . of tattered hordes of fleeing refugees, strung across strange and rugged landscapes; of marauding Oriental troops; of bearded, unkempt American fighters inhabiting alien hovels in alien lands and dauntlessly improvising devices and designs as they go—all have a timely appearance."[30] Movietone news showed scenes from the Korea battlefront, but as a main feature, the Korean films never performed well at the box office.[31]

Nevertheless, several movies about the war were produced while it was being fought. The first and only enduring film was made in October 1950 over the course of ten days of low-budget shooting on sound stages and, for the outdoor scenes, in Griffiths Park, Los Angeles.[32] *Steel Helmet* was directed by Samuel Fuller, a veteran of World War II and apparently as sick of war as he was certain the country would continue to fight them. On only one occasion is the reason for the war mentioned in the film and then in terms so abstract they would serve any country in any war at any time. "When your house is attacked," says a soldier who had been a conscientious objector during WWII, "you have got to defend it." The explanation can hardly be heard because it is spoken over the chatter of a machine gun. There was a larger problem: the audience first had to believe that America's house was located everywhere and anywhere in the world, or it would not be clear how the North Koreans could otherwise have attacked it.

Two other patriotic moments in the film were also problematic. A North Korean prisoner of war appeals to a black soldier on the basis of racial solidarity, pointing out that he can eat with whites only when there's a war on and must always ride in the back of the bus. The soldier staunchly replies that one hundred years ago his people weren't allowed on the bus, in fifty years he expected to get to the middle, and in another fifty all the way to the front. He is clearly willing to wait, but his answer leaves something to be desired as a defense of the values for which it is presumed the war is being fought. The Japanese-American soldier in the unit similarly rejects the prisoner's reminder of wartime internment. Internment had been wrong, but he was an American and America solved its own problems. A critical reviewer for the army's Motion Picture Section worried that "the Red PW" had the better arguments.[33]

The movie ends with a straggling line of soldiers walking slowly away from the camera as the words "there is no end to this story" scroll onto the screen. The implication that Korea might be only one of a potentially endless series of American wars made *Steel Helmet* an unlikely vehicle for national mobilization.

I Want You, released on Christmas Eve in 1951, was meant to overcome what the *New York Times* movie critic Bosley Crowther called the average American's resistance to "the necessity of facing up to another war and then finally standing still for it because that is the patriotic thing to do." *I Want You* opens with an aerial shot of an average American town, "the way it would look," the narrator intones, "to a bird or to a bomber pilot straightening out for his run over the target" or, he hastens to add, "to a low-flying angel." The narrative connects three stories of reluctance to serve: the first about a businessman, played by Dana Andrews, a married man with two children; the second about his younger brother; the third about the son of a worker in the business Andrews owns whose father seeks to have him exempted from the draft.[34] Andrews volunteers for Korea, less out of a sense of patriotism than of obligation. How otherwise will he be able to face his children in the future when they ask, "What were you doing, Daddy, when the world was shaking?" His wife, played by the ideal housewife and mother, Dorothy McGuire, puts his decision in domestic terms. In the words of Crowther's acerbic review, she explains that he is going so as "to defend his kiddies and his home." "All in all the running crisis of the cold war,'" Crowther concluded, "has been absorbed in the cotton padding of sentiment. A straight recruiting poster would be more convincing and pack more dramatic appeal."[35]

However, the movie wasn't as straightforward as a poster; in fact, it was radically ambivalent. A picture-perfect family dinner party explodes when Dorothy McGuire, not known for raising her voice, denounces her young brother-in-law's professed preference for a nuclear war that would settle everything once and for all without his having to serve. She despises him, she says, for his readiness to incinerate the world, but she despises him equally for his selfish desire to avoid the military. The political message is clear: preemptive nuclear war is as unacceptable as pacifism, and that leaves "limited war" the only alternative. What McGuire insists upon is not belief in the specific war in Korea but rather acquiescence in whatever war is on hand.

This message is briefly questioned by McGuire's hitherto meek and submissive mother-in-law, who, having lost one son to World War II, is desperate to keep her remaining two sons safe at home. Standing in her living room, surrounded by her husband's World War I trophies, she suddenly turns on him. She raises her arm and, with one violent sweep, cleanses the mantelpiece of military paraphernalia, pulls sabers and helmets and unit citations off the walls, declaring that she has always hated this room. Turning to her astonished husband, she reminds him that he had not been a hero after all but only a general's orderly, who had nevertheless raised his sons on war stories. "You were *proud* when our son died," she charges, and for a moment the obscenity of taking pride in such a death is evident.

Yet, in the end, the worker's son is drafted, then dies, and the younger boy goes to war, spurred by his girlfriend's admiration and, if not persuaded, at least not protesting his draft board's claim that he would be fighting for his freedom to choose where he worked and not to be afraid of a "knock at the door in the middle of the night." In the closing frames of the film, Dorothy McGuire turns her back to the camera and shepherds her two children into their large white house. The house, the children, the town, have all been made safe by war.

Even those who claimed to have liked the film, like the editor of the *Los Angeles Daily News*, praised it in language that revealed the fragility of its argument. The editorial acknowledged that, of course, "a poor little citizen's" instincts are to "seek a snug harbor for himself and his family" as a storm rages outside the door. His sense of duty may tell him that he has to help fight the storm, but his "intelligence tells him about the doubts that beset millions in the United States today." The greatness of *I Want You* lay in its demonstration that "the citizens must accept their responsibility for the war."[36] Thus it was obedience that the film championed, not intelligence.

A DIFFERENT SORT OF WAR

But blind obedience was a totalitarian demand. Americans, it was presumed, fought in the name of the reasoned morality of the cause. President Truman laid it out for reporters in an informal speech after lunch at the Muehlebach Hotel in Kansas City, Missouri. He called for a worldwide mobilization against the "menace" of the "inheritors of Genghis Khan and Tamerlane, who were the greatest murderers in the history of the world."[37] Yet in the early days of the war, there were warnings that murderousness was not confined to the other side. In August 1950, John Osborne wrote a long essay that ran in both *Life* and *Time*.[38] From the outset, Osborne confessed his distress at what he felt he had to report: "This is a story that no American should ever have to write," he began. "It is the ugly story of an ugly war." Before telling it, however, he gave the good news: U.S. troops were superb. They may have been raw when they arrived and even abandoned positions they should have held, but "in a land and among a people that most of them dislike, in a war that all too few of them understand and none of them want, they became strong men and good soldiers—fast." U.S. firepower and the ability to coordinate and use it had been "thrilling" to observe.

In Korea, these fine soldiers were having forced upon them "acts and attitudes of the utmost savagery." By this Osborne meant not the "inevitable savagery of combat in the field, but savagery in detail—the blotting out of villages where the enemy *may* be hiding; the shooting and shelling of refugees who *may* include [the enemy] or who *may* be screening an enemy march upon our positions." Even harder to witness was the "savagery by proxy, the savagery of [our ally]. . . . They murder to save themselves the trouble of escorting prisoners to the rear; they murder civilians simply to get them out of the way or to avoid the trouble of searching and cross-examining them. And they extort information . . . by means so brutal that they cannot be described."

Osborne was told that U.S. soldiers had seen North Korean soldiers change out of their uniforms into ordinary Korean peasant garb, and so, he suggested, their suspicion of refugees was not surprising: "Every time they see a column of peasants coming toward them they reach for their guns, and sometimes they use their guns."[39] He was present at a particularly tense moment when a call came through to the regimental command post that a column of three hundred to four hundred refugees was moving right into the lines of a company of U.S. soldiers. "Don't let them through," the major in command ordered the regimental commanders. And if they won't go back, a staff officer asked? Then fire over their heads, came the answer. And then? "Well, then, fire into them if you have to. *If you have to,* I said." "From the command post," Osborne wrote, "an urgent and remonstrating voice speaks over the wire into the hills. 'My God, John. It's gone too far when we are shooting at children.'" And then in response to the unheard voice from the outpost, the same officer said, "'Watch it, John, watch it! But don't take any chances.'"[40]

Osborne's point was that Korea was a different sort of war, one fought "amongst and to some extent by the population of the country." A purely military approach would not work; the problem had to be engaged at a political level. Otherwise, Osborne warned, the U.S. effort was doomed, and along with it, the American soldier, who had then to fight in ways Osborne could not bear to describe in too great detail.

Korea was not the first time the U.S. military had fought a war "amongst and to some extent by the population of the country." But few Americans remembered the suppression of insurgencies in the Philippines or Nicaragua. The image of war perfected and perpetuated by combat reporting in World War II had encouraged Americans to believe their wars were without ambiguity, against regular troops on the ground and clearly marked enemy territory from the air. Osborne did not name what he described as a guerrilla war, nor did he name his description of the appropriate response counterinsurgency. His effort in this article was to warn readers about the peculiar nature of this new, "savage" war.

On October 9, 1950, over the caption "U.S. Fighting Man: Winner— and Still Champ," a *Newsweek* cover photo showed an exhausted soldier, helmet askew, holding at gunpoint a Korean soldier, whose arms are raised high in the air. The American looks dazed; the Korean terrified. Inside was the story of the capture of Seoul, which had been, General Douglas MacArthur assured the world, "conducted in such a manner as to cause the least possible damage to civil installations." The *Newsweek* correspondent's gloss was laconic: "He could tell that to the Marines." The city had been 60 percent "burned, wrecked or damaged. . . . American artillery and flame-throwers turned concrete buildings into hollow shells and slums into ashes." The accompanying pictures were stark: a small child, seated amidst the ruins of some building, another group of children searching the wreckage, a group of "Red POWs cowering in a ditch," and two Korean women, naked from the waist up, arms clutching at their pants while somehow also attempting to cover their breasts. They are surrounded by heavily equipped American soldiers and one man, an officer or perhaps an interpreter, with a notebook. The caption called their expression "sullen" and identified them as "Red 'nurses'" who had been captured while "firing guns."

There were two letters of protest, both by women. Joan Aida Waterson, "College Student," felt some comment from the "'home front'" was called for. She had been distressed by the picture of the women, who should not perhaps, as nurses or as women, have been engaged in combat, but who nevertheless deserved more dignity than they were given. The second letter, from a nurse in Middleboro, Massachusetts, was harsher. "We as Americans criticize the way the Reds treat the American prisoners of war," Helen McDonald wrote. But the picture of the nurses "partially disrobed at the mercy of four 'men'" made McDonald "thoroughly ashamed of our forces in their treatment of POWs." "It's no wonder the Reds treat our soldiers, nurses, etc., the way they do," she went on, "when they see pictures like this." As a nurse, "I'm sure if I happened to be in their shoes I'd fire a gun to protect myself against such a predicament, too." Why, she asked, had they been made to strip? Because, the editors explained, "GIs have learned from bitter experience that North Koreans often conceal hand grenades in their clothing. Hence, all prisoners are stripped and searched."

Several readers wrote to denounce McDonald for her excessive concern for enemy captives, and in a later issue she clarified her position. *Newsweek* had edited the original letter without her permission. The full text made abundantly clear that her protest was against not the treatment of the nurses but the publication of the picture: "Won't you do your part in keeping such pictures out of your magazine," she asked the editors. "The UN and we Americans could emphasize the 'Golden Rule' just a little bit more by banning the publication of atrocity pictures. It only embitters the enemy and gives them ideas to do likewise."[41]

Stories of North Korean and Chinese atrocities against American troops were graphically reported, giving the reader a sense that the country was fighting an especially barbarous enemy. Yet a Manichean view of the war was difficult to sustain. In early July, a story detailing the treatment accorded suspected guerrillas caught behind South Korean lines led Telford Taylor, former chief counsel at Nuremberg, to warn against oversimplified judgments of the enemy: "We will make ourselves appear ridiculous and hypocritical if we condemn the conduct of the enemy, when at the same time troops allied with us are with impunity executing prisoners by means of rifle butts applied to backbones."[42] In late October 1950, Charles Grutzner reported on the state of things in Seoul following the recapture of the city by UN forces. Suspected political prisoners, including 1,200 women and 300 children, were being held in "severe conditions." About 200 had been found guilty at trials "in which they were not permitted to face their accusers." The warden of the prison confessed that he was unable to feed or properly care for such numbers; moreover, he believed "many prisoners, especially the women, are innocent of Communist charges." Despite the overflowing jail, large numbers of people continued to be arrested. "Among the less pleasant sights in this oriental metropolis," Grutzner wrote, "is a man with hands tied walking with a downcast head, while tied to the rope behind him is his wife, her hands also bound, and a baby in a cloth wrapping on her back."[43]

In November, Grutzner described in detail the killing of some of these prisoners, and in December the wholesale execution of political prisoners in Seoul by the Rhee government was widely reported. "The executions were not brought to public notice," the New York Times reported, "until United States and British units happened to move into an area bordering the execution ground. . . . [They] were horrified upon seeing truckloads of old men, women, youths, and several children lined up before open graves and shot down by South Korean military policemen with rifles and machine guns." Although American military authorities refrained from interfering, British soldiers did physically block further executions.[44] A generally supportive Time condemned the shootings as a disgrace to the South Korean government.[45] Finally bowing to the bad publicity, Rhee ordered a review of all death sentences, decreed that henceforth executions would be individual rather than en masse, and released all prisoners sentenced to less than ten years in jail. An outraged letter to the New York Times demanded to know why American forces had not prevented the executions from the start. "Why did we hesitate to interfere? Are we not in Korea against precisely this sort of lawlessness and violence? . . . As an American, as a veteran, as a teacher, and as a simple human being, I demand that we act in this matter. If moral survival means anything—and it should mean everything—our hands must be clean."[46]

The impossibility of keeping one's hands clean, which Osborne had warned about almost a year earlier, was occasionally made clear by front-line reporters. Buried in a New York Times story on the interference of ham radio operators in the shelling of Seoul in March 1951, George Barrett described what it was like to be on the receiving end of American firepower. He wrote of a napalm raid on a village of about two hundred people where the dead were left unburied "because there is nobody left" to do the job. He had come across a sole survivor, an old woman whom he found "dazedly hanging up some clothes in a blackened courtyard filled with the bodies of four members of her family." Elsewhere in the village, the dead had "kept the exact postures they had held when the napalm struck—a man about to get on his bicycle, fifty boys and girls playing in an orphanage, a housewife strangely unmarked, holding in her hand a page torn from a Sears-Roebuck catalogue crayoned at mail order number 3,811,294 for a $2.98 'bewitching bed jacket—coral.'"[47]

In a report published in April, Barrett warned that the immense firepower of U.S. forces was responsible for growing bitterness among Koreans of all political persuasions. UN forces withdrawing from Pyongyang had employed a scorched-earth policy, "leaving blackened paths of their own whenever they have been forced to withdraw along their sectors." No one questioned the need to deny military equipment to the enemy, but "many of the ruins created by the United Nations troops do little or nothing" to hamper the Chinese or North Koreans. Korean civilians fled with the UN forces "not so much to get away from the Communists but to get out of the path of the shelling and bombing." Then, without naming names, Barrett went on: "There seems to be a growing feeling that if a general policy of 'preserve Korea' wherever militarily possible could be laid down more emphatically, the troops in the field and the pilots in the planes would be more selective and careful in their choice of targets." Barrett understood that a soldier, sensing a sudden movement, could not be blamed "if the figure darting behind a distant barn turns out later to be a woman carrying her child." "But," he continued, without further comment, "there are cases of infantry-men resting for a short break, putting matches to a straw hut to get warm."[48]

When he returned from his two-year stint as a war reporter, Barrett reflected on the behavior of American troops in a lengthy essay for the *New York Times Magazine* that focused on Sgt. William A. "Ned" Nedzweckas, grabbed from easy duty in Hokkaido, Japan, to fight in Korea. The hardest phase of the war, Barrett reported, was the fight back up the peninsula to drive Chinese troops north of the thirty-eighth parallel. Guerrillas behind the lines were a constant threat, and one of the "nastiest jobs" Ned had to do was "to take it out on the civilians" as, Barrett at once added, "the Communists were also taking it out on the civilians." When a village was suspected of sheltering "Red bands," Ned's unit was ordered to go in "and burn down all the houses to check the guerrillas." Ned would enter shouting "Okay, Sayonara! Sayonara!" Then, as flames consumed their houses, the "startled cries of the villagers as they dashed out of the huts would fade quickly into staring silence as they huddled together, frightened, in a paddy field."[49]

Ned had few questions about *how* he had to fight. "To veterans of the last two World Wars, who experienced deep personal feelings against the Germans and Japanese," Barrett wrote, "there is an eerie character about the professional, calm, and almost disinterested way men in Korea kill and get killed. . . . There is one phrase the G.I. in Korea has taken as his own: 'That's the way the ball bounces.' It spells out the fatalistic acceptance that characterizes the combat man in Korea." The combat man did, however, wonder *why* he was fighting. "'What are we doing over here?' is about the only question that gives real concern to Ned," Barrett wrote, "and it's a question that none of the high-sounding declarations put out by generals and morale groups . . . has been able to answer for most G.I.s." Not that it mattered: "Understand it or not," Ned was "prepared to finish the job." In spite of his "confusion," Barrett wrote, "he vaguely senses, when nailed down on the subject, that Communist aggression in Korea is aggression everywhere."

Vagueness was acceptable. What the administration could not afford was a specific sense that the United States should not be in Korea at all, and it could generally count on senior news executives to cooperate. In August 1950, Edward R. Murrow sent a disheartening report from Tokyo. "This is a most difficult broadcast to do," he began, in a tone reminiscent of John Osborne's dispatch. After talking extensively with troops and officers, he concluded that a recent offensive he had witnessed was "meaningless," although it had cost "hundreds of lives and drained vital supplies." The battle had been fought solely because, as one officer put it, "We decided we needed a victory." He went on: when he walked through "dead valleys, through villages to which we have put the torch by retreating, what then of the people who live there? . . . Will our occupation of that flea-bitten land lessen, or increase, the attraction of Communism?"[50] CBS did not broadcast the program.

AN INVISIBLE WAR

By the fall of 1952, as the cease-fire talks dragged on and the war settled into a deadly routine, as public support sank to 37 percent, the war became invisible to everyone except to those who continued to fight it—forgotten before it had ended. Charles Cole, on leave from the Navy, found no Korean War news in his hometown newspaper: "Korea just didn't seem to exist."[51] David Hackworth returned from Korea in 1952 to a "country without a cause." It was "as if Korea, that distant battlefield, did not exist at all, or that Killed; Missing, or Wounded in Action were words reserved for someone else's son. To date, more than 105,000 Someone Else's Sons."[52]

James Michener complained in a series of articles for the *Saturday Evening Post* that the men fighting the war had become "forgotten heroes."[53] Reflecting on his service as a public information officer during 1951, Lee Judge described his frustration "over a war the world seemed to have forgotten."[54] A week in which there had been 2,200 American casualties was reported by *US. News & World Report* under the headline "Korea: The 'Forgotten' War." Ground battles, the journal reminded its readers, were as intense as in any previous war; air battles had grown to WWII size; casualties had doubled. Yet the headlines were dominated by news of domestic shortages of beef and new cars, strikes, and government scandal. Korea was "half forgotten," receding in the public mind "to the status of an experimental war, one being fought back and forth for the purpose of testing men, weapons, materials, and methods, on a continuing basis." While men died at an ever-increasing rate, "the war [is] almost forgotten at home, with no end in sight."[55]

Max Ascoli, editor of *Reporter* magazine, observed in sorrow and anger that there has "never been a great fuss made about those who have fought and who still are ready to fight in Korea. Few entertainers have volunteered to go to the dismal peninsula. Blood donations have lagged pitiably." Korea, Ascoli wrote, was a "peripheral suburban war," which had lost its "news value" because of "repetitiousness."[56]

The people Samuel Lubell interviewed, as he traveled the country in the months before the 1952 presidential election, were entirely focused on the war; people cursed at the very mention of Truman's name. There was widespread agreement that the war had staved off a recession or worse, but the Democratic Party's campaign slogan, "You never had it better," left people feeling guilty. In Weatherford, Texas, an Adlai Stevenson supporter observed to a neighbor that if the Republicans won, they'd all be "selling apples again," to which his friend replied: "Maybe so, but at least it won't be a bloody apple." Voters in Iowa, Detroit, and Los Angeles used the term "blood money" to describe the current economic good times.

Public reaction to Korea, Lubell wrote, punctured the myth that "'the people only have to be told the facts to do what is expected of them.' The expression 'We don't know what the War is all about' was voiced most frequently by persons with sons or husbands in Korea. Clearly they did not lack information; but emotion had stopped their ears to all explanations of why we were fighting in Korea."[57]

Lubell predicted that the era of limited war was over; the 1952 election amounted to a public repudiation of such policies. "The same dread that the American people might not support a prolonged attrition," he wrote in 1956, "which would prompt our politicians to try to avoid involvement could be expected to spur them to get any war over with quickly once we're engaged."[58] His prediction held for barely five years.

The war did not so much end as stop. "It has been a strange war," an editorial in the *Wall Street Journal* observed. "It came with sudden stealth in an unsuspected place. Now it seems to end in a whimper. In the strange quiet that follows the silenced guns, none of us feel great transport; we have too often been brought to hope only to meet disillusion. Rather, we feel a numbness. Tomorrow we may have to pick up our arms again—if not in Korea, then elsewhere. But we know that even if this truce vanishes tomorrow, or if it should be followed by a greater trial, neither we nor our enemies can any longer doubt our resolution. That is the victory of the truce of Panmunjom."[59] *Life* was similarly low-key. "It was plain that the end of fighting in Korea . . . did not promise either surcease from anxiety or lasting peace. . . . Since there was no real victory, there was no occasion for celebration."[60]

Throughout the war, the Truman administration had labored against the immense reluctance of the country to go to war again, especially for reasons they found less than compelling. Equally, throughout the war, it could count on acquiescence, however sullen. William Styron, who had been called up in the summer of 1950, two years later published a novella based on his experience that captured the public mood. The narrator, Lieutenant Culver, speaks for all those men actually mobilized for Korea and symbolically for the nation as a whole: "It had all come much too soon and Culver had felt weirdly as if he had fallen asleep in some barracks in 1945 and had awakened in a half-dozen years or so to find that the intervening freedom, growth, and serenity had been only a glorious if somewhat prolonged dream. A flood of protest had welled up in him, for he had put the idea of war out of his mind entirely, and the brief years since Okinawa had been the richest of his life." But the protest only wells up—it has no issue.[61]

A passive public did not notice other aspects of this first of the limited wars. During World War II, American dead and wounded came to almost one million men, a significant number even when compared with countries that suffered greater losses. In Korea, the disparity of casualties between the United States and Korea was so enormous one might have expected considerable commentary.[62] Instead, the numbers seem to have been taken as more or less ordinary: 2–3 million Koreans to 33,000+ Americans. (Later, 3–4 million Vietnamese to 58,000+ Americans, 100,000 + Iraqis to 5 Americans; over 4,000 Americans—and counting as of September 2009— and to between 100,000 and 600,000 Iraqis—and counting.) Generally speaking, the press during the Korean War protected the public from a too concrete knowledge of what U.S. military power had wrought later. From the very beginning, bombing runs were described as precision targeting, and the targets identified were always military. There was acknowledgment that noncombatants did get hurt, but the issue was always cast in terms of intention. "The issue of intention," Sahr Conway-Lanz has written, "and not the question of whose weapons literally killed civilians or destroyed their homes, became the morally significant one for many Americans. If soldiers and officials did not intend the harm inflicted on noncombatants, Americans decided that their country's methods conformed to the humanitarian notions that undergirded the norm of noncombatant immunity."[63]

The war had been unpopular, although opinions varied on how to end it: as many, or more, Americans urged an all-out nuclear war against China or the Soviet Union as wanted a quick negotiated peace. In its aftermath, there was no investigation of how the war had been fought, but only of American prisoners of war who, by dying in unprecedented numbers, collaborating with the enemy, and choosing to remain among the communists, had failed to embrace the war sufficiently.[64] The main political expression of public dissatisfaction was the resounding defeat of the Democratic Party. Succeeding administrations would remember the political price and work to avoid it, but Korea seemed to hold few general lessons for the future.[65] The larger goals of U.S. foreign policy and its war-fighting practices remained largely unexamined. Perhaps for that reason, the country slipped easily, without undue protest, into another limited war in Asia, one which none of the presidents who fought it were ever able to sell for very long.

NOTES

1. I am thinking here of the homeopathic post-Vietnam wars: Operation Urgent Fury (Grenada), Operation Just Cause (Panama), Operation Uphold Democracy (Haiti), Operations Desert Shield and Desert Storm (Iraq), Operation Restore Hope (Somalia), Operation Deliberate Force (Bosnia), and Operation Allied Force (Kosovo). Of these, only Restore Hope, during which eighteen American soldiers were killed and their bodies mutilated, drew sustained public ire.

2. As George C. Marshall remarked after World War II, maybe a king could indulge in a long war, "but you cannot have such a protracted struggle in a democracy in the face of mounting casualties." Quoted in Mark A. Stoler, "Selling Different Kinds of War: Franklin D. Roosevelt and American Public Opinion during World War II," in *Selling War in a Media Age: The Presidency and Public Opinion in the American Century*, ed. Kenneth Osgood and Andrew K. Frank (Gainesville: University of Florida Press, 2010), 82. Stoler makes it clear that selling an *unlimited* war, even after Pearl Harbor, even by a master politician like FDR, was no easy matter.

3. See Steven Casey, "White House Publicity Operations during the Korean War, June 1950–June 1951," *Presidential Studies Quarterly* 35, no. 4 (2005): 691–717. Casey argues the case at meticulously documented length in *Selling the Korean War: Propaganda, Politics, and Public Opinion in the United States, 1950–1953* (New York: Oxford University Press, 2008).

4. Editors' note: When this essay was first published, Marilyn Young referred here to other essays in the volume in which "Hard Sell" was published: *Selling War in a Media Age: The Presidency and Public Opinion in the American Century*, ed. Kenneth Osgood and Andrew K. Frank (Gainesville: University of Florida Press, 2010).

5. The single best source on the literature, film, and memorialization of the Korean War is James R. Kerin Jr., "The Korean War and American Memory" (PhD diss., University of Pennsylvania, 1994). See also W. D. Ehrhart and Philip K. Jason, eds., *Retrieving Bones: Stories and Poems of the Korean War* (New Brunswick, N.J.: Rutgers University Press, 1999). Paul M. Edwards has compiled a useful bibliography that includes literature, *The Korean War: An Annotated Bibliography* (Westport, Conn: Greenwood Press, 1998). An excellent collection of essays on the subject is Philip West and Suh Ji-moon, eds., *Remembering the "Forgotten War": The Korean War through Literature and Art* (Armonk, N.Y.: M.E. Sharpe, 2001).

6. Samuel Hynes, *The Soldiers' Tale: Bearing Witness to Modern War* (New York: Allen Lane/Penguin Press, 1997), xiii. Editors' note: In the original version of this essay, Young briefly discusses W. D. Ehrhart, "Soldier-Poets of the Korean War," *War, Literature and the Arts* 9, no. 2 (1997): 8.

7. See Susan Moeller's book *Shooting War: Photography and the American Experience of Combat* (New York: Basic Books, 1989) for an interesting analysis of the changing nature of war photography from WWII through Vietnam.

See also David Donald Duncan's *This Is War! A PhotoNarrative in Three Parts* (New York: Harper, 1951) and Charles and Eugene Jones, *The Face of War* (New York: Prentice-Hall, 1951) for a taste of just how disturbing the photographs got. Note that Duncan and the Jones brothers published while the war was still being fought. Correspondents like John Osborne (*Time, Life*) and George Barrett (*New York Times*) wrote some especially vivid dispatches, and Horner Bigart (*New York Times*) became the bane of MacArthur's existence in the early months of the war, as he reported, in the most unadorned prose, the flight/ retreat of U.S. troops before the North Koreans' advance.

8. William Styron, *This Quiet Dust and Other Writings* (New York: Vintage Books, 1993), 334.

9. Hanson W. Baldwin, "A New Era in Air?" *New York Times*, May 1, 1952, 16. Part 1 of this two-part series was subtitled "'Mutiny' of Reservists Who Refuse to Fly Dramatizes a Menace to Aviation Power." Part 2 appeared the next day and was subtitled "Reasons for Decline of Interest in Flying Are Listed—Youth Is Seeking Security." Among the reasons for the decline, Baldwin listed the increasingly technological nature of flying, which reduced the glamour. On the other hand, he reported that the marines were also having trouble recruiting. The Korean War, he concluded, left younger people "cold." *New York Times*, May 2, 1952, 9.

10. About the difficulty of naming, see Richard Rovere, "Letter from Washington," *New Yorker*, August 5, 1950, 48. A Marine Corps marching song took the metaphor a step further: "We're Harry's police force on call / So put your pack back on / The next stop is Saigon." Quoted in Kerin, "The Korean War and American Memory," 54.

11. Rovere, "Letter from Washington," 48.

12. Paul G. Pierpaoli Jr., *Truman and Korea: The Political Culture of the Early Cold War* (Columbia: University of Missouri Press, 1999), 29.

13. "Say, Joe, what does a North Korean *look* like?" a carnival game operator in a *New Yorker* cartoon asked his friend as he set up the target for a game. *New Yorker*, July 15, 1950, 18.

14. "Skiers in Northwest United as Defense 'Guerrillas,'" *New York Times*, December 19, 1950, 20.

15. Russell Porter, "Red 'Peace' Rally Defies Court," *New York Times*, August 3, 1950, 1. Later that evening, five hundred demonstrators were dispersed when they tried to rally at Madison Square Park. Seven hundred policemen were on hand to monitor the behavior of "persons known to be Communist sympathizers" in the area of Times Square. The *Times* was gentler toward the newly organized American Women for Peace, seven hundred of whose members held a brief demonstration at the White House and then sent a delegation to lobby Congress and the State Department for peace in Korea. It reported the gathering in a straightforward manner, including the "shock" expressed by the acting president of American Women for Peace at a press conference in the face of "clever questions trying to prove us a Red delegation." Dr. Clementina J. Paolone described herself as an Italian American, "of Roman Catholic

upbringing, and one of the 'good loyal American women that shout for peace.'" But the newspaper offered its readers, without comment, Dr. Paolone's office address. The headline was "700 Women Besiege Capital for Peace; Largely from New York City," August 8, 1950, 19. In December, about one thousand women demonstrated at the UN. David Anderson, "Youthful 'Peace' Gathering Stages a Protest Sit Down at Lake Success," *New York Times*, December 1, 1950, 7. Note that the *Times* always put the word *peace* in quotation marks. On this occasion, 150 teenagers, led by Paul Robeson Jr., sat down in the morning, and twenty-one buses carrying one thousand members of American Women for Peace arrived that afternoon, packing the Economic and Social Council room.

16. "Man on the Street Says: 'Try for Peace, Arm for War,' Reported from Webster City, Iowa," *U.S. News & World Report*, December 15, 1950, 24–25. The National Opinion Research Center reported in February 1951 that 57 percent of those polled would be in favor of seating the People's Republic of China in the UN if that would bring peace in Korea. Hugh Garland Wood, "American Reaction to Limited War in Asia: Korea and Vietnam, 1950–1968" (PhD diss., University of Colorado, 1974), 141.

17. Quoted in D. M. Giangreco and Kathryn Moore, *Dear Harry: Truman's Mailroom, 1945–1953: 'The Truman Administration through Correspondence with "Everyday Americans"* (Mechanicsburg, PA: Stackpole Books, 1999), 323. Mrs. Evans signed herself "A mother with a heart full and her hands full also." Hers was among the few answered on this subject—a letter hoping she would be sustained by pride in her sons' service. See also the letter from Mrs. Culbertson, 346–47.

18. "The Good War," in Studs Terkel, *An Oral History of World War Two* (New York: Pantheon, 1984), 137.

19. "Bravo, Lieutenant," *NewsSentinel*, March 29, 1951, 6; Giangreco and Moore, *Dear Harry*, 349–50.

20. "For Halt in Korean War," *New York Times*, May 18, 1951, 3; May 21, 1951, 6; *Congressional Record*, May 15, June 17, 1951, 5424, 7192. A few congressmembers spoke for the resolution, including Senator John Butler, R-MD, Senator Warren Magnuson, D-WA, and Representative Thor C. Tollefson, D-WA. The Senate never acted on it. See Edwin Mantell, "Opposition to the Korean War: A Study in American Dissent" (PhD diss., New York University, 1973), 159.

21. Ronald J. Caridi, *The Korean War and American Politics: The Republican Party as a Case Study* (Philadelphia: University of Pennsylvania Press, 1968), 133.

22. Caridi, *The Korean War and American Politics*, 223.

23. David Detzer, *Thunder of the Captains: The Short Summer of 1950* (New York: Crowell, 1977), 153.

24. Thomas Doherty, *Projections of War: Hollywood, American Culture, and World War II* (New York: Columbia University Press, 1993), 276.

25. Although not always. Howard Hughes, director of the 1952 big budget *One Minute to Zero*, refused to remove a scene in which the hero, played by Robert Mitchum, orders his troops to fire point-blank at a mass of approaching refugees. The rest of the movie is dedicated to proving that he had no

choice (there were North Korean soldiers hiding among the civilians) and that communist atrocities were far worse. See Lawrence H. Suid, *Film and Propaganda in America: A Documentary History*, vol. 5 (Westport: Greenwood Press, 1993), microfiche, documents M-442 to M-450.

26. Jose Ferrer and Judy Holliday also won Oscars and, the following week, were reported by *Time* as near the top of the House Un-American Activities Committee's "Pink List," *Time*, April 16, 1951.

27. *Variety*, January 24, 1951, 6.

28. See Lary May, "Reluctant Crusaders: Korean War Films and the Lost Audience," in *Remembering the "Forgotten War": The Korean War through Literature and Art*, ed. Philip West and Suh Ji-moon (Armonk, N.Y.: M. E. Sharpe), 117. John Steelman, who was on Truman's White House staff, cooperated with Darryl F. Zanuck on the film.

29. Peter Gietschier, "Limited War and the Home Front: Ohio during the Korean War" (PhD diss., Ohio State University, 1977), 221.

30. Bosley Crowther review, *New York Times Film Reviews*, vol. for 1950, 2466.

31. May, "Reluctant Crusaders," 127. May has calculated that no Korean War film "reached the top five moneymaking productions during the 1950s. Instead, thirty-two failed to reach the top fifty grossing films in any year." The majority of anticommunist/Korean War films were financial failures. May's conclusion is that the "effort to create a cold war consensus and voluntary support for the war failed on all fronts."

32. Portions of these reflections on the movies have appeared in my essay "The Korean War: Ambivalence on the Silver Screen," in *The Korean War at Fifty: International Perspectives*, ed. Mark F. Wilkinson (Lexington, Va.: John A. Adams '71 Center for Military History and Strategic Analysis, Virginia Military Institute, 2004).

33. Suid, *Film and Propaganda*, vol. 5 (microfiches supplement). See documents M-436 to M-441.

34. Andrews was the star of the 1946 Oscar-winning movie *Best Years of Our Lives*. In a sense, *I Want You* was the sequel.

35. *New York Times Film Reviews*, vol. for 1951, 2574–75.

36. May, "Reluctant Crusaders," 121–22.

37. Paul P. Kennedy, "Truman Calls Reds Present-Day Heirs of Mongol Killers," *New York Times*, December 24, 1950, 1. "I have been trying to mobilize the moral force of the world," Truman went on. "Catholics, Protestants, Jews, the Eastern church, the Grand Lama of Tibet, the Indian Sanskrit code—I have been trying to organize all these people to the understanding that their welfare and the existence of decency and honor in the world depends on our working together instead of trying to cut each other's throats." Truman kept an office in the hotel, which was close to Independence.

38. John Osborne, "The Ugly War," *Time*, August 21, 1950, 20–22. Osborne was the senior correspondent in the Pacific for *Time* and *Life*.

39. Scenes of North Korean soldiers doing exactly that appeared in two Korean War films: *Steel Helmet* and *One Minute to Zero*. Both films also show, and

justify, American soldiers committing war crimes. In *Steel Helmet,* an unarmed prisoner of war is executed; in *One Minute to Zero,* the hero orders a heavy artillery barrage against a column of refugees.

40. See Charles J. Hanley, Martha Mendoza, and Sang-hun Choe, *The Bridge at No Gun Ri: A Hidden Nightmare from the Korean War* (New York: Henry Holt, 2001) and Sahr Conway-Lanz's *Collateral Damage: Americans, Noncombatant Immunity, and Atrocity after World War II* (New York: Routledge, 2006) for details on U.S. policy toward refugees.

41. *Newsweek* cover photo, October 9, 1950. Inside, the editors explain this somber black-and-white photograph: a "U.S. Marine orders captured North Koreans to keep their hands up—and, in effect, tells the rest of the world that America not only will fight future aggression but will also win." Perhaps to balance this one, the full-color cover of the October 23 issue is of a very different sort of soldier: one hand is clenched into a fist, the other holds aloft his rifle; his eyes smile; his mouth is wide open in a yell of defiance. "New Army: Bullets and Guts," the caption reads. Inside we learn what may be responsible for this particular soldier's excellent spirits: he isn't in Korea but rather on his way to Virginia for further training as an engineer. The letters about the nurses appear in the November 6 issue on pp. 4–6. The letters attacking McDonald appeared first on November 20, p. 24; more letters, including McDonald's self-defense, are in the December 4 issue, pp. 4–6.

42. Telford Taylor, et al., "Letter to the Editor: "Atrocities in Korea," *New York Times* (New York, N.Y.), July 16, 1950. Taylor acknowledged the difference between conventional and guerrilla warfare as well as the differences between the "traditions and practices of warfare in the Orient" and the West. "The laws of war and war crimes," he wrote, "are not weapons like bazookas and hand grenades to be used only against the enemy. The laws of war can be 'law' in the true sense only if they are of general application and applied to all sides."

43. Charles Grutzner, "Communist Suspects Jam Cells of War-Smashed Prison in Seoul," *New York Times,* October 28, 1950, 3.

44. Charles Grutzner, "27 Executed in Seoul Cemetery for Collaboration with Red Foe," *New York Times,* November 3, 1950, 0–1. The article began: "A Kiisang girl, the equivalent of Japanese geisha girl, died today with a love song on her lips." For the December reports, see "Seoul Executions Stir Westerners," *New York Times,* December 17, 1950, 6; "9,330 Tried in Seoul as Red Supporters," *New York Times,* December 18, 1950, 2; "British Troops Bar Executions," *New York Times,* December 19, 1950, 4.

45. "A Matter of Convenience," *Time,* December 25, 1950, 19. The title was in response to a comment by General Lee Ho, vice chief of Martial Law Head-quarters, reported by the *New York Times* in its December 17 account of the execution. The general observed that civilians sentenced to death were usually hanged in prison, "but we have found that shooting by firing squad is more convenient."

46. "Rhee Terms News of Killings Untrue; Denies Wholesale Execution," *New York Times,* December 19, 1950, 4; United Press, "Seoul Halts Execution of Political

Prisoners," *New York Times*, December 21, 1950, 5; Richard J. H. Johnston, "Seoul to Mitigate Prisoners' Terms," *New York Times*, December 22, 1950, 2; Marius Livingston, "Letter to Editor: Korean Executions Protested," *New York Times* (Princeton, N.J.), December 28, 1950, 22.

47. George Barrett, "Radio Hams in U.S. Discuss Girls, So Shelling of Seoul Is Held Up," *New York Times*, February 9, 1951, 1:3–3:2.

48. George Barrett, "UN Losing Favor by Korean Damage," *New York Times*, March 3, 1951, 2.

49. George Barrett, "'That's the Way the Ball Bounces,'" *New York Times*, November 23, 1951, 66–67. The quotes that follow are from this article.

50. Robert A. Rosenstone, *In Search of Light: The Broadcasts of Edward R. Murrow, 1938–1961*, ed. Edward R. Bliss (New York: Knopf 1967), 167–69. Bliss's headnote states that it "was not used because, in the judgment of CBS, it might hurt the war effort" (166).

51. Charles F. Cole, *Korea Remembered: Enough of a War; The USS* Ozbourn's *First Korean Tour, 1950–1951* (Las Cruces, N.M.: Yucca Tree Press, 1995), 212, 273.

52. David Hackworth and Julie Sherman, *About Face: The Odyssey of an American Warrior* (New York: Simon and Schuster, 1989), 211.

53. James Michener, "The Forgotten Heroes of Korea," *Saturday Evening Post*, May 1952, 19–21, 124–28.

54. Lee Judge, *Reporter Magazine*, June 14, 1952, 22.

55. "Korea: The Forgotten War," *U.S. News & World Report*, October 5, 1951, 21.

56. Max Ascoli, *Reporter*, January 22, 1951, l; June 24, 1952, 1. The polls in the spring of 1952 indicated immense impatience with the war. In the spring of 1952, Gallup showed 51 percent believed the war had been a mistake. But only 16 percent urged withdrawal, and 49 percent thought the United States should launch an all-out attack on China. See Wood, "American Reaction," 222, 154; and Benjamin C. Schwartz, *Casualties, Public Opinion, and U.S. Military Intervention: Implications for U.S. Regional Deterrence Strategies* (Santa Monica, Calif.: RAND, 1994).

57. Samuel Lubell, *Revolt of the Moderates* (New York: Harper and Bros., 1956), 41, 42, 265n5. He draws here on material first published in his report for the *Saturday Evening Post*, June 7, 1952: "Is America Going Isolationist Again?" 19–21, 48–54. What struck Lubell most forcibly was the uneven distribution of risk: the contrast between those who had relatives in the war or were themselves subject to the draft and those protected, largely by economic circumstances, from such dangers.

58. Lubell, *Revolt of the Moderates*, 45. It would take the Vietnam war to fulfill his prediction, the Gulf War to implement it, and Operation Iraqi Freedom to demonstrate that the American state has always found a way to sell a war.

59. "The Truce," *Wall Street Journal*, July 27, 1953, 6.

60. Quoted in Susan Moeller, *Shooting War: Photography and the American Experience of Combat* (New York: Basic Books, 1989), 321.

61. William Styron's novella *The Long March* appeared in the first issue of *discovery* [*sic*] magazine in 1952 and was then republished in a Modern American Library

edition in 1956. Page numbers refer to that edition (but note a more recent edition: *The Long March and In the Clap Shack* (New York: Vintage, 1993), 7. The one character who rebels does so in a form that is at once self-defeating and the fulfillment of what the marines have asked him to do.

62. It wasn't totally absent. See, e.g., Freda Kirchwey, "Liberation by Death," *Nation*, March 10, 1951, 215–16.

63. Conway-Lanz, *Collateral Damage*, 184.

64. On prisoners of war, see Raymond B. Lech, *Broken Soldiers* (Urbana: University of Illinois Press, 2000), Susan Carruthers, *Cold War Captives; Imprisonment, Escape, and Brainwashing* (Berkeley: University of California Press, 2009); Charles S. Young, "Name, Rank, and Serial Number: Korean War POWs and the Politics of Limited War" (PhD diss., Rutgers University, 2003); Ron Theodore Robin, *Making of the Cold War Enemy* (Princeton: N.J.: Princeton University Press, 2001).

65. There were many specific lessons: a new Uniform Military Code of Conduct was issued, designed to stiffen the spine of future prisoners of war, and everyone agreed that China should never be provoked into participating in a new war in Asia.

3

U.S. OPPOSITION TO WAR IN KOREA AND VIETNAM

By the numbers, Korea was a more unpopular war than Vietnam. If popularity ended wars, the Korean war should have been over before it began. "The data suggests," John E. Mueller concluded in an essay comparing popular support for the two wars, "that while *the opposition to the war in Vietnam may have been more vocal than that in Korea, it was not more extensive.*"[1] An opposition that is heard means that attention, on the part of the press, politicians, pundits, had to be paid. And once attention was paid, questions could be asked, questions that led to the unraveling of some, though hardly all, of the dominant ideology of the day. Senator William J. Fulbright had shepherded the Gulf of Tonkin resolution, authorizing the war in Vietnam, through the Senate just over a year earlier. By 1966, he was ready to hold public hearings on the war. The hearings, in turn, provided the antiwar movement with an abundance of information and an evident respectability.

The most obvious difference between opposition to the Korean and Vietnam wars lies here. The possibility that organized, vocal opposition to the Korean War would be heard had been stilled at least two years before it began. In 1946, those who supported a conciliatory approach to the Soviet Union were already being rendered marginal by the press and both political parties. I say *rendered* marginal, because it is difficult to know the degree to which their ideas were rejected by the American public at

Marilyn B. Young, "Hong Kong Workshop," n.d. (unpublished essay), box 1, hard copy HK/Korea Dissent folder, Marilyn Young Papers, Tamiment Library and Robert F. Wagner Labor Archive, Elmer Holmes Bobst Library, New York University. The editors are unable to precisely date this manuscript, but it appears to have been written in 2000 or shortly after. This essay has been lightly edited to minimize overlap with other works in this volume.

large. By 1948, the position had been wholly demonized. After Henry Wallace was forced to resign from Truman's cabinet in the fall of 1946 he launched a nation-wide speaking tour, preaching against what he called Truman's policy of "unlimited aid to anti-Soviet governments."[2] The State Department's Division of Public Studies tracked his trip in a confidential memorandum. In May 1947, Wallace had toured the Middle and Far West "speaking to large, enthusiastic crowds who paid as much as $3.60 to hear and see him." The press estimated total attendance at about one hundred thousand. "The size of the audience," the memo noted, "has amazed many commentators." Wallace's program defied the gathering Cold War consensus at every point. The Truman Doctrine might not lead directly to war, but "it will never lead to peace," and the "bipartisan bloc" that supported it was simply "undemocratic, one-party government." He urged large-scale loans to the Soviet Union, international control of atomic energy, a broad policy of disarmament, the "final liquidation of fascism, the settlement of the civil war in Greece and China according to the principles of the UN charter," a ten-year program of world economic reconstruction, funded by the United States but administered by the UN "for the sole purpose of raising standards of living and serving the general welfare of the world." He asked for "food for the starving, not guns for decadent governments." And if the Soviet Union refused to cooperate with the United States, then the administration must "give the people proof by honestly trying to meet with the Russians and talking over all of our problems." The memo noted that the press had paid "considerable—but not particularly sympathetic" attention to his tour.[3]

The elections of 1946, which gave the Republican Party a majority in both houses of Congress, galvanized anticommunist liberals into action. "In Europe," James Wechsler complained, "there was a growing 'third Force.'" But in the United States there was only a void between "a rising Republican reaction" and a "procommunist Left." Into the void stepped the Americans for Democratic Action (ADA), an expanded version of the anticommunist, antifascist Union for Democratic Action founded in 1941 by Reinhold Niebuhr. Its explicit goal was to oppose the recently established Progressive Citizens of America (PCA).[4]

In November 1947, Clark Clifford, confident Wallace would lead a third party in 1948, outlined electoral strategy and tactics to Truman in a forty-three-page memo, focusing attention on the importance of maintaining labor, minority, and liberal support for the Democratic Party. (The memo was actually written by John Rowe and sent to Truman by Clifford. Nevertheless, the messenger is generally given the credit.) Liberals, like businessmen on the Republican side, were "numerically small," but "far more influential than mere numbers entitle them to be." The "right," the memo argued, "may have the money," but the left "has always had the pen. If the 'intellectual' can be induced to back the President, he will do so in the press, on the radio, and in the movies. He is the artist of propaganda. He is the 'idea man' for the people." One way to detach liberals from any lingering affection they might have for Wallace was to firmly "identify him in the public mind with the Communists."[5] The perfect instrument to carry out the tactic was the ADA.

The Communist Party itself, which had never achieved legitimacy in the United States no matter how effective its participation in the trade union movement or even at high levels in the government bureaucracy, was thus well on its way to full expulsion from the body politic. "By the late 1940s," Ellen Schrecker notes, "almost anything a Communist did could be the pretext for a criminal prosecution. The specific crime was irrelevant; Communism in and of itself was, or many prosecutors believed, should have been against the law."[6]

The ADA proved an able instrument of Clifford's tactics. Despite considerable dissent within the ranks, the organization embraced the president and his foreign and domestic program. Though initially weaker than the PCA in both membership and funding, the ADA rode the twin horses of domestic and international anticommunism to organizational expansion and strength through its vigorous engagement in the 1948 campaign. According to one national board member, "there was an agreement very early in the campaign . . . that *the* job that the ADA would take on would be the fight against Henry Wallace."[7] In April 1948, the research department produced a thirty-four-page pamphlet, *Henry A. Wallace: The First Three Months*, charging that the Progressive Party was entirely a creature of international communism. To the pleasure of its authors, the pamphlet was widely cited in the press and Arthur Schlesinger Jr., a founding member of the ADA, was delighted. "This is a brief and official note," he wrote the organization's director of publicity, "to say that the Wallace effort seems to me excellent—a most valuable contribution to virtue and enlightenment, which I hope will provoke some redbaiting millionaires into action."[8]

George Gallup, reflecting on the most recent poll data indicating that 51 percent of the voters thought the Progressive Party was communist dominated, concluded that "politicians of both major parties have tried to pin the Communist tag on the followers of Henry A. Wallace since his party was launched six months ago. Apparently their efforts have succeeded."[9]

Wallace's ability to reach the public was increasingly limited. According to Curtis MacDougall, a participant and chronicler of the Progressive Party, a list of the cities in which Progressive Party leaders "found it difficult or impossible to find adequate meeting places would mean to virtually compile a Postal Guide."[10] Wallace was banned from speaking on a number of university and college campuses; when he did speak, he often faced hostile crowds, and when violence broke out, it was generally the Wallace supporters the police rounded up. Passing out a Wallace leaflet could get you charged with disorderly behavior; or your name, address, and place of employment published in the local paper along with a suggestion to the FBI to check you out; it could even serve as evidence against you in a child custody case. Senator Glenn Taylor, Wallace's running mate, was seriously beaten, jailed, and fined in Alabama when he tried to give a speech at the Southern Negro Youth Conference, and the Mayor of Charleston, South Carolina, defended the murderer of a Wallace supporter on the grounds that in addition to raising "unrest among the colored people in the South," the victim had been the chairman of the Wallace committee and one of the "despicable, slick, slimy Communists" troubling Charleston's civil peace.[11] And yet, the Progressive Party convention in July sold thirty-two thousand seats and filled Shibe Stadium in Philadelphia to capacity with supporters who had come to hear Wallace and Taylor accept the nomination.

Wallace's acceptance speech rehearsed the trajectory of the country since he had, four years earlier, put Roosevelt's name in nomination at the 1944 Democratic Convention. Four years, he proclaimed, of betrayal, disillusion, threats of war. "Instead of the promised years of harvest, the years of the locust are upon us. In Hyde Park they buried our president and in Washington they buried our dreams." As Truman entered the White House, he was accompanied by the "ghosts of the Great Depression, the banking house boys, and the oil-well diplomats." Boldly, given the propaganda victory Truman was reaping from the Soviet blockade of Berlin, Wallace insisted that the United States had divided Germany and that the Berlin crisis "did not happen. Berlin was caused. . . . I say the peace of the world is too fragile to be shuttled back and forth through a narrow air corridor in freighter planes."[12] No less than his opponents, Wallace placed the United States at the center of the world, the embodiment of all mankind's dreams as well as its nightmares: "The American dream is the dream of the prophets of old, the dream of each man living in peace under his own vine and fig tree; then all the nations of the world shall flow up to the mountains of the Lord and man shall learn war no more. We are the generation blessed above all generations, because to us is given for the first time in all history the power to make dreams come true."[13]

In the election of 1948, an alternative foreign policy, composed of an internationalism open to accommodation with the Soviet Union, dedicated to domestic social welfare, antiracist, and opposed to the remilitarization of Europe or Asia, was effectively crushed. Henry Wallace and the Progressive Party barely make an appearance in the general historiography of the period. The party no doubt earned its resounding electoral failure, but the consequence was the near total association of any dissent from Cold War foreign policy with international communism.

Lawrence Wittner, among others, has discussed the impact of the defeat of the Progressive Party. What I'd like to underline here is that while people felt free to express their dislike, even detestation, of the Korean War to newspapermen, in letters to President Harry S. Truman, in petitions (Truman received 850 peace petitions with 72,750 signatures between June and July 1952) to their representatives in Congress or UN Ambassador Warren Austin, any organized dissent was tainted by immediate association with communism. Mobilization, therefore, seems to have been out of the question. The way one antiwar rally was reported by the *New York Times* is typical. "Red 'Peace' Rally Defies Court; Routed by Police; 14 Held, 3 Hurt," read the headline on August 3, 1950. In late July 1950 the New York Labor Conference for Peace applied for and was refused permission to hold a peace rally in Union Square Park. The police ban was upheld by the State Supreme Court, which declared that a rally would "interrupt traffic, making control impossible, and seriously inconvenience many thousands of homegoers." Moreover, Judge Eugene L. Brisach observed, "This meeting is one which would provoke incidents. . . . The right of public assembly is a paramount one, but its application does not require the destruction of the balance of the public." On the day of the rally, a crowd, estimated by the sponsors as 15,000 strong, gathered in defiance of the ban, and 1,000 policemen were on hand to meet them. (The police counted 2,000 demonstrators and 8,000 "spectators and bystanders.") "On the whole," the *Times* reported, the police "used restraint," although demonstrators who refused to disperse were "severely beaten" and mounted police "rode onto crowded sidewalks." Fourteen people were arrested on various charges of assault, including calling a policeman a "Cossack," and "trying to bite a policeman." Their names and addresses were published in the paper. Later that evening, a group of 500 demonstrators were dispersed when they tried to rally at Madison Square Park and some 700 policemen were on hand to monitor the behavior of "persons known to be Communist sympathizers" in the area of Times Square.[14]

The *Times* was gentler with the newly organized American Women for Peace, seven hundred of whom held a brief demonstration at the White House and then sent a delegation to lobby Congress and the State Department for peace in Korea. It reported the gathering in a straightforward manner, including the "shock," expressed by the acting president of American Women for Peace at a press conference in the face of "clever questions trying to prove us a Red delegation." Dr. Clementina J. Palone described herself as an Italian-American, "of Roman Catholic upbringing, and one of the 'good loyal American women that shout for peace.'" Still, the *Times* also offered its readers, without comment, Dr. Paolone's office address and noted that she was an adjunct assistant in obstetrics at the New York Infirmary.[15]

Rallies against the Vietnam war also faced police harassment; demonstrators were beaten, arrested, and no doubt at least one of them tried to bite a policeman. But while hostile spectators might have yelled "Commie" at protesters and President Lyndon B. Johnson tried hard to link the antiwar movement to an international conspiracy, the charge had lost its power to frighten. Under Johnson and then more intensely under Nixon, anti–Vietnam war groups were subject to FBI surveillance, infiltration, and, in the case of African American groups in particular, literally murderous violence. But, unlike the FBI, incessant congressional investigations humiliated and silenced individuals and shut down organizations altogether.

Organized opposition to the Korean War suffered a serious blow when Henry Wallace split with the party he had founded and endorsed the war. Wallace's endorsement of the war was not unqualified:

I want to make it clear that when Russia, the United States, and the United Nations appeal to force, I am on the side of the United States and the United Nations. . . . I hold no brief for the past actions of either the United States or Russia but when my country is at war and the United Nations sanctions that war, I am on the side of my country and the United Nations. The United States will fight a losing battle in Asia as long as she stands behind feudal regimes based on exorbitant charges of land lords and money lords. Russia is using a mightier power than the atom bomb as long as she helps the people get out from under their ancient aggressors.[16]

Wallace's action was greeted with pleasure on the front page of the *Times*: "Wallace Supports Our Fight in Korea," and in an editorial noting that while "in some respects" his thinking might "still be confused," the editors were now certain Wallace was "what we always hoped he would remain, a loyal American at heart."[17]

Any organized effort to urge disengagement in Korea was read for its communist affiliation and treated accordingly. At the end of January 1951, for example, a member of Warren Austin's staff at the UN wrote a lengthy memorandum in which she tried to analyze the large volume of mail that had been received in the preceding year. "The first mail," Mary Politzer wrote, "generally expressed support of the United Nations action in Korea and seemed to be almost completely spontaneously written." After Chinese entry into the war, however, Politzer thought the mail was largely organized, and to that degree, she seemed not to take it seriously. The largest percentage of letter writers were members of "peace groups," whom Austin's office "presumed to be Communist-front organizations." These urged an immediate end to the war, negotiations, and admission of China into the UN. "It is unfortunate," Politzer went on, that "several well-intentioned individuals have lined up in support of those 'peace' campaigns, evidently unaware of their sponsorship." Moreover, the Methodist Church, the American Friends Service Committee, and the Women's International League for Peace and Freedom, "although obviously . . . not in any way affiliated with Communists," have "followed the same line."[18]

No one could make that charge against the merchants, businessmen, lawyers, farmers, and housewives of Webster City, Iowa, as described in the December 15, 1950, issue of *US News & World Report*. "Down at the grass roots," the anonymous reporter wrote, "what people want is peace, if they can get it." Many people "are quite willing to give up in Korea, permanently." Nor was there much objection to Chinese admission into the UN. "If we mean to shut out all representatives who don't agree with us," a group of farmers agreed, "there's no reason to have a world organization." Indeed, the people of Webster City were all for a negotiated peace, the sooner the better. They thought there was no "real quarrel" between the United States and China, that the Chinese had been "engineered" into the Korean War by the Russians and few wanted to drop atom bombs on anyone. And while most had supported Truman's initial intervention, the overwhelming majority now saw it as a mistake. They were not isolationists ("I can't conceive of the U.S. as operating on a purely national or Hemisphere basis. The world is not that simple any longer," a spokesman for a group of farmers told the reporter) nor pacifists ("It's foolish to fight little fires until Russia is ready to launch an all-out attack. We should classify areas. Where they are minor, as Korea is, let them go"), and they were all for increasing the pace of mobilization and arms production. The reporter's conclusion, much like that reached by Samuel Lubbell in his public opinion survey two years later, was that people wanted peace; if they couldn't get it, "they will accept war, preferably a decisive war."[19]

During the Vietnam war, those who called for getting all the way in or pulling out entirely were generally classified as prowar. I wasn't sure that was a correct interpretation then; I'm certain it is wrong-headed about the Korean War. The note that is consistently struck in all the interview material I read is of a longing for peace, an assumption that peace was a normative state, and, on occasion, that longing for peace was translated into a desire for the sort of war people had imagined WWII to have been: a total war to be followed by total peace. Sometimes both views were expressed simultaneously, as in a heavily underlined letter to Truman from Mrs. Steve Evans of Forbus, Texas. "I am pleading with you *not to drop the A Bomb*," she wrote.

> I have five sons in the service. Three are in Korea. And at the moment I don't know if the other two have been sent there or not. One is missing since July. . . . Deep down in my heart something tells me he is a prisoner in China. If you order the A Bomb dropped, that will cause a civil war here because mothers and fathers won't sit back and let their sons be

killed when it could have been prevented. Order the Chinese to give our prisoners up and tell them you will draw our troops out, and then let the A Bomb drop. But first it should be dropped on Russia.

Please help our boys first and dear God, send my darlings back to me. And *give us peace once more.*

More temperately, Mrs. Jane Culbertson, of St. Louis, Missouri, whose husband was a prisoner of war, urged Truman to sign a ceasefire as soon as possible: "We, the little people, did not send our boys to Korea—it is time the men responsible bring them back."[20]

The Fort Wayne *News-Sentinel* published marine lieutenant Gale C. Buuck's questions for Truman in the spring of 1951. He wanted to know, "How many more of my men must die on account of your stubborn refusal to pull out of Korea? . . . None of us know why we are here and none of us can understand why we stay." The Sentinel agreed with the lieutenant: "Having no clearly defined purpose, Mr. Truman has no clearly defined answer." The editors firmly opposed any renewed effort to carry the war into North Korea for a second time. "None of us wants to appease Russia, Lieutenant, but is the reckless provocation of war that could leave the world in chaos and without victory the answer?" Meanwhile, the Chinese, knowing a good thing when they saw it, reproduced Buuck's letter as a propaganda leaflet, with a safe-conduct pass on the reverse side.[21]

The only political expression available to people, however, was electoral. In 1952, as in 1964 (and even, I would argue, in 1968), the public voted for the party they thought would end the war. Individual congressmen occasionally called for peace, but there was nothing resembling the concerted congressional actions against the Vietnam war, however slow these may have been in coming. In May 1951, Edwin Johnson, Democratic senator from Colorado, introduced a cease-fire resolution in the Senate. After a serious of rhetorical "whereas's," which condemned the "hopeless conflict of attrition and indecisiveness, the immorality of "slaughtering additional millions of human beings" so as to force an "uneasy peace upon the vanquished," Johnson called for an immediate cease-fire, a return to the status quo ante, a full exchange of prisoners and the withdrawal of all non-Korean forces from the peninsula." A week after this speech, Johnson was interviewed on the popular radio program "Pro and Con." Most of the press, he pointed out had "shied away" from any discussion of his resolution, and some had accused him of being a "defeatist, an isolationist, an appeaser," but the response from his constituents had been overwhelmingly positive. The *New York Times* reported Johnson's resolution in a single paragraph; it reported the Soviet response far more prominently.[22] When asked if he were troubled that *Pravda* had praised his resolution, Johnson responded that it was "good news. There can be no peace in the world unless Russia agrees to it." Predictably, the Republican right attacked, with Senator Knowland leading the charge. But Johnson's speech represented an eloquent version of an increasingly popular position.[23]

Republican opposition to the war, on the other hand, was consistent only in its incoherence. Having greeted news of the administration's intervention in Korea with approbation, it took a while to gather grounds for partisan attack. Privately, Senator Robert A. Taft expressed concern that the United States was in danger of becoming an "imperialistic nation;" publicly he insisted the Korean War was entirely a consequence of Truman's failure to ensure victory for Chiang Kai-shek in China. As that had already occurred, it was unclear what to do now. Over the course of the next three years, Republicans veered between calls for total withdrawal and equally impassioned calls for policies that threatened a vast expansion of the war. The closest approach to a coherent policy was Herbert Hoover's call for the United States to transform America into a Gibraltar for the defense of Western civilization: "We can," Hoover declared in December 1950, "without any measure of doubt, with our own air and naval forces, hold the Atlantic and Pacific Oceans with one frontier on Britain (if she wishes to cooperate), and the other on Japan, Formosa and the Philippines."[24] But nothing in Hoover's speech indicated what to do, immediately, in Korea. Nevertheless, Republican understanding of the depth of public disaffection runs all through the 1952 presidential campaign. In another era, Senator Everett Dirksen's speech putting Taft's name in nomination at the 1952 Republican Convention would have been considered a moving call for peace: "Once it was deemed the primary duty of government to keep the nation at peace. In the last twenty years those in power have given us the biggest, costliest, bloodiest war in the history of Christendom. They have given us more. They have given us an undeclared, unconstitutional one-man war in Korea, now in its third year. As one Korean GI put it, 'We can't win, we can't lose, we can't quit.' He might have added, 'We can only die.'"[25]

The terms of organized African American opposition to the Korean War were constricted by the decision of the NAACP to support Truman's foreign policy in exchange for such gains in civil rights as the Democratic Party offered. In a July 1946 essay for *Life* magazine, Arthur Schlesinger Jr. had warned that the CPUSA was "sinking tentacles into the NAACP,"[26] but any danger this charge might have entailed was eliminated by the departure of W.E.B. Dubois from the organization, thus cleansing it of any communist taint. The Civil Rights Congress opposed the war from the outset, but its influence, compared to that of the NAACP, was slight. The black press, like the white press, grew more critical of the war the longer it continued, but letters to the editors sounded a different, more challenging note. A letter to the *Amsterdam News* early in the war condemned the all-black Twenty-Fourth Infantry Regiment, whose members "should be ashamed of themselves. Here America treats Negroes as dogs yet, at the first opportunity, they fight and die for their segregators."[27] A letter to the editor of the *California Eagle* in the late summer of 1950 suggested that if "the Negro people are going to fight, they should take up arms against the KKK rather than against the Korean people in order to bring jim-crow to that country." African American support for the war dissipated radically when the Twenty-Fourth Infantry Regiment was accused of "bugging out" in the early days of the war. The accusation was reinforced by a spate of arrests and convictions of black soldiers, including Lieutenant Leon A. Gilbert, one of the very few officers in the regiment. Gilbert, charged with "misbehavior in the face of the enemy," was sentenced to death, but a major campaign by the NAACP reduced his sentence to twenty years of hard labor. It should be noted that the *Times* report on the petition campaign for Gilbert—signed by six hundred thousand people—appeared on the last page of the paper, in a tiny, easy to miss, box.[28]

In January 1951, the attorney for the NAACP, Thurgood Marshall, initiated an investigation of the disproportionate number of courts martial among black troops. Although there were four times as many whites as blacks in the Twenty-Fifth Infantry Division, twice as many blacks had been charged and tried by all-white military juries. He uncovered a pattern of hasty trials, unproven charges, draconian sentences, and open racism. After weeks of interviewing, Marshall concluded that the "*high rate of casualties among officers made it necessary to blame someone. The Negro soldier was the convenient scapegoat.*" Nevertheless, Marshall noted, black troops had remained loyal, "turning a deaf ear to Communist propaganda."[29]

My argument has been that once we note the difference between the expression and the existence of opposition, opposition to the Korean War was as great as that to the Vietnam war. (A corollary to this argument, which I will not elaborate here, is that the wars themselves were more alike than most Vietnam antiwar protesters assumed.) But by 1947, as Lynn Hinds and Theodore Windt point out, anticommunism "had been rhetorically constructed into a universal political reality." Those who challenged any of its fundamental tenets were branded naive, idealistic, or, with the Korean War, subversive, possibly traitorous. Strategic or tactical criticism was possible, but only after the critics had paid "homage to the metaphysical structure and basic premises of the anticommunist reality."[30] Organized protest against the Korean War was all but impossible; in its place there was passive acceptance and such vengeance on the war party as elections could offer.

I want to turn very briefly to the Vietnam antiwar movement, which for some time now has become a footnote in essays, documentaries, novels, and films, which prefer to focus on that proper noun, the Sixties. In contrast to Johnson and Nixon, who recognized the power and broad base of the political movement that annually deposited tens of thousands of citizens on their doorstep, the latter-day media and popular historical treatment of the Sixties trivialize and depoliticize them, representing the decade largely in terms of styles of consumption. The war, insofar as it has any presence at all in these renderings, is reduced to a peace sign, preferably in multicolored ink on the lean, undulating belly of a topless young woman swaying to the music at an endless Woodstock festival. More generous critics, themselves often veterans of the era, suggest that the Sixties were best characterized by utopian politics that died of their own excesses: factionalism, romantic revolutionary violence, blind anti-Americanism. Their only legacy, the identity politics, individualism, and consumerist greed of the decades that followed.

The separation between political and cultural movements these analyses insist upon distorts the history of the period. The two movements overlapped in terms of personnel, practices, anticapitalist yearnings, and occasional tactics, and they were mutually reinforcing. Skepticism about constituted authority—medical, governmental, philosophic, historical, political, pedagogical—marked both the counterculture and such political groups as Students for a Democratic Society or, more broadly, the New Left.

But what was the source of the skepticism? The political and the cultural movements of the 1960s preceded the antiwar movement, and both continued after the war had ended. One of the most interesting interpretations of post-1945 American history is Tom Engelhardt's *The End of Victory Culture*. Engelhardt argues that in the great mobilizer of American national consciousness has been the war story—victorious, of course, and always just. In 1945 the United States had won the war (as Americans liked to put it to themselves), and yet over the next five years the world had become an ever less safe place: fear of domestic depression was widespread; young men were being recalled to service; and the news was full of reports of unprecedented military defeats in Korea, rapidly escalating casualties, savage tactics, and the unthinkable, but obsessively thought about, likelihood of nuclear world war.[31] The possibility of an alternative foreign or domestic policy had been decisively defeated in 1948. The collapse of the Progressive Party and the successful representation of its remnants as communist dupes meant that the language of protest was tainted. The mildest expression of doubt about the Korean War was subject to sharp criticism, even repression. Cultural repression went hand in hand with political repression, as the recent literature on the dreary history of 1950s gender, sexual, and familial constrictions, which paralleled and supported America's policy of containment abroad, has made abundantly clear.

Politically, the stalemate truce in Korea was not a satisfactory substitute for victory, and in its aftermath there remained a herd of scapegoats who could be blamed: the press, the cowardly and/or treasonous Democratic administration, the cowardly and/or treasonous behavior of American prisoners of war, the failure of a generation of soft, coddled young men, communist spies. There was a strong sense of an enemy within, not only Marx's mole, but more problematic forces born of America's very success. David Riesman, in his best-selling *The Lonely Crowd*, described the United States in 1950 as a society in a "phase of incipient decline" due to the eclipse of the sort of American who had made the country great, the nineteenth-century "inner-directed" individualist, and his replacement by conformist, peer-pleasing "other-directed" men.[32]

For students and young people in general, there was no political language in which to challenge the status quo directly. Movements for civil rights and against racial intolerance (as it was then called) were couched in the rhetoric of the Cold War and containment. The vision of the Founding Fathers, eternally renewed, endowed the country with an inalienable ability to correct its course and reform itself.

Yet, by 1957, Allen Ginsberg decried the fate of the best minds of his generation and suggested that something was fundamentally wrong with the country. The music, drugs, styles of consumption, anti-Protestant work ethic, contempt for capitalism and its values, and polymorphously perverse sexuality of the late 1950s received a media name (and temporal restriction): the Beat Generation. I think the Beats mark the beginning of the Sixties, and what they offered those who read their work, like the much larger audience who watched the more ambiguous products of Hollywood (James Dean in *Rebel without a Cause*, for example), was the language in which to question the world of Mamie and Ike and Lawrence Welk. At about the same time, the civil rights movement was beginning to introduce the country to a set of tactics and the images that went with them that raised connected but different questions. What was the nature of the federal government's commitment to universal suffrage? Would it use federal troops to enforce equal rights for all its citizens? Questions about contemporary racial arrangements led inevitably to historical ones and an uneasy recognition of the contradictory nature of the vision of slave-holding Founding Fathers.

Another strand in the rope from which the standard American national narrative would later be hung in effigy was the different responses of the government and of significant sectors of the population to the revolution in Cuba.[33] Castro addressing thousands of people at Soldier's Field in Cambridge, eating fried chicken in the Hotel Teresa, speaking the language of a noncommunist political, social, and cultural revolution, could not be dismissed persuasively as just another Soviet clone. In addition, there was the more sedate movement, also with international connections, to end nuclear testing, with its implicit suggestion that a foreign policy of global anticommunist containment was no longer self-evidently justifiable. In both the civil rights movement and the test ban movement, the efficacy of an older American tradition of protest, nonviolent civil disobedience, was rediscovered. The word "communist" might still be flung as an epithet, but its power to wound, to humiliate, to threaten one's job, was spent. Among the last people in America to believe in its incantatory power was Lyndon Johnson, who kept hoping that the FBI would uncover evidence connecting the antiwar protesters to purveyors of Moscow gold.

Perhaps the best, if most complicated, example of the way the social movements that preceded the Vietnam war fed those who would oppose it is the way in which the two came together. Some elements of the civil rights movement made the connection very early. Malcolm X, for example, denounced the war in December 1964, and before the year was out, he was joined by James Forman, executive secretary of the Student Non-Violent Coordinating Committee. In 1965 the McComb, Mississippi, branch of the Freedom Democratic Party explicitly called for draft resistance:

> No one has a right to ask us to risk our lives and kill other Colored People in . . . Vietnam so that the White American can get richer. We will be looked upon as traitors to the Colored People of the world if Negro people continue to fight and die without a cause. . . . We can write our sons and ask if they know what they are fighting for. If he answers Freedom, tell him that's what we are fighting for here in Mississippi.
> And if he says Democracy tell him the truth—we don't know anything about Communism, socialism, and all that, but we do know that Negroes have caught hell under this American democracy.[34]

Chicano draftees, like African Americans, with far fewer options than their white counterparts, nevertheless joined the ranks of resisters. Ernesto Vigil was the first, refusing to fight against his "brown brothers in Vietnam."[35] And by 1967, white America's favorite civil rights leader, Martin Luther King Jr. had not only endorsed draft resistance but had expressed an unexpected empathy for the "desperate, rejected and angry young men" who had set ghettoes from Watts to Washington, D.C., on fire: "As I have walked among [them] I have told them that Molotov cocktails and rifles would not solve their problems. But they asked—and rightly so—what about Vietnam? Their questions hit home, and I knew that I could never again raise my voice against the violence of the oppressed in the ghettos without having first spoken clearly to the greatest purveyor of violence in the world today—my own government."[36]

The movement against the war in Vietnam was the culmination of the powerful protests of the preceding decade, and for a time it swallowed them all. To those, like the members of the Weather Underground, for whom the war was only a symptom, the goal was to end the war, and presumably all future wars, by ending the capitalist system itself. For them, the move-ment's narrow focus was a source of disdain and anger. "Two, three, many Vietnams," Che Guevera had promised when he set off to bring the Cuban revolution to Bolivia. Well then, why not in America too? The victory cul-ture, Tom Engelhardt has written, lived on in those segments of the antiwar movement that celebrated Third World revolution and appropriated a vast array of familiar patriotic images, from counterparades (demonstrations), to counterflags (the bold red, blue, and yellow of the National Liberation Front), to a new set of Founding Fathers (Fidel Castro, Ho Chi Minh, Mao Zedong).[37] Equally familiar was the combination of rhetorical internation-alism and solipsism. The eyes of the antiwar movement—perforce but also by preference—were largely fixed on the United States. America, the exem-plary Christian nation, had become the home of the Anti-Christ.

But for the overwhelming majority of the antiwar movement it was enough to try to end the slaughter. In the event, Ho Chi Minh did win. His colleagues and heirs had defeated the world's preeminent military power. And the antiwar movement had succeeded as well, if not in ending then at least in limiting the destruction done to Indochina. It took over a decade to achieve this, but the legacies of the antiwar movement, like the legacies of the war itself, linger. Postwar administrations have labored to make their wars exceedingly brief, yet they seem still to look nervously over their shoulder.

NOTES

In the original manuscript, the majority of sources are fully cited, but a number of endnotes have informal notes only, and there were no citations for some quotations. When Young's sources were clear from the text and notes, the editors did their best to locate and cite to them. Some sources could not be identified. In those cases, Young's original informal notations appear in the notes. Editors' comments in the notes are identified by "Eds."

1. John E. Mueller, "Trends in Popular Support for the Wars in Korea and Vietnam," *American Political Science Review* 65 (June 1971): 358–75 (italics in original).
2. John C. Culver, *American Dreamer: The Life and Times of Henry A. Wallace* (New York: W.W. Norton, 2000), 443.
3. Eds: The source Marilyn Young relied on for this passage is unclear. Her informal cite is June 6, 1947; fiche 1975–136D. The State Department memo is discussed in Culver, *American Dreamer*, 445–46. Culver's citation is Depart-ment of State, internal memorandum, June 6, 1947, Harry S. Truman Library.

4. Steven M. Gillon, *Politics and Vision: The ADA and American Liberalism, 1947–1985* (New York: Oxford University Press, 1987), 15.

5. Allen Yarnell, *Democrats and Progressives: The 1948 Presidential Election as a Test of Postwar Liberalism* (Berkeley: University of California Press, 1974), 34.

6. Ellen Schrecker, *Many Are the Crimes: McCarthyism in America* (Princeton, N.J.: Princeton University Press, 1999), 120.

7. Gillon, *Politics and Vision*, 52.

8. Eds: The source Marilyn Young relied on for this passage is unclear. Her informal endnote cite is Weg, 1 8, 24. The memo is quoted and cited in Allen Yarnell, *Democrats and Progressives: the 1948 Presidential Election as a Test of Postwar Liberalism* (Berkeley: University of California Press, 1974), 99, 133n42. According to Yarnell, the original memo is in the Americans for Democratic Action Papers, Historical Society of Wisconsin. Young's source for the Arthur Schlesinger, Jr. quote is unclear.

9. Eds: Marilyn Young's informal citation for this passage is Walt, 231. The editors have been unable to confirm the full citation.

10. Curtis Daniel MacDougall, *Gideon's Army: The Decision and the Organization*, 2 vols. (New York: Marzani & Munsell, 1965), 2:202.

11. MacDougall, *Gideon's Army*, 2:407.

12. Culver, *American Dreamer*, 489.

13. Culver, *American Dreamer*, 490.

14. Russell Porter, "Red 'Peace' Rally Defies Court," *New York Times*, August 3, 1950, 1.

15. "700 Women Besiege Capital for Peace," *New York Times*, August 9, 1950, 19.

16. Culver, *American Dreamer*, 508.

17. James Haggerty, "Wallace Supports Our Fight in Korea," *New York Times*, July 16, 1950, 1; "The Return of Henry Wallace," *New York Times*, August 10, 1950, 22.

18. Eds: A citation did not appear in the original manuscript.

19. "Try for Peace, Arm for War," *US News & World Report*, December 15, 1950, 24–25.

20. Eds: Citations for these letters did not appear in the original manuscript. It is likely that Marilyn Young's sources come from archival research at the Harry S. Truman Presidential Library, which holds many letters like these. Evans's and Culbertson's letters also appear in D. M. Giangreco and Kathryn Moore, *Dear Harry—Truman's Mailroom, 1945–1953: The Truman Administration through Correspondence with Everyday Americans* (Mechanicsburg, Pa.: Stackpole Books, 1999), 323, 346–47.

21. Eds: A citation did not appear in the original manuscript. This correspondence is reproduced in Giangreco and Moore, *Dear Harry—Truman's Mailroom*, 349.

22. "For Halt in Korean War," *New York Times*, May 18, 1950, 3; "Russians Play Up Johnson Peace Bid," *New York Times*, May 21, 1950, 6.

23. Senator Edwin Johnson, "Cease Fire in Korea," *Congressional Record*, 82d Cong., 1st sess., June 27, 1951, vol. 97, pt. 5, p. 7192.

24. Ronald J. Caridi, *The Korean War and American Politics: The Republican Party as a Case Study* (Philadelphia: University of Pennsylvania Press, 1969), 133.

25. Caridi, *The Korean War and American Politics*, 223.

26. Arthur Schlesinger, Jr., "The U.S. Communist Party," *Life*, July 29, 1946, 88–90; David Levering Lewis, *W.E.B. DuBois, 1919–1963: The Fight for Equality in the American Century* (New York: Henry Holt & Co., 2000), 517.

27. The cite in Young's manuscript appears to be to Gerald Gill, "Dissent, Discontent and Disinterest: Afro-American Opposition to the United States Wars of the Twentieth Century" (PhD. diss, Howard University, 1985), 299–300.

28. "Pardon Petitions Pushed," *New York Times*, September 5, 1951, 29. The Civil Rights Congress, which had initiated the campaign to save Gilbert's life, gracefully withdrew when it became clear their support would hurt more than help him.

29. Thurgood Marshall, *Report on Korea: The Shameful Story of the Courts Martial of Negro GIs* (New York: NAACP, 1951; italics in original).

30. Lynn Boyd Hinds and Theodore Windt, *The Cold War as Rhetoric: The Beginnings, 1945–1950* (Westport, Conn.: Praeger, 1991), 250–51.

31. Tom Engelhardt, *The End of Victory Culture: Cold War America and the Disillusioning of a Generation* (New York: Basic Books, 1995).

32. David Riesman, with Nathan Glazer and Reuel Denney, *The Lonely Crowd: A Study of the Changing American Character* (New Haven, Conn.: Yale University Press, 1950).

33. See Van Gosse, *Where the Boys Are: Cuba, Cold War America, and the Making of the New Left* (London: Verso, 1993).

34. *Black Protest, History, Documents and Analysis, 1619–Present*, ed. Joanne Grant (New York: Fawcett World Library, 1969), 415–16.

35. Ramon Ruiz, "Another Defector from the Gringo World," *New Republic*, July 27, 1968, 11. See also early issues of the Chicano journal *La Raza*. See also George Mariscal, *Aztlan and Vietnam: Chicano and Chicana Experiences of the War* (Berkeley: University of California Press, 1999).

36. *I Have a Dream: Writings and Speeches That Changed the World*, ed. James Melvin (New York: HarperCollins, 1992), 135–52.

37. Engelhardt, *The End of Victory Culture*.

4

"THE SAME STRUGGLE FOR LIBERTY": KOREA AND VIETMAN

Sometimes Americans seem to know themselves by what they are not. During the Cold War, the United States was not the Soviet Union. It was not a nation of conformists, despite David Riesman's cries and alarums about "other-direction." Nor was it militaristic, despite its defense budget, foreign bases, and foreign wars. Freedom of speech and association were secure, despite loyalty oaths, blacklists, and congressional committees investigating subversion. Above all, unlike its Soviet enemy (or some of its retrograde European allies), the United States was not and, by definition, could not be an imperialist nation. The contradictions between U.S. policy and its essential self-understanding, however sharp, have seldom cut to the bone, although every now and then there are problems.

The French insistence that their war in Indochina was the same as the war in Korea, for example, was potentially troubling. What could the reimposition of French colonialism in Indochina have to do with the struggle for democracy against communist aggression on the Korean peninsula? The connection, French officials repeatedly explained as they sought an increase in U.S. aid, was the common enemy, Soviet imperialism. With the conclusion of the Elysée Agreements in 1949, Indochina had been granted all the independence it could reasonably want. In the words of General Jean-Marie Gabriel de Lattre de Tassigny, the fight now was against "red colonialism," and in this, surely, Washington and Paris

First published in *The First Vietnam War: Colonial Conflict and Cold War Crisis*, ed. Mark Atwood Lawrence and Frederik Logevall (Cambridge: Harvard University Press, 2007), 196–214.
Copyright © 2007 by the President and Fellows of Harvard College.

were united. Unless, as the French suspected, the United States wished to replace France in Southeast Asia altogether. For many in Washington, red colonialism could not effectively be fought so long as the French variety of colonialization continued to cooperate in heightening the appeal of communism. Neither side could afford to push the other too hard: France must be kept in the war, and the United States must continue to finance the French war without taking it over. This essay is a brief examination of what has been, until recently, a persistent American dilemma: how to acquire, manage, or subcontract an empire without naming it, or better, in the name of the right of self-determination for all people. If, as the French argued, the U.S. war in Korea was indeed the same as the French war in Indochina, was it because the French had abandoned imperialism or because the United States had embraced it?

"ONE FRONT" OR TWO?

Jacques Soustelle, secretary general of the Gaullist Rassemblement du peuple français and former minister of colonies, posed the issue bluntly in a long essay with the title "Indo-China and Korea: One Front," published in *Foreign Affairs* in the fall of 1950. "The glow from the Korean battlefields," Soustelle wrote, "lights up the whole Asiatic front from Manchuria to Malaya." Communist success in China, the insurgencies in Malaya and Indochina, and North Korea's invasion of the South were all expressions of "the expansion of Soviet power toward the sea, pushing its satellites ahead, and exploiting against the West the nationalism, even xenophobia, of the Asiatic masses." After extolling the benevolent record of France in Indochina ("no one, even the Indo-Chinese themselves, could have done for Indo-China what France has done"), Soustelle explained the military situation this way: "The Viet-Minh forces . . . are inferior in number to the French and Viet-Nam troops, but they benefit by the tactical advantages of guerrilla warfare in a tropical country full of dense vegetation and marshes." Since U.S. troops were also tied down in Asia "for an unforeseeable length of time," it seemed obvious to Soustelle that "the entire strategy of the West in Asia must be conceived as a whole and that it would be foolish to consider Korea and Indo-China separately." The United States must declare its "common purposes" with France, he urged, "publicly before world opinion, above all in a way that the Asiatic people themselves will hear and understand them."[1]

Soustelle's urgent desire that Asian nationalists see the French war in Indochina as a Franco-American endeavor was exactly what worried Washington. In addition to the issue of colonialism, the French seemed to be losing. Two U.S. survey missions were dispatched to Southeast Asia in June 1950 to assess the Indochina situation. The report of the first mission, led by Robert Allen Griffin, the former deputy chief of the economic aid mission to China, focused on the political problem, fearing "a repetition of the circumstances leading to the fall of China" if the French failed to satisfy Vietnamese demands for independence.[2] However, should the French throw themselves "passionately" into making Bao Dai's government work, China's fate might yet be avoided. The second mission, a joint state-defense effort led by John F. Melby and Major General Graves B. Erskine, concluded that only the "proper application of sufficient military force, plus goading the French into a more offensive spirit can hold the lid on the Indochinese kettle" and then only for a limited period of time. In the long run, the French would have to commit themselves to ultimate independence ("with a specified period of five, ten, twenty, or thirty years").[3] Recollecting in tranquility half a century later, George Allen, an intelligence analyst for the army, noted that the function of any survey mission was to "propose a solution no matter how intractable the problem." Usually, he observed, "such study groups seem to listen selectively, to minimize negative factors, and to find reasons for doing *something*, rather than proposing that *nothing* be done."[4] In this case, the something the survey missions urged was that the French fight fiercely for the total independence of Indochina. Of course, as Allen observed, "France lacked the resources and the determination to wage war in the Far East merely for the sake of containing communism; if there was to be no French Union, there need be no war in Indochina."[5] The conclusion, although evident to Allen, proved elusive to both the Truman and Eisenhower administrations.

In the fall of 1950, General Douglas MacArthur, basking in the prospect of a quick and total victory in Korea, reflected on the French in Indochina. He found their situation "puzzling." The French had twice the forces at their command that MacArthur had had at the outbreak of hostilities in Korea and faced about half the number of enemy troops he had faced. "I cannot understand why they do not clean it up. They should be able to do so in four months." Was the French army any good at all, MacArthur wondered: "If the French won't fight we are up against it because the defense of Europe hinges on them. . . . They have the flower of the French Army in Indo-China, and they are not fighting. If this is so, no matter what supplies we pour in they may be of no use." Admiral Arthur Radford ventured an explanation: "The French seem to have no popular backing from the local Indo-Chinese." But he did not dwell on this insight. Rather, he insisted: "We must stiffen the backbone of the French." President Truman was discouraged: "We have been working on the French in connection with Indo-China for years without success." Averell Harriman, in mild defense of French martial prowess, remembered hearing from officers who were there that the French had fought well in Italy. General Omar Bradley agreed but pointed out that those Frenchmen "were selected people who had escaped from France to continue the fight. We cannot judge the fighting of all French troops by them." This observation depressed Truman, who said it was "the most discouraging thing we face." Every effort had been made to persuade the French to do the decent thing, like the Dutch in Indonesia, but, asserted Truman, "the French have not been willing to listen." Should the French prime minister come to Washington, Truman swore, "he is going to hear some very plain talk. I am going to talk cold turkey to him. If you don't want him to hear that kind of talk, you had better keep him away from me."[6] Radford chimed in. He had seen some French ships in Hawaii and had the impression that "they were not anxious to go to Indo-China and were dragging their feet."[7]

In public session, MacArthur praised the French commander in chief, General M. M. Carpentier, as a military man "enjoying the highest reputation." Later, when Truman, MacArthur, Harriman, and Dean Rusk, then assistant secretary for Far Eastern affairs, met to continue the discussion, Carpentier expressed his doubts. Asked his opinion of the essence of the problem in Indochina, MacArthur said the French needed to "get an aggressive General" and that such a man could "clean up the Viet-minh forces with French Union troops now available in Indochina."[8]

It was with considerable relief, therefore, that Washington greeted the news of the appointment of General de Lattre as both high commissioner and commander in chief of French Union forces in Indochina in December 1950. De Lattre, a heavily decorated, multiply wounded veteran of World War I and the colonial war in Morocco in 1925, had escaped a Vichy prison to join de Gaulle's Free French forces in 1943.

From the moment his appointment was announced, de Lattre received excellent press coverage in the United States. A steady stream of upbeat articles reported a surge in French morale. Tillman Durdin, a reliable weathervane of official U.S. opinion, reported from Saigon that although "informed persons realize that the situation basically remains critical . . . both French and Vietnamese, nevertheless, have been infused with a new spirit and energy." De Lattre had banished "defeatism" and with his "Napoleonic jaw and Roman nose has stirred widespread enthusiasm by a rare combination of showmanship, charm, energy and forcefulness." He "swept" from one end of Vietnam to the other, by plane and by car, delivering speeches in a "husky voice that ranges from a whisper to a fortissimo," making "heart-stirring points," talking to the Vietnamese "of their independence, of the coming strength and greatness of their country, of France's determination to help in building a powerful Vietnam Army and of French sincerity in establishing the new Vietnamese state."

In effect, Durdin justified the French war to the American public by identifying it with the charismatic figure of de Lattre. His profile of the general in the Sunday *New York Times Magazine*, for example, credited de Lattre with having wrought a "miracle" and quoted his speeches with enthusiasm: "Within a week [de Lattre] had visited by air all the major cities of Indo-China and everywhere he declaimed: 'the days of looseness are over! We shall not yield another inch of territory.'" There were more details of de Lattre's physical appearance: his "quick smile," his war wounds, his "typically French" shoulder shrug, and the fact that, "like MacArthur," he preferred to be photographed with his hat on so as to conceal his thinning hair.[9]

In addition to his energy and his qualities as a tactician, de Lattre was the sort of Frenchman an American could admire. He wasn't much for reading, instead placing "prime emphasis on the human factor." Rather than deciding on the basis of reports or documents, he liked "to call in someone and talk things over."[10] According to a Reuters dispatch, de Lattre preferred orange juice to "choice French wines," served broiled chops and mashed potatoes for lunch, and although he came from a "long line of fighting men who served the French kings," his "tastes are strangely simple." His public demeanor verged on the "flamboyant," but he was democratic, as shown by a propensity to admonish anyone, from a sergeant major to a local priest, whose performance was not up to par. Nicknamed "D.D.T." after his initials, the general had expressed pleasure at the

implication that his arrival had signaled the "cleaning up" of the dangerously deteriorating French position in Vietnam. Finally, his "spectacular
'strong man' characteristics" appealed to the "Asian temperament"; he had
become a "rallying point for those bewildered by war and adversity."[11] In
late August 1951, a feature article in the *New York Times Magazine* carried
a picture of the general, staring in three-quarter profile into the distance,
a cigarette between his lips, his expression determined. Once more, de
Lattre's capacity to inspire his troops was described. He lectured the men
that Vietnam was their opportunity to redeem French defeat in 1940. "In
the army, and especially in the professional army," Michael James wrote,
"[guilt over the defeat] has taken on the aspect of a psychosis. Every little
victory against the Viet-minh is an answer to the world."[12] Neither James
nor Durdin said much about the issue that most concerned Hanson Baldwin, the military correspondent for the *Times.* Baldwin acknowledged de
Lattre's energy but doubted it was enough. "The French must yield more
in substance, rather than merely in form, to the Vietnamese Government
if the taint of 'colonialism' is to be avoided."[13]

Other close observers were less sanguine that an aggressive general
would do the trick, but they had difficulty making their voices heard over
the passionate advocacy of the U.S. embassy in Paris. Charlton Ogburn,
public information officer in the Bureau of Far Eastern Affairs, complained
of an American embassy official who dismissed all expressions of concern
over the suppression of nationalist movements in Asia as products of an
unnecessary preoccupation with the "patter of naked brown feet." Ogburn
mused parenthetically that this patter should "by now have drummed its
way into the hearing even of people in Paris." The United States was left
with two "ghastly" choices: to let the communists take over Indochina or
to "continue to pour treasure (and perhaps eventually lives) into a hopeless cause . . . and this at a cost of alienating vital segments of Asian public opinion." Ogburn argued that it was time to relieve "hostile Senators"
of the illusion that Indochina was a clear case of communist aggression
that must be met "in a hard-hitting, two-fisted manner." This might work
"in the short run," but he feared it was "sowing the whirlwind" unless,
Ogburn warned, "we intend when the time comes to commit American
ground forces in Indochina and thus throw all Asia to the wolves along
with the best chances the free world has."[14] John Ohly, deputy director of
the Mutual Defense Assistance Program, was equally worried: "We are

certainly dangerously close to the point of being so deeply committed that we may find ourselves committed to direct intervention. These situations, unfortunately, have a way of snowballing."[15]

Ogburn's hostility to the embassy in Paris was more than matched by the hostility of French officials, including de Lattre, to Americans in Vietnam. "The French have been viewing United States economic aid activities . . . with suspicion and some disapproval," Durdin reported without further comment from Hanoi. "[They] appear to want United States aid, but without the Americans, the American label or any augmentation of American influence here."[16] To be sure, the U.S. minister in Saigon, Donald Heath, reported to the State Department, the French were grateful for American military aid. But economic aid was something else again, a wound to French amour propre, making them look, de Lattre complained, "like a poor cousin in Viet eyes." Deeply irritated, de Lattre banned any mention of American economic aid in the leading French language newspaper in Vietnam, lashed out in public against American missionaries, religious and secular, and refused to provide sufficient housing for the American military mission. "Yours is a rich country," de Lattre told Heath, "why don't you build houses. Or get rid of some of your ECA [Economic Cooperation Administration] men and your Amer[ican] missionaries, then we [could] house MAAG [American Military Advisory and Assistance Group]."[17] Disturbed by the ferocity of his attack, Heath wrote a long, three-part telegram to the State Department, expressing his conviction that tension over U.S. economic aid had become a serious obstacle overall to U.S. policy in Indochina.[18]

Much of Heath's concern drew upon a long private conversation he had had with the acting French diplomatic counselor in Saigon. French grievances focused, in particular, on the activities of STEM (Special Technical and Economic Mission), and Heath's telegram reported the complaints in detail. First, the counselor explained, France had never asked for economic aid but instead had been compelled to accept it in order to get the military aid it wanted.[19] Second, the publicity STEM projects received, along with U.S. efforts to negotiate direct, bilateral agreements with the Associated States, undermined the French Union. Americans seemed to think Indochina had been "discovered in 1950 and that history of civilization in Indochina began with arrival of US aid. If [a] water pump or tractor [is] delivered [to] Indochina, it becomes, in STEM publicity, [the] first water pump and first tractor that Indochina has ever had. If medical first aid station opened, it is inauguration of public health in IC." No attention was paid to what the French had been doing for generations and continued to do at "25 times the volume and with 1/25 the publicity."

Even worse than STEM self-aggrandizement, according to the French counselor, were the activities of the U.S. Information Exchange (USIE), whose popular English-language classes reminded the French of nothing so much as the Russians, whose first step toward gaining influence was "to open Russian courses in blind belief that all that is good is in Russia." The French were particularly outraged by the fact that so many Vietnamese were learning English when so few of them "know French well and their time and effort might be better spent in acquiring really useful knowledge of French which will be much more important to them." Unless, the counselor observed suspiciously, "America expects Vietnam not to remain in French Union." USIE's translation projects were equally upsetting. The first book translated was a history of the United States: "This seems either absurd or offensive to most French who have found that even literate Viets know little of history of their own country and almost nothing of history of France . . . To expect them to read American history seems height of national egotism on part Americans."[20] Despite de Lattre's claim that the fight against red colonialism joined France and the United States, the Saigon legation reported dissatisfaction with USIE's translation of books that were either "violently pro-US or anti-USSR, issues which have little meaning for most Viets." And why, Heath was asked, were there five times as many Americans in Vietnam as all other foreigners combined? Clearly, America looked forward to the day when Indochina, absent the French, would become a "zone of US influence." Basic to this angry litany, Heath concluded, was the fear that American policy looked to the ultimate departure of Indochina from the French Union.[21] Heath was not entirely sympathetic to French strictures, but he was clear about the bottom line: "our most immediate concern in Indochina today is the mil[itary] def[ense] of its terr[itory] and that def[ense] today rests solely on the Fr[ench]." In "other less troubled parts of the world" it might be possible to dismiss what they said; not in Indochina. De Lattre, Heath thought, agreed with much of this criticism.[22]

"OUR FIRST CONSIDERATION IS REAL ESTATE"

Toward the end of June, Heath asked for a full-scale policy review. The directive under which he had operated since his arrival in 1950 required U.S. policy to "supplement but not to supplant" the French, on the assumption that French policy was "evolutionary and designed to perfect" the independence of the Indochinese states within the French Union. There was no alternative to the French: "Present-day Vietnam returned to peace by an international agency and given a coalition [government] as a result of some form of internationally observed free election [would] fall to the Commies no less surely, no less slowly, and perhaps rather more cheaply than did the East Eur[o-pean] states of the immed[iate] postwar period." All the French asked, in return for the lives and treasure spent in averting such a disaster, was loyal support from the United States. In the future, Heath intended to make it clear to all American personnel in Vietnam that "they must not listen or give encouragement to improper criticism of Fr[ench] sacrifices and intentions and that violation [of] this rule will be regarded as insubordination."

Heath was not insensible to the underlying causes of local American attitudes toward the French, and his summary of their views reads like an indictment of the French record. Some Americans, he observed, argued that "central facts IC problem are the rising tides of Asian nationalism and embittered hatred of Viet people for Fr[ance]; they maintain that enemy here is regarded as the Fr[ench] rather than [the Viet Minh] or Commies, that all sections of opinion unite on proposition [that] Fr[ance] must go and differ only as to means of their expulsion." Moreover, proposals for Vietnam's position in the French Union seemed to lack any provision for trade unions, independent political parties, or a parliament while retaining the French secret police, censorship, French domination of the economy, opium, a relaxed attitude toward corruption, and "the omnipresence of Fr[ench] officials, names and culture"—in other words, "the most sordid and restrictive colonialism." Some Americans in Vietnam urged total U.S. withdrawal from "this pestilence"; others wanted the United States to replace the French in the conviction that "all social ills will depart with the Fr[ench]." Only history would decide whether these negative impressions had any merit. But at that moment in time, Heath argued, they were irrelevant: there was no Third Force for Americans to adopt and support; there was no alternative to the French.[23]

In a strongly worded telegram from Paris, Ambassador David Bruce wholly endorsed Heath's effort to discipline American aid workers who sided with the Vietnamese. "Vietnamese [should] never be permitted to forget essential irreplaceable contribution French are making toward their independence and fate they wld meet if French were to withdraw. Nor must we ourselves forget ever present danger of having Vietnamese play us off against the French."[24] Heath had been careful to exempt Robert Blum,[25] who headed the ECA mission in Vietnam, from any breach of protocol, and Blum was equally delicate in his response to Heath's complaints, expressing his full agreement that U.S. policy was to "supplement but not supplant" the French. That said, there were real problems: "Basically the Fr[ench] are not very sympathetic with our program and [would] much prefer to see our money used for other purposes," wrote Blum. The consultation the French demanded would not change this fundamental difficulty. Moreover, Blum acknowledged there was a deeper contradiction between the short-term necessity of supporting the French and the long-term importance of strengthening "local anti-Commie aspirations." Indeed, "in this part of the world only [a] break with past offers a firm foundation for the future."[26]

In Washington, the assistant director for non-European affairs in the Office of International Security was more direct. The notion of instructing American personnel to avoid criticizing the French, Jonathan Bingham maintained, "would seem to put United States personnel in Indochina in the position of the 'Hear No Evil' monkey." It was hard to believe Heath really meant what he said, for if his instructions were followed, "it would promptly get around Indochina that United States officials would 'not even listen' to Vietnamese complaints about the French, no matter how well founded they might be." Heath's recommendations would gravely damage "our standing in Asia as a whole by identifying us with colonialism." Moreover, Heath had said nothing in his telegram about the importance of getting the French to move with greater speed toward full independence for the Associated States. "It should be possible to convince the French that such a course in the long run offers them the only way to escape from the crushing military burden they now carry in Indochina and at the same time avoid the kind of an upheaval which could result in their losing Indochina altogether."[27]

De Lattre's unhappiness with the Americans intensified over the course of the hot Saigon summer, as did the dissatisfaction of U.S. economic aid administrators in Saigon with both the French and their American superiors. In a personal, "eyes only" telegram to the secretary of state in late July, Heath laid out his understanding of all the bottom lines: "Our primary objective in Indochina at the present time, our first consideration, is real estate. . . . We are interested above all else in seeing to it that the strategic position, the rice, the rubber, and the tin of [Southeast Asia] shall be denied, as long as possible, to the Commie world." Anything that advanced that end should be encouraged; anything that detracted from it should be junked. The United States in Indochina was neither for nor against the French or the Vietnamese: "We have no permanently fixed ideological position in Franco-Vietnamese politics. . . . For the immed[iate] future . . . Fr[ench] arms and Fr[ench] resources will have to do the job of def[ense] if it is to be done at all." It followed, therefore, that all efforts must be bent to support French policy, including the "nascent" French Union. The tension between officials in STEM and the French must be resolved in favor of the French. Indeed, with the possibility of an armistice in Korea it was likely that pressure would mount in France for "negotiated appeasement in Vietnam," leaving the United States in the position of urging the French not to "intervene less in IC but to continue their exertions beyond politically popular level."[28]

Livingston Merchant, deputy assistant secretary of state for Far Eastern affairs, summarized the controversy for Dean Rusk. Heath was convinced that the fundamental U.S. goal of keeping Indochina and thus all of Southeast Asia out of the hands of the communists could only be realized through single-minded support of France. Both military and economic aid should be channeled solely through France. The U.S. stake was concrete and material—tin, rubber, and rice—not in any sense ideological. The ECA, by contrast, wanted to give economic, although not military, aid directly to the Associated States in an effort to strengthen their independence. For Robert Blum and his associates, what the United States stood for mattered. It could not and should not stand for the continuation of French colonialism. Merchant thought Heath was probably right to suspect that the STEM staff allowed themselves to become allies of the Vietnamese against the French. "For one thing," he reasoned, "it is hard for me to believe that ECA or anyone else could persuade a doctor or an engineer, or a technical expert in almost any field to go to Indochina under present conditions unless he possessed a strong humanitarian motivation, which almost by definition would place his sympathies on the side of the native people and against their colonial ex-masters." The real question, he asked, was, "How best do we assure the preservation of Indochina from Communism?" If support for the French so alienated people that they joined the other side en masse, the country would be lost "just about as easily as a military victory over De Lattre by an invading Chinese Communist army."[29]

Still, Merchant warned, undermining the French could lead to their withdrawal and a similar rapid loss of Indochina. A proper assessment of the problem required a judgment as to the "sincerity of French intentions" and this boiled down to an analysis of de Lattre's intentions. Merchant noted that Heath clearly was enamored of de Lattre's "flamboyance, vigor and Napoleonic character," which had given heart to "French colonials and stoked the fear of Vietnamese who never believed French promises to begin with." But Merchant contended that the fundamental issues had to be solved in Washington, not in the field; de Lattre's forthcoming visit would be an opportunity to test the sincerity of his commitment to ultimate independence for the Associated States. The real hope lay in the creation of a national army, to which U.S. military aid should be channeled, while economic aid must be directed toward the strengthening of the "native regimes and not the French." At the same time, Merchant added, French sensibilities should be protected through consultation and an avoidance of excessive publicity.[30]

The U.S. legation in Saigon, meanwhile, was tireless in its promotion of de Lattre. In a long telegram to the State Department, the second-ranking official in the U.S. embassy, Edmond Gullion, expressed his admiration for the general, who worked ceaselessly to "confront divided and listless Viets" hoping to "inspire and drive Viets out of their hesitancy in spite of themselves. He leads passionately this effort with wholly sincere faith, tremendous energy and unbounded will which has galvanized French Union forces and may yet transform political picture." Of course, Gullion hedged, when it came to Indochina, "imponderables" had often intervened to destroy the best-laid plans. "The imponderables," Gullion explained, "constitute the spiritual order of battle of opposing forces in which the will and genius of De Lattre is arrayed against Stalinist dynamic. The critical imponderable is the extent to which De Lattre's spark can light the tardy flame of Viet's patriotism and fuel the ardor of the Fr[ench]."[31]

Americans had the opportunity to observe de Lattre directly in mid-September 1951. He arrived in the United States on board the *Ile de France*, holding his own, *Time* magazine reported, with fellow passengers like Humphrey Bogart and Lauren Bacall, themselves returning from the discomforts of filming *The African Queen* on location.[32] In response to de Lattre's request, press photographers took his picture as the ship sailed past the Statue of Liberty: "[De Lattre], impeccable from kepi to pigskin gloves, turned his hawklike profile to the lenses and pointed theatrically toward his country's copper gift to the U.S." His sense of the moment was rewarded by a cover photo in *Time*, a full-face portrait, lips pressed together in an expression both confident and determined, against a background of flooded rice paddies in which a military stockade flying the tricolor was reflected. "The war in Indo-China," de Lattre told a press conference in New York, "is not a colonial war, it is a war against Red colonialism; as in Korea, it is a war against Communist dictatorship. . . . We are fighting on a world battlefield, for liberty and for peace."[33] As *Time* approvingly summarized his views, Korea, Indochina, and Malaya were only "different battles of the same war." De Lattre understood that Americans resisted the comparison between the French in Indochina and the British in Malaya, and he tried to address that resistance directly. France "is not fighting in Indo-China with any idea of profit," he insisted. On the contrary, the war was costing the French billions a year. "We are there," he went on, "because we have promised to protect the Associated States." "A great many Americans do not know the truth about our position in Indo-China," he acknowledged to a friendly reporter in New York. Somewhat more mysteriously he promised to "bring them proof they cannot deny. I shall also bring them proof that the war in Indo-China is the same as the war in Korea."[34]

AMERICA TAKES THE LONG VIEW

To *Time* and *Life* he was a "formidable Frenchman," the "French MacArthur," but "younger . . . and strictly non-fading."[35] An editorial in *Life* embraced de Lattre's message whole: strategically, Indochina was more important than Korea and "of all the new battlefronts where American troops may soon be fighting . . . the likeliest;" de Lattre's claim that French colonialism was a dead letter had become "increasingly true"; and, perhaps most important, he had banished neutralism in Indochina—"those who are not with Ho are now against him." The United States could further reduce those who supported Ho Chi Minh by "giving their Asia-front hero the support he needs." If the war became a United Nations effort, it might well be that de Lattre would command American troops, as Matthew Ridgway commanded European troops in Korea. "Why not? It's the same war. And he is another general who likes to win."[36]

The comparison between the wars in Korea and in Indochina preoccupied the editors of *Time* as well as de Lattre and his Washington colleagues. To win the support of the American public for increased levels of aid to the French in Indochina, it was necessary to demonstrate that the French, like the Americans in Korea, were resisting a war of aggression launched by communists against the legitimate government. Before making the case, the differences between Korea and Indochina had to be acknowledged. The situation in Indochina, *Time* explained to its readers, had begun as a "slow guerrilla nuisance" rather than the "dramatic shock of the Red attack in Korea." To most of the world, including most Frenchmen, it was a "dubious cause" in a distant country of little interest. The arrival of de Lattre had changed everything. He had inspired the troops, cleaned the slackers out of saloons and brothels, shipped the incompetents home, and, unlike his predecessors, had "grasped at once the importance of a U.S. weapon ideal for jungle fighting: napalm." In a manner that would become familiar during the U.S. war in Vietnam, *Time* believed de Lattre's battlefield successes would persuade the public of the importance of Indochina, where "the battle lines of Asia and Europe merge." The possibility of victory had transformed a dubious cause into a worthy one.

Along with arguing the centrality of France's war to the overall struggle against communism, *Time* was anxious to restore the reputation of France to an American public that thought of the country in terms of "falling cabinets and rising black-marketeers," an "envious France," and a "timid" one. De Lattre's France, by contrast, was "a country so large that all the men of Western civilization have a home there." Above all, *Time* sought to sell the war in Indochina to the American public by merging it with the person of de Lattre himself. He was moody, impatient, touchy on issues of honor, intensely dramatic, a meticulous dresser, and a stickler for high sartorial standards in others (observing to a stenographer as he fired her, "You don't know how to dress, Miss, and your hair is dirty"). "Around him all women must be beautiful," a reporter who knew him told *Time*, "all men handsome and intelligent, all motorcars sleek and fast, all public appearances impressive." And yet, for all his force and drive, there was as well a humanizing sadness about the man, which the reporter attributed to the death of his son Bernard in combat in Vietnam: "Sometimes a sudden memory will wring from him an uncontrollable sob." At heart, de Lattre, like MacArthur, was "essentially an old-fashioned man who believes in the old-fashioned virtues," above all "duty—to France, duty to end all this killing, duty to end all this chaos in the world." Best of all, with sufficient help from the United States, de Lattre promised a quick victory in Indochina. The editors failed to comment that in this too he resembled General MacArthur in Korea.[37]

In public talks as in private conversations with officials, de Lattre insisted that the war France fought in Vietnam was not in any sense a colonial war or a war for profit. President Truman, according to the *New York Times*, believed him: "Truman Justifies War in Indo-China," the headline announced. The fight in Korea and the battle in Indochina were "the same fight for liberty."[38] In Washington, de Lattre opened his discussion at the State Department somewhat disingenuously: "Since there was mutual agreement that colonialism was a dead issue, there was no reason to discuss the issue further." The real problems lay in the failure of the United States to deliver military supplies on time and in sufficient quantities. "Korea received practically everything," he complained, "Indochina what was left." Acheson and Truman agreed that Indochinese needs were indeed very important but would nevertheless be acted upon only after those in Korea had been fulfilled. De Lattre dropped the subject for the time being but returned to it, in different forms, throughout the meeting. He asked, he said, only for a simple yes or no: "Did the U.S. admit that Indochina was the keystone in Southeast Asia? If the answer was No, nothing more could be accomplished, if Yes, the U.S. must provide the weapons to make resistance possible." He would continue to fight in Indochina because that was his duty, he said, "but it must be remembered that it was the American battlefield as well as the French."

Several days later, after a successful appearance on *Meet the Press*, de Lattre met with the Joint Chiefs of Staff and Secretary of Defense Robert Lovett. De Lattre appealed to them to understand that if he lost Indochina, then "Asia is lost." If northern Tonkin fell, so would Vietnam and with it all of Southeast Asia and India. There was worse to come: having ingested Southeast Asia and India and now lapping at the waters of the Suez Canal, the entire Muslim world might be engulfed. Then "the Moslems in North Africa would soon fall in line and Europe itself would be outflanked." This invocation of a future war of civilizations in addition to the struggle against communism already underway did not have its intended effect.[39] Lovett praised de Lattre for his presentation and agreed that his theater of operations was the same as that of the United States in Korea in one sense, but—and it was a crucial but—"the United States has a primary obligation in other theaters, whereas your primary obligation is in your own theater." De Lattre, in turn, suggested that unless the United States delivered the supplies it had promised, on time and in good order, there was not much point to his continuing. He could not tell his countrymen to proceed "without hope of victory." General J. Lawton Collins hastened to explain why some deliveries had been late, but de Lattre was not appeased. He hated to feel, as he sometimes did in the United States, that he was a "beggar." He said he would like to feel instead that "I am your man just as General Ridgway is your own man. Your spirit should lead you to send me these things without my asking." Lovett protested: "We all regard General de Lattre as a comrade in arms and will do everything possible for his theatre within our capabilities." The general shot back: "Do not say *my* theatre. It is not my theatre; it is *our* theatre."[40] The end result of de Lattre's trip was a speed up in military deliveries and an abiding sense of irritation caused by de Lattre's subsequent boasting that he had succeeded in changing U.S. policy.[41]

A few weeks after the visit, Dean Rusk, in a formal address before the Seattle World Affairs Council, felt obliged to clarify, once more, the nature of the struggle in Indochina. "Many Americans," Rusk conceded, "have been troubled in the past about the issue of colonialism in Indo-china." But the issue was well on its way to solution despite the reasonable doubts felt by people in Indochina and other Asian countries. There was only one issue in Indochina, and that was whether its people would be allowed "to work out their future as they see fit or whether they will be subjected to a Communist reign of terror and be absorbed by force into the new colonialism of a Soviet Communist empire."[42] Nevertheless, some U.S. press reports continued to describe Vietnam as only semi-independent. The "average Vietnamese," one correspondent wrote, "still does not regard himself as independent. Much of the Communist appeal is based on the 'independence' issue and 'anti-colonial' propaganda." Despite communist "ruthlessness," the "young intellectuals with whom this correspondent talked . . . seemed to be more concerned about the presence of the French than about the threat of communism."[43]

Every now and then a report to the State Department suggested the full complexity of the situation in Vietnam. Robert Allen Griffin, for example, wrote to Acheson from a stopover in Singapore during a late November tour of Asia. What was going on in Vietnam was not just an anticolonial movement but rather a revolution. Moreover, the revolution would continue, along with communist popularity, for as long as the "independence" movement supported by the French consisted solely of "native mandarins who are succeeding foreign mandarins. . . . The present type of govt in Vietnam is a relic of the past as much as Fr[ench] colonialism." The conflict went beyond nationalism and Francophobia, and it was one with which the United States was already familiar: "It is old Asian issue that destroyed the Kuomintang in China, Communist opportunity to exploit insecurity, and hunger and wretchedness of masses of people to whom their [government] has failed to make an effective appeal."[44] Heath responded from Saigon that, yes, Griffin was right about the "native mandarins," but unfortunately he knew of "no leaders with 'grassroots' support' who [would] join [a government] constituted on [the] basis of existing Franco-Vietnamese relations." Moreover, "if there were such persons, doubtful if Fr[ench] wld accept them or that they would be proof against Asiatic neutralism or Viet Minh infiltration."[45]

In late December 1951, State and Defense Department officials met to discuss where things stood in Vietnam. General Hoyt Vandenberg raised the central question: Was the United States prepared to see the French lose in Indochina? Lawton Collins disputed the idea that if Indochina fell, all of Southeast Asia would be lost. From a strictly military point of view, the British could hold Malaya even if the French withdrew from Indochina, and in terms of resources, Malaya and Indonesia were far more important than Indochina. Omar Bradley thought it would be impossible to "get our public to go along with the idea of our going into Indochina in a military way." But Paul Nitze wondered whether public reaction might not be worse if Indochina went communist.[46]

The possibility of Chinese intervention in Indochina, especially in the wake of a truce in Korea, loomed over all considerations of U.S. policy.

The French and the British worried that this time the United States might take the opportunity to expand the war into China proper and insisted that even in the event of Chinese intervention, military action remain confined to Indochina itself. The Joint Chiefs of Staff, on the other hand, opposed any prior constraint. At a cabinet meeting in March 1952, British prime minister Winston Churchill observed that "the Americans would like to extend the area of conflict beyond the actual point of aggression by bombing ports and communications, and possibly by mining rivers in China, and instituting a naval blockade of the China Coast." This would lead to total war or, of equal importance to Churchill, endanger Hong Kong and Malaya. Moreover, Churchill remarked, mixing the practical and the ethical, "It would be silly to waste bombs in the vague inchoate mass of China and wrong to kill thousands of people to no purpose."[47]

The gulf that divided the United States from the Europeans, including the British, was more fundamental than the choice of weapons or targets. What most frustrated the French was the resistance of American officials to the logic of the French situation. They were as eager to fight red colonialism as the Americans but insisted on the necessity of ongoing ties between Indochina and France. Why else were the French fighting? Why should the French public support the war? Indeed, successfully building the French Union would constitute the defeat of red colonialism. De Lattre put it with the utmost clarity at a National Press Club luncheon during his visit to the United States: "The war declared by the Vietminh six years, ago," he told the assembled reporters, "did not have independence as its real objective, but rather the installation of communism. This war tried to eliminate all that was French in order to enslave Indo-China in the most terrible of dominations."[48] Washington understood this. At a National Security Council meeting in late December 1953, Vice President Richard Nixon, fresh from a world tour, warned that if the French withdrew "the only capable leadership at the present time in Vietnam is Communist leadership."[49] "What people want," Nixon told the National Security Council, "we all know—independence and peace." Sadly, "we have got ourselves in the position of being 'against peace' and 'against independence'. . . . Sometimes an anti-Communist line isn't the best line."[50] The United States might have to settle for half of Korea, but more was possible in Indochina if only the French would cooperate by offering, at the very least, independence within a reformed French Union.

The Americans, intent on defeating red colonialism, were convinced that the only way to do so was by opposing colonialism of any color through the creation of a pliant, reliably anticommunist, independent Indochina under U.S. supervision. In 1953 and for the next two decades, this remained the American definition of Vietnamese independence. Of course, nationalists would try to "eliminate all that was French" as part of their quest for full sovereignty. In contrast no genuine nationalist would ever wish to eliminate all that was American.

Decades later, in a discussion between American and Vietnamese policy makers and historians, Nicholas Katzenbach, who had worked on Vietnam in both the Kennedy and Johnson administrations, explained to the Vietnamese that "it should have been clear to everyone that the United States was opposed to colonialism after World War II, even if some of the policies of the United States tended to support the colonial powers in some parts of the world." Yet, he complained, his Vietnamese interlocutors seemed to think that the United States was "precolonial . . . even though everything that we did and said opposed colonialism in most parts of the world."[51] Colonel Herbert Schandler, who served two tours of duty in Vietnam, was more sympathetic to the Vietnamese point of view. Listening to a Vietnamese historian describe U.S. policy in 1950, Schandler, who now teaches at the U.S. National Defense University, said he could "sense how confusing it must have been, in 1950, for you to try to figure out why this country . . . had for some reason decided to become your enemy. But— and this seems to be something that was very hard for you in Vietnam to grasp, for obvious reasons—the United States was taking a *world* view of all these issues."[52] In this first decade of the twenty-first century, the notion that the worldview to which Schandler appealed was at the same time an imperial, even an imperialist, view is no longer shocking. These days, de Lattre would have had less difficulty reaching an understanding with Washington.

NOTES

1. Jacques Soustelle, "Indo-China and Korea: One Front," *Foreign Affairs* 29, no. 1 (October 1950): 56, 61, 64, 65, 66.
2. Quoted in *The US Government and the Vietnam War: Executive and Legislative Roles in Relationships, Part I, 1945–1961* (Washington, D.C.: U.S. Government Printing Office, 1984), 68.

3. John F. Melby, "Memoir, Vietnam—1950," *Diplomatic History* 6, no. 1 (Winter 1982): 108.
4. George W. Allen, *None So Blind: A Personal Account of the Intelligence Failure in Vietnam* (Chicago: Ivan R. Dee, 2001), 20.
5. Allen, *None So Blind*, 22.
6. "Substance of Statements Made at Wake Island Conference on 15 October 1950," *Foreign Relations of the United States, 1950, Korea* (hereafter *FRUS, 1950, Korea*), 7:957–58. Truman referred specifically to the trip Philip Jessup had just completed: a fourteen-country tour of Asia in March 1950. Jessup had found the French sadly wanting in Indochina. They were "failing to put over their viewpoint" on Indochina and Asia. They are conspicuously lacking in a sense of public relations." They were making "somewhat the same mistakes that the British General Braddock made in the French and Indian Wars." Bao Dai's government "would be deficient in competent personnel even if all elements rallied to his side." *FRUS, 1950, Korea*, 6:69, 6:71.
7. "Substance of Statements Made at Wake Island," 957–58.
8. "Substance of Statements Made at Wake Island." According to MacArthur, it wasn't much of a problem to begin with: "He contrasted the Indochinese situation sharply with Korea and left the impression that our problem in Korea was more difficult from a military point of view than the problem faced by the French in Indochina." Rusk, perhaps recalling Radford's offhand comment, asked MacArthur, "How seriously popular opinion should be weighed as a military factor in such operations as Indochina and Korea." Would, for example, a hostile population have interfered with the landing at Inchon? "He replied that a hostile population could, of course, have made the task more difficult but it would not have been a decisive factor," because armed men passing through a village in Asia are treated with the highest respect." It was more of an annoyance than anything else, due to the "logistic support which it gives the enemy" such as "food, water, care of wounded and, particularly, intelligence." The plain talk and cold turkey Truman promised French prime minister Rene Pleven turned out to be rather mild so far as the French were concerned but very tough about the Chinese. There would be no recognition of the communist regime. "They have been very mean to all Americans," Truman informed Pleven. "They have mistreated our people every time they had a chance, and we have been their friends ever since the Open Door Policy, and a long time before that. I don't appreciate that." Pleven acknowledged that France had been slow to see the Chinese as aggressors, but once they crossed the thirty-eighth parallel into South Korea, "we reached the same conclusion about the Chinese communists that you did." France would, therefore, support a U.S. resolution on Chinese aggression in the United Nations. Memorandum for the President, January 30, 1951, Secretary's File, Harry S. Truman Library, Declassified Documents Research Service. As Washington braced for the opening of hearings on General MacArthur's recall, a leak to the *New York Times* made public not only the general's doubts about the possibility of China entering the Korean War but also his strictures on the quality of French troops in Indochina. The reporter

added, in brackets, "The French there have made considerable progress since." See Anthony Leviero, "Wake Talks Bared," *New York Times*, April 21, 1951, 1. The following week, Tillman Durdin reported on the "pained surprise" with which the report was read in Hanoi. "Americans here [in Hanoi]," Durdin wrote, "are inclined to agree with the French reactions." An American officer attached to French troops ranked the French soldier in Indochina above his American counterpart. Tillman Durdin, "MacArthur Report Pains Frenchmen," *New York Times*, May 1, 1951, 6.

9. Tillman Durdin, "De Lattre Cheers French in Vietnam," *New York Times*, January 11, 1951, 4. De Lattre returned the compliment. "De Lattre Credits U.S. Aid in Tongking," read a headline in the *New York Times* shortly after his appointment, "French Chief Says American Supplies Played Big Part in Successful Defense," January 24, 1951, 6. Hardly a week went by without a puff piece on de Lattre by Durdin. See, for example, "French Are Heartened by Gains in Indo-China," *New York Times*, January 28, 1951, E-4. Durdin was cautious. In careful subjunctive clauses he pointed out that it was necessary to "emphasize that many basic realities of the situation might well continue to warrant a contrasting mood of gloom and pessimism." These included the increased strength of the Viet Minh and the possibility of Chinese intervention. For Durdin's profile, see "Fighter on a Mission," *New York Times*, February 18, 1951, 152.

10. Durdin, "Fighter on a Mission," 152.

11. "Far East General Is 'D.D.T.' to French," *New York Times*, August 19, 1951, 23. Irvin Wall observed that only "the pressures of war and desperation over the possibility of losing both Korea and Vietnam can explain the American infatuation with the general, who had previously been highly regarded in Washington, but also suspected for his alleged flirtation with Communism." Wall, *The United States and the Making of Postwar France, 1945–1954* (New York: Cambridge University Press, 1991), 243.

12. Michael James, "De Lattre of Rhine, Danube and Tonkin," *New York Times Magazine*, August 26, 1951, 59.

13. Hanson Baldwin, "The Crisis in Indo-China," *New York Times Magazine*, January 5, 1951, 4. Baldwin described de Lattre as a man of "much temperament and little tact.... He proved to be one of the most difficult French officers with whom Americans had to deal during the last war."

14. "Memorandum, Charlton Ogburn to Dean Rusk, August 18, 1950," *FRUS, 1950*, 6:863–64. In the same memorandum, Ogburn pointed to the central contradiction, one which would not change over the entire course of the French war in Indochina: "The French, who have been telling us every few days for many months that the French Army cannot be expected to fight for Vietnamese independence, have now decided that we should build up a Vietnamese Army to fight for the French Union." Ogburn's prescience—and his open contempt for the quality of many of his fellow State Department officers—was apparent in an earlier memorandum. In March he noted the absence in Saigon of anyone who knew anything about the country. It was not, therefore, surprising that the

legation should imagine that American aid would have much of an impact on the military situation:

> My hunch is that Ho Chi-minh's cohorts having stood off 130–150 thousand French colonial troops for four years (during which time they must have conceived a blazing hatred for France and France's friends), are not going to wilt under the *psychological* impact of American military assistance. They might on the other hand give way under the *physical* impact of American weapons—if we send enough. Should things get too hot for them, they will, I suppose, do what the Indonesian Republicans used to tell us they would do—i.e., go underground until a more propitious occasion presented itself. So unless the French are prepared to police Vietnam indefinitely or are enabled by the magnitude of our assistance actually to kill off a hundred thousand of the more ardent Vietnamese rebels, it may well be that a military decision now—even if it can be achieved—will be followed a couple of years hence by a take-over by Ho's party.

"Ogburn to Walton Butterworth, March 21, 1950," *FRUS* 6:767 (italics original).

15. John Ohly to Dean Acheson, November 20, 1950, quoted in *The US Government and the Vietnam War: Executive and Legislative Roles in Relationships, Part l, 1945–1961* (Washington, D.C.: Government Printing Office, 1984), 84.

16. Durdin, "M'Arthur Report Pains Frenchmen."

17. "Donald Heath to Secretary of State, May 15, 1951," *FRUS* 6, pt. 1:419. Heath called the general's tone "impertinent."

18. "Heath to Secretary of State, June 14, 1951," *FRUS* 6, pt. 1:425–28.

19. This charge was immediately refuted in a telegram, "Ambassador David Bruce to the Secretary of State, June 19, 1951," *FRUS* 6, pt. 1:428–29.

20. "Ambassador David Bruce to the Secretary of State, June 19, 1951"; "Heath to Secretary of State, June 14, 1951," *FRUS* 6, pt. 1:425–28. Acheson's response to French complaints was acerbic. One of USIE's main functions was to teach English; the Vietnamese wanted it, and, if they were to make use of American aid, needed it. Of course, French should continue to be Vietnam's second language, but teaching it was hardly a USIE task. Similarly, it was "entirely appropriate" that the first book USIE had translated was on U.S. history. "If the Viets 'know nothing or little' of their own history or that of France, this is a problem for the Ministry of Education and incidentally one which should have been taken up long ago." It was not an American problem. "Acheson to Heath, July 13, 1951," *FRUS* 6, pt. 1:453.

21. "Heath to Secretary of State, June 14, 1951," *FRUS* 6, pt. 1:425.

22. The U.S. consul in Hanoi thought there were additional explanations for de Lattre's angry mood: "De Lattre looked old and worn-out, spoke very low, almost in reverie but very bitterly." The cause was the death of his son Bernard in combat. "What price all this sacrifice," de Lattre had asked, "if those ostensibly on our side refuse to believe in our sincerity? If this constant sacrificing of our youths' flower does not prove us sincere in desire to give Vietnam

independence, what further is necessary to drive the idea home?" In a "bona fide war," he would have had the consolation of knowing Bernard had died a hero's death. Instead, his son had "been offered up on behalf of an ungrateful people," who not only had not warned the French unit there were Viet Minh in the area but had "booed and hissed *'vendus'* (sold out)" at the Vietnamese soldiers accompanying them." There was no comment on this indication that French sincerity was widely in doubt nor on the "typical first reaction" of Vietnamese officials to the news—fear that de Lattre would order napalm reprisal raids. Bao Dai was also worried, telling Heath he feared that de Lattre "might now conceive war as one of revenge." "Wendell Blancke to Secretary of State, May 31, 1951," *FRUS* 6, pt. 1:424, 425.

23. "Heath to Secretary of State, June 29, 1951," *FRUS* 6, pt. 1:433–39.

24. "Bruce to Secretary of State, July 5, 1951," *FRUS* 6, pt. 1:443.

25. Blum was also a CIA agent. See *The US Government and the Vietnam War*, 91.

26. "Robert Blum to Secretary of State, July 12, 1951," *FRUS* 6, pt. 1:450, 451.

27. "Jonathan B. Bingham to Secretary of State, July 12, 1951," *FRUS* 6, pt. 1:448, 449.

28. "Donald Heath to Secretary of State, July 20, 1951," *FRUS* 6, pt. 1:457–59.

29. "Livingston Merchant to Dean Rusk, July 27, 1951," *FRUS* 6, pt. 1: 462–64.

30. "Livingston Merchant to Dean Rusk, July 27, 1951," *FRUS* 6, pt. 1: 462–64.

31. In August, Heath left for consultations in Washington, Paris, and London, and the charge, Edmond Gullion, took over. "Gullion to Secretary of State, August 18, 1951," *FRUS* 6, pt. 1:480–84.

32. "The French MacArthur," *Time*, September 24, 1951, 32. "Africa is a good place to stay away from," Bogart told the press, "but I suppose that statement will burn up all the Africans."

33. "The French MacArthur," 32.

34. "The French MacArthur," 32, 35; Michael James, "De Lattre Cites Indo-China Peril," *New York Times*, September 14, 1951, sec. 3, 5.

35. Editorial, "De Lattre and His Message," *Life* 31, no. 13, September 24, 1951, 52.

36. "De Lattre and His Message," 52.

37. "The French MacArthur," 32, 33, 34, 35, For all its adulation of de Lattre and, in particular, his appeals to the Vietnamese to fight for their country, *Time* admitted that according to U.S. observers, "half the Indo Chinese would still vote for Ho rather than French supported Bao [Dai]" in free elections.

38. "Truman Justifies War in Indo-China," *New York Times*, September 15, 1951, 2.

39. De Lattre made the same point at a National Press Club luncheon: "Once Tongking is lost there is really no barrier before Suez, and I will leave to your imagination how defeatism and defeat would swell up as time passes, how Communist fifth columns would get into the game in every country as strong external Communist forces apply pressure on their frontiers." "Asia Called Stake of Indo-China War," *New York Times*, September 31, 1951, 3.

40. "Minutes to Meeting at the Pentagon, September 20, 1951," *FRUS* 6, pt. 1:517–21.

41. Memorandum of conversation by William M. Gibson, Office of Philippines and Southeast Asian Affairs. Members of de Lattre's staff confided to a reporter that while the talks had been cordial enough, they felt the United States had

"a tendency to underestimate the Viet minh forces. 'They do not seem to fully understand the problems of guerillas,' this officer asserted. 'You have to fight in Indo-China to know about that kind of Communist.'" Michael James, "U.S. Asked to Assay Indo-China's Peril," *New York Times*, September 16, 1951, 5.

42. *U.S.-Vietnam Relations: 1945–1967: Study Prepared by the Department of Defense* (Washington, D.C.: U.S. Government Printing Office, 1971), book 8, November 6, 1951, 459.

43. Henry R. Lieberman, "Report on the 'Little Wars' of Southeast Asia," *New York Times*, September 9, 1951, B-4.

44. "Robert Allen Griffin to Richard Bissell, Nov. 30, 1951," *FRUS* 6, pt. 1:549.

45. "Donald Heath to Secretary of State, Dec. 9, 1951," *FRUS* 6, pt. 1:558–59.

46. "Substance of Discussions of State—Joint Chiefs of Staff Meeting at the Pentagon Building, Dec. 21, 1951," *FRUS* 6, pt. 1:569–70. When asked if France could hold on in Indochina if the Chinese stayed out, General Collins answered that they could, "but there is no chance that they really can clean up the situation." Nitze then wondered what it would take, and Collins responded, "A lot." Two things worried him: the lack of able native leadership and the fact that "as of now the Indochina thing is clearly a one man show. If anything should happen to De Lattre, it might all go to pieces."

47. Geoffrey Warner, "Britain and the Crisis over Dien Bien Phu, April 1954: The Failure of United Action," in *Dien Bien Phu and the Crisis of Franco-American Relations, 1954–1955*, ed. Laurence S. Kaplan, et al. (Wilmington, Del.: SR Books, 1989), 56.

48. "Asia Called Stake of lndo-China War," *New York Times*, September 21, 1951, 3.

49. Memorandum of the discussion at the 177th Meeting of the National Security Council, December 24, 1953, 13 (DDRS).

50. Memorandum of the discussion at the 177th Meeting, 19. Nixon hoped the United States could convince the Indochinese that independence within the French Union was indeed possible.

51. Robert S. McNamara et al., *Argument without End: In Search of Answers to the Vietnam Tragedy* (New York: PublicAffairs, 1999), 53.

52. McNamara, *Argument without End*, 82. Luu Doan Huynh, a Vietnamese historian, reflected that American after American explained that the United States did not intend to attack Vietnam in the mid-1950s. "But really," he said, "your bullets are the killers of our people. We see that this is America's gift to Vietnam—allowing the French to kill our people. This is the most convincing evidence we have of America's loyalties in this affair . . . please try to understand me when I say: *Blood speaks with a terrible voice!*"

5

COUNTING THE BODIES
IN VIETNAM

> When all else is forgotten about statistical reporting in the
> Vietnamese war, the body count will be remembered.
>
> —Brigadier General (ret.) Douglas Kinnard, *The War Managers*

> Well, we don't do body counts on other people.
>
> —Secretary of Defense Donald Rumsfeld on *Fox News*,
> November 2, 2003

> The body counts are back. For the first time since Vietnam, the military has
> begun regularly reporting the number of enemy killed in the war zone—in
> contradiction, apparently, to prior statement by its own top brass.
>
> —Mark Benjamin, "Return of the Body Count," *Salon*,
> June 11, 2001

> Not everything that counts can be counted.
> Not everything that can be counted counts.
>
> —Albert Einstein, quoted in Lawrence Kaplan,
> "Vietnamization," *New Republic*, March 24, 2011

The first reference to the phrase *body count* on Google is the American heavy
metal band of the same name. The lyrics of their most famous song, "Body
Count," describe the war on the streets of Los Angeles in 1991: "I hear it every
night / another gunfight / the tension mounts / on with the Body Count."

First published in *Body and Nation: The Global Realm of U.S. Body Politics in the Twentieth Century*, ed. Emily Rosenberg and Shannon Fitzpatrick (Durham, N.C.: Duke University Press, 2014), 230–40. Copyright © 2014 by Duke University Press. All rights reserved. Republished by permission of the copyright holder. www.dukepress.edu.

Ice-T, who served four years in the U.S. Army (1979–83), no doubt first heard the phrase in reference to the Vietnam war, where daily body counts were how the military tracked success for the public and for itself. As a way of measuring progress, the body count had the virtue of simplicity and apparently scientific certainty; before long it also became the focus of criticism of American military tactics at home and abroad. As in so much else that once marked the Vietnam war as exceptional, from civilian massacres to massive bombing, the body count was common practice in the Korean War, starting in 1951, when the war stabilized at or near the thirty-eighth parallel. "We want maximum casualties on the enemy," General James Van Fleet instructed the commanding officers of the Eighth Army in the spring of 1951. "Terrain in itself doesn't mean much." Decades later General Bruce Palmer observed that in both Korea and Vietnam the absence of any territorial objective meant that "it was not possible to demonstrate or assess progress in terms of territory gained and held." Counting the enemy dead was one of the only ways of indicating "how the war was going. . . . At one point in the Korean War, the explicit, if crudely stated, military objective was to kill as many Chinese ('Chinks') as possible."[1]

The war of attrition in Korea seems not to have been a matter of public concern in the United States. Some congressmen did wonder what U.S. objectives were and were told they were "to kill as many Chinese Communists as possible without enlarging the war at the present in Korea." Ultimately, the reasoning went, such punishment would "bring them to the negotiating table."[2] The number of bombing sorties was reported daily, but unlike in Vietnam, there was no daily toll of the enemy dead. Nor, given that at this point in the Korean War the enemy consisted of regular troops rather than guerrillas, was there as great a possibility of counting civilian as military dead, except when death was the result of aerial bombing. In these cases the things that were counted were "structures."

In Vietnam, by contrast, counting bodies began early in the U.S. war effort. In 1963 George Tanham, a researcher for the RAND Corporation, went to Vietnam to assess progress. RAND (Research and Development) was itself the perfect instrument for Secretary of Defense, Robert S. McNamara, committed to advanced management techniques. Founded in 1945 by the Douglas Aircraft Company, Project RAND reported directly to General Curtis LeMay. In 1948 it separated from Douglas and, with the help of Ford Foundation funding, became an independent, nonprofit research organization whose mission was to "further and promote scientific, educational, and charitable purposes, all for the public welfare and security of the United States of America." *Pravda*, with some justice, called it the "academy of science and death."[3] Tanham checked in with General Rollen "Buck" Anthis, commander of the Second Air Force Division, whose approach to the issues was numerical: the combination of U.S. and Vietnamese air operations was responsible for two-thirds of all enemy casualties that year. Mai Elliott, in her study of RAND, has observed, "Measuring progress by tracking statistics was the general tendency of the U.S. military in Vietnam. In a war without a front line, in which the enemy's objective was not to capture and hold territory and in which the U.S. goal was to grind down the enemy, the key measure of progress was the number of enemy killed in action—known as the *kill ratio*, or, later, as the *body count*." Tanham was not persuaded that "achievement by numbers" was an adequate measurement and worried about the practice, already in use, of establishing an "enemy zone" in which anything that moved was a legitimate target. But concerns about civilian deaths were dismissed by Anthis as isolated incidents and in any case the responsibility of the South Vietnamese officials who told him whom and what to bomb.[4]

By 1964 the military had established a system for counting bodies. The Operations Division of the Military Assistance Command in Vietnam counted weapons captured, sorties flown, and enemy bodies, and of these, according to Brigadier General Douglas Kinnard, the body count was "regarded as one of the most important indicators of progress." As more and more U.S. troops arrived in Vietnam and General William Westmoreland's war of attrition expanded, statistics from various sectors of the country were incorporated into monthly measurement of progress reports, which showed both the absolute numbers killed and the kill ratio comparing American deaths to National Liberation Front (NLF) and North Vietnamese deaths. Kinnard recalls his surprise when he attended a briefing in the spring of 1969: "The first seven charts concerned body count and kill ratio: this unit compared with that unit; this year compared with last year; night compared with day, and so on."[5]

The goal was to reach a "crossover point" at which more enemy soldiers were being killed than could be replaced. Only body counts would indicate when that point had arrived. Moreover, body counts satisfied Secretary McNamara's passion for measurements, for statistics, for production. When he expressed his displeasure with the low body count of one unit during a visit to Vietnam in 1966, the message was clear: the way to advance one's career was to produce more bodies. The Battle of the Ia Drang Valley in 1965 was the sort of engagement Westmoreland and McNamara had in mind. There, in only a few days, Lieutenant Colonel Harold Moore's troops had killed 1,894 men; early in the next year Moore's score was even more impressive: a kill ratio of 40:1.[6]

One problem was finding the enemy so as to be able to use U.S. firepower and then count the results. The overwhelming majority of combat engagements were initiated by the enemy, leaving the U.S. military to send out patrols—bait, really—to search for and then destroy whomever they found. Soldiers remembered the exhilaration, "like that experienced when one's football team scored a touchdown," of a countable kill. There were contests among platoons, a point system with a sliding scale of value, an "efficiency index" based on the kill ratio (enemy to U.S. dead or wounded).[7] To count the dead, you've got to, in the words of the helicopter tail gunner in the film *Full Metal Jacket*, "get some." It was sometimes difficult to record precise numbers. After one engagement in the Central Highlands, the military historian S. L. A. Marshall observed that it was difficult even to estimate how many had been killed because the bodies "had been brayed [sic] apart by the blast and arms, legs, and heads had been scattered over a wide space."[8]

Often bodies could be collected without any combat at all. David Bressem, a helicopter pilot, told an ad hoc congressional committee that his unit had equipped their helicopters with sirens. "Anyone taking evasive action could be fired on," he said, by which he understood "someone running or trying to evade a helicopter or any fire." His unit flew over a group of farmers who failed to scatter: "We then hovered a few feet off the ground among them with two helicopters, turned on the police sirens and when they heard the police sirens, they started to disperse and we opened up on them and just shot them all down."[9] The massacre of over four hundred civilians at My Lai in the spring of 1968 was initially reported as a successful operation yielding 128 enemy dead. My Lai was not an aberration but rather, as Ron Ridenhour, the solider who worked hard to expose it, wrote, "an operation."[10] The shift from Westmoreland's war of attrition to General Creighton Abrams's "accelerated pacification" did not mean an end to the body count. General Julian Ewell, known within the military by his nickname, the "Butcher of the Mekong," was congratulated by Abrams on the success of Operation Speedy Express, which lasted from early December 1968 to the end of May 1969.[11] Ewell's pressure on his commanding officers to increase the kill ratio spurred them to exceed even Moore's record, achieving a ratio of 40.8:1. Units with low body counts were told they would have to remain in the field until they improved, and officers were given 3 × 5 index cards on which to record their monthly totals. One American military observer witnessed the strafing of a group of boys and the water buffalo they tended, which had turned the paddy field in which they stood "into a bloody ooze littered with bits of mangled flesh. The dead boys and the water buffalo were added to the official body count of the Viet Cong."[12] A reporter for *Newsweek* observed that despite a body count of almost eleven thousand, only 748 weapons had been collected in the Speedy Express operation. The use of firepower, Kevin Buckley concluded, was "indiscriminate" but "quite discriminating . . . as a matter of policy, in populated areas." One after-action report offered a dubious explanation: "Many individuals in vc guerrilla units are not armed with weapons."[13]

The Phoenix Program, the showcase counterinsurgency effort that occupied the waning years of the American effort in Vietnam, did not change the statistical focus on piling up bodies. Robert "Blowtorch Bob" Komer led the effort, which was intended to directly contest NLF control of villages and hamlets throughout the country by imitating the tactics of the guerrillas as Komer understood them. In addition to welfare projects, teams of Vietnamese with their American advisors would gather information so as to target and eliminate the "Viet Cong infrastructure (VCI)," the network of people, soldiers, and political cadres that RAND and other American analysts credited with sustaining the NLF in the face of American firepower. Komer set a quota of three thousand VCI to be "neutralized" each month. From 1968 to mid-1971, twenty-eight thousand VCI were captured, twenty thousand assassinated, and seventeen thousand persuaded to defect. How many of these people were actually affiliated with the NLF is anyone's guess, for the program was an extortionist's paradise, with payoffs available for denunciation on the one hand or protection on the other. K. Barton Osborne, a military intelligence officer, recalled, "Bringing these people in and interrogating them, the process of even considering legal recourses, was just too overpowering, considering the mania for the body count and the quotas assigned for V.C.I. and neu-tralization. Quite often it was just a matter of expediency just to eliminate a person in the field rather than deal with the paperwork."[14]

Morley Safer, who had been a CBS news reporter in Vietnam, described the effort to locate and "neutralize" local NLF cadres as "a monster child with its computer brain and assassin's instinct [that] would make the Vietcong wither from within": "So out into the countryside went teams of accountants and case officers, Vietnamese assassins and their Amer-ican counterparts, with bags and bags of money, the whole effort teth-ered to a computer in the United States Embassy in Saigon. And from the embassy came reports again and again that the program was work-ing. Body count became our most important product. The bodies turned out to be just about anyone who got in the way, sometimes even genu-ine, certifiable 'infrastructures.'"[15] The disparity in the piles of bodies, the lack of weapons collected, and the lack of notable progress in winning the war gradually brought the practice of counting bodies into disrepute. Some criticism was simple skepticism about the numbers: Were all of the dead really armed enemy soldiers? But skepticism moved readily into an appalled realization: If they weren't enemy soldiers, who were they? With the withdrawal of all American troops in 1973, counting dead Vietnamese was left to those who lived there.

All along, in Korea as in Vietnam, the bookkeeping had been double entry: the fewer American bodies the better; the more enemy bodies the better. American bodies had names, and every effort was made to recover the dead and ship them home along with their personal effects.[16] After the war the American bodies left in Vietnam became a major political issue, and in the effort to restore relations with the United States, the Vietnam-ese government, in the words of Senator John Kerry, launched "the most significant remains retrieval and identification effort in the history of war-fare."[17] As Michael Allen pointed out, by the standard of other wars, the numbers were modest, about 5 percent of those who had died in Vietnam. By contrast, 20 percent "of all Americans killed in World War II—over 78,000 were never found and 8,500 more were never identified. More than 8,000 Americans are still missing from the Korean War, nearly a quarter of American losses." In each of these wars, some effort was made to recover the dead, but "nothing so extensive as the post-Vietnam accounting effort had ever been attempted." Talk of these "lost warriors," Allen explains, "became a way to talk about a lost war, and the effort to account for them was as much a means to establish accountability for their loss as it was a search for their remains."[18] The government had betrayed its citizens, not by sending its young men to fight in Vietnam but by leaving their bodies behind. Americans, not Vietnamese, were the true victims of the war. By 1993 the U.S. government was spending $100 million on recovery efforts, which, given the paucity of results, came to approximately $1.7 million per recovery. Neil Sheehan observed that there was something "bizarre, perhaps even morally obscene—and an insult to the bravery of the dead, to spend so much money searching for bones in a country where children die for want of anti-biotics and thousands of amputees from the war, many of them former Saigon-government soldiers . . . hobble on crutches or go armless, because they cannot afford prosthetic devices."[19]

Vietnamese bodies had no names and were left where they lay, gathered in great nets and helicoptered to mass graves, dragged behind a departing tank, mutilated, their ears trophies for their killers, or left marked with a playing card thought to terrify Vietnamese peasants, the ace of spades.[20] After the war the three hundred thousand Vietnamese missing in action were not considered an American problem. For many Vietnamese, these unburied dead are doomed to wander the earth, grieving, angry, a constant reproach to the living.[21]

For some American veterans, however, the Vietnamese dead were an American problem, or in any case, their problem. George Evans, a poet who had served as a combat medic in Vietnam in 1969, returned thirty years later ready to bear what he thought would be the deserved hostility of the village he was visiting. According to his companion on the trip, Wayne Karlin, Evans was perhaps "remembering the children he told me he had seen early in his tour, when he went into the emergency room and saw two dead Vietnamese children—run over by an American truck engaged in a game the drivers called 'gook hockey,' betting on whether or not they could run down the kids on the roads—lying on gurneys, 'like little dolls.' Their mother came in screaming, running back and forth between them, beating at George's chest, her spittle wetting his face, hysterical, lost, her face burned into his mind. They were not the last dead children he saw." Walking through the village, Evans felt he was "running a grief gauntlet—faces twisted in pain, moans and keening sounds." Grief, and also "pure anger." Later he remembered thinking, "Now they have me, finally and now I pay." He braced to face it, telling himself, "Take it, be strong, they deserve to give it and you deserve to get it, it's your responsibility, their pain belongs to you." Karlin, walking beside him, felt no hostility and wondered whether they had each seen what they needed to see.[22]

Karlin's book, *Wandering Souls*, is an account of the effort of one veteran, Homer Steedly Jr., who had fought in Kontum province in 1969, to return the belongings of the young Vietnamese soldier he had killed to the soldier's family.[23] Steedly never explains why he went through the pockets of the man he had just shot, removed the documents he found there, and sent them home to his own mother for safekeeping. Years later, in the course of putting together a website on his war experience, Steedly examined them for the first time. Hoang Ngoc Dam had been trained as a medic, and his notebooks were full of carefully drawn anatomical studies. "I realized that I wanted to try and get those back to whoever they belonged to, just simply because it belonged to them."[24] With Karlin's help Steedly returned to Dam's village and, in an elaborate ceremony, carried a tray of fruit for the family altar. "I'm Homer Steedly," he told the assembled villagers. "I'm a farmer's son that got sent halfway around the world and wound up killing people that I didn't mean to." Later he traveled with the family to retrieve Dam's bones for reburial. In a mystical moment, stopping casually on the trip back north with what were presumed to be Dam's bones, Steedly found himself at the very spot on the trail where Dam had died. He does not feel forgiven. Only Dam himself can offer that, Steedly believes, and perhaps will, should they indeed meet after death.[25]

In the main, however, neither American soldiers nor the American public knew the names of the Vietnamese killed by American arms. Yet every now and then a photograph would inscribe a particular face on public consciousness; later the face might be named. Kim Phuoc, the young girl, her clothes burned off by napalm, her face frozen in shock, was one. Over time, rather like the "Hiroshima maidens" brought to the United States for plastic surgery in 1955, Kim Phuoc came to symbolize all the unnamed Vietnamese dead. Kim Phuoc was treated for her injuries in Saigon; after the war, having studied in Cuba and emigrated to Canada, she established a foundation to assist child victims of war. In a ceremony at the Vietnam Veterans Memorial in Washington in 1996, she accepted an apology from a U.S. serviceman who claimed he may have helped target the bombing raid that burned her. Other faces and other names from those years of war, however, have remained in the shadows of a past the American public wants to forget.

The war continues to mark Vietnamese bodies. The United States had so liberally seeded Vietnam with land mines that they have killed and maimed some 105,000 people between 1975 and 2000. And then there is Agent Orange, as liberally sprayed over South Vietnamese forests and fields. From 1962 to 1971, nineteen million gallons of herbicide were sprayed over six million acres in South Vietnam. Eleven million of those gallons, stored in drums with an orange stripe at the top, contained a highly toxic by-product, 2,4,5-T, Agent Orange. Put another way, some 12 percent of the population of what was then South Vietnam was exposed to this toxic spraying. According to a recent estimate by Fred Wilcox, three million Vietnamese continue to suffer the effects of the chemical warfare the United States conducted during the war, and a "third and even fourth generation of Agent Orange babies have been born." The deformities, recorded in a book of photographs by Philip Jones Griffith, are extreme: not only blind, but eyeless; not only paralyzed, but limbless; not only a misshapen head, but two heads.[26]

It was hardly surprising that the military decided to give up on countless bodies, although not on war itself. Initially General Tommy Franks and Secretary of State Donald Rumsfeld were both firm: there would be no body counts in Iraq after the 2003 invasion. Until a successful Freedom of Information request in 2007, the official number of Iraqis killed by American forces was classified information. According to Lawrence Kaplan, some units in Afghanistan did publicize their kill ratios, but "the practice remained controversial."[27] As the war in Afghanistan began its tenth year, however, the body count returned, with regular reports of the numbers killed, divided into "leaders" and "rank and file."

The new American way of war, which shifts the burden of combat to contract soldiers, Special Forces, and drones, has reintroduced a problem familiar from the Vietnam war: Exactly whose bodies are they? The precision with which drones and Special Forces hunter-killer teams operate depends on the quality of the targeting intelligence available. With some regularity, the targets turn out to be wedding parties, Pakistani military units, Afghani military and police, even, on one occasion, American Marines. Moreover, the quota system returned with a capitalist twist. The contractors who operated some of the targeting programs had quotas. As Joshua Foust has reported, this means that "their continued employment depends on their ability to satisfy the stated performance metrics. So they have a financial incentive to make life-or-death decisions about possible kill targets just to stay employed."[28]

Kaplan wrote that counting bodies meant that the United States was losing the war. The trouble with body counts, he concluded, was the "lack of strategic underpinnings, its tenuous moral legitimacy."[29] That's one way of looking at it. The other is to observe what it reliably reveals: whose bodies count.

NOTES

1. Quoted in Scott Sigmund Gartner and Marissa Edson Myers, "Body Counts and 'Success' in the Vietnam and Korean Wars," *Journal of Interdisciplinary History* 25, no. 3 (Winter 1995): 386, 388–89. So far as I know Gartner and Myers were the first to point out the use of body counts as a marker of success in the Korean War.

2. Gartner and Myers, "Body Counts and 'Success,'" 386, 393.

3. See Alex Abella, *Soldiers of Reason* (New York: Mariner Books, 2009), 92.

4. The mission statement appears in the official "About" section of the online history of RAND, *https://www.rand.org/about/history.html.* Duong Van Mai Elliott, *RAND in Southeast Asia* (Santa Monica, Calif.: RAND Corporation, 2010), 36, 37.

5. Douglas Kinnard, *The War Managers* (Annapolis, Md.: Naval Institute Press, 2007), 73.

6. Gregory A. Daddis, *No Sure Victory: Measuring U.S. Army Effectiveness and Progress in the Vietnam War* (New York: Oxford University Press, 2011), 99–108. As Daddis explains, Westmoreland was convinced that the NLF were the proper concern of the South Vietnamese Army; Americans should be engaging main force North Vietnamese units, while behind the security lines thus established, the South Vietnamese would take care of "pacification" (91–92). For Ia Drang, see 79–85. Daddis also summarizes Hanoi's very different assessment of the battle and its meaning.

7. Daddis, *No Sure Victory*, 96.

8. Quoted in Daddis, *No Sure Victory*, 102–3.

9. Testimony before the Dellums Committee, quoted in Marilyn Young, John J. Fitzgerald, and A. Tom Grunfeld, *The Vietnam War: A History in Documents* (Oxford: Oxford University Press, 2002), 113.

10. Seymour Hersh, "Lieutenant Accused of Murdering 109 Civilians," *St. Louis Post-Dispatch*, November 13, 1969, reprinted on Candide's Notebooks, http://pierretristam.com/Bobst/ library/wf-200.htm. This site contains all of Hersh's original dispatches. [Eds: This site is no longer accessible.] For Ridenhour, see Nick Turse, *Kill Anything That Moves: The Real American War in Vietnam* (New York: Metropolitan, 2013).

11. See Austin Long, "Doctrine of Eternal Recurrence: The U.S. Military and Counterinsurgency Doctrine, 1960–1970 and 2003–2006," RAND Counterinsurgency Study, Paper 6, prepared for the Office of the Secretary of Defense (Santa Monica, Calif.: RAND Corporation, 2008), 18.

12. Nick Turse, "A My Lai a Month," *Nation*, November 13, 2008. The title refers to the estimate made by a soldier who took part in Operation Speedy Express. Turse also discusses his use of the cache of official U.S. documents, declassified in the 1990s and subsequently reclassified, that have revealed how body count drove a blindness to civilian casualties and undercut any claim that the killings at My Lai were a one-time aberration. See also Nick Turse and Deborah Nelson, "A Tortured Past," *Los Angeles Times*, August 20, 2006, and the second in their series, "Civilian Killings Went Unpunished," August 25, 2006.

13. Daddis, *No Sure Victory*, 164–66; Young, et al., *The Vietnam War*, 223. See also Turse, *Kill Anything That Moves*.

14. See Young, et al., *The Vietnam War*, 213. This account of Phoenix is drawn from 212–13, 240–41.

15. Morley Safer, "Body Count Was Their Most Important Product," review of Douglas Valentine's book *The Phoenix Program, New York Times*, October 21, 1990.

16. When this is violated, as occurred recently with respect to what the air force has been doing with the bodies of the unidentifiable American dead in Iraq and Afghanistan, there was a serious public outcry. Bodies that proved difficult to identify had been cremated and then dumped in landfills. A report by Brad Knickerbocker quoted from a CNN account: "Backtracking on initial information about how it handled the remains of American service members killed in Iraq and Afghanistan, the Air Force now says the cremated body parts of hundreds of the fallen were burned and dumped in the landfill. . . . The Air Force also said that 1,762 body parts were never identified and also were disposed of, first by cremation, then by further incineration and then buried in a landfill." The practice is said to have ended in 2008. Brad Knickerbocker, "Remains of Hundreds of Fallen American Soldiers Sent to Landfill," *Christian Science Monitor*, December 8, 2011.

17. Quoted in Michael J. Allen, *Until the Last Man Comes Home* (Chapel Hill, N.C.: University of North Carolina Press, 2009), 286. See also Neil Sheehan, "Prisoners of the Past," *New Yorker*, May 24, 1993, 46–51.

18. Allen, *Until the Last Man Comes Home*, 2, 4.

19. Sheehan, "Prisoners of the Past," 46. Total U.S. aid for prosthetic devices came to $1 million.

20. One can buy "Ace of Spades Death Card Patches" on eBay for a song.

21. Memorialization of the dead in Vietnam is complicated by state politics and local religious practice. See Heonik Kwon, *The Ghosts of War in Vietnam* (Cambridge: Cambridge University Press, 2008).

22. Wayne Karlin, *Wandering Souls* (New York: Nation Books, 2009), 218, 219.

23. Karlin, *Wandering Souls*, 218.

24. Karlin, *Wandering Souls*, 176.

25. Karlin, *Wandering Souls*, 256, 286, 305.

26. See Fred Wilcox, "'Dead Forests, Dying People': Agent Orange and Chemical Warfare in Vietnam," *Asia-Pacific Journal: Japan Focus* 9, no. 3 (December 11, 2011). In 2007 a congressional earmark introduced by Senator Patrick Leahy (Democrat, Vermont) to a huge Bush administration appropriation for the War on Terror promised $3 million to clean up dioxin storage sites in Vietnam and support public health programs in the surrounding countryside. It should be noted that this was less than half the amount appropriated by the Ford Foundation for dioxin-related projects in Vietnam.

27. Lawrence Kaplan, "Vietnamization," *New Republic*, March 24, 2011, 9. The Freedom of Information Act suit was brought by the American Civil Liberties Union.

28. Joshua Foust, "Unaccountable Killing Machines: The True Cost of U.S. Drones," *Atlantic*, December 30, 2011.

29. Kaplan, "Vietnamization," 9. Kill ratios are less frequently cited, perhaps because on the whole the disparity between Afghan and U.S. dead is so great. An article in the *Toronto Globe and Mail* quoted the former chief of the defense staff of Canadian forces Rick Hillier, who succinctly stated the military's objective, "to kill 'scumbags,'" but noted that the enemy's "kill ratios are uncomfortably high and growing." Michael Bell, "Afghanistan, Iraq and the Limits of Foreign Intervention," *Globe and Mail*, July 23, 2010. Of course, with drones doing much of the killing, the ratio is pure sci-fi: man against machine.

PART **2**

UNLIMITED WAR,
LIMITED MEMORY

6

THE BIG SLEEP

In order to sleep soundly, Americans will believe anything.
—Joseph Stalin

War is the health of the state.
—Randolph Bourne

In the last forlorn days of America's occupation of Saigon, an American reporter pressed a reluctant diplomat for the "lessons of the war." "They will be whatever makes us think well of ourselves," he replied, "so that our sleep will be untroubled."[1] In seeking to ensure the national repose, the United States is hardly unique. To help their countrymen sleep better, defeated aggressors have always worked to transform their aggression into something more palatable. Abetting this effort is the fact that in wars even aggressors are victims. For many Japanese, the atomic bombing of Hiroshima and Nagasaki balanced, or even erased, the moral onus of Pearl Harbor, the war against China, and their invasion of other Southeast Asian countries; for many Germans, the fire bombings of Hamburg and Dresden, the flood of German refugees from the East, and the rape of German women by the Soviet Army, helped ease the guilty memory of the blitzkrieg and the Holocaust.

First published in *Red Badges of Courage: Wars and Conflicts in American Culture,* ed. Biancamaria Pisapia, Ugo Rubeo, and Anna Scacchi (Roma: Bulzoni Editore, 1998). This essay has been lightly edited to minimize overlap with other works in this volume.

After the Vietnam war, its angry veterans served as surrogate victims for America at large. There was a schizophrenic element in this, since veterans were understood to be victims not only of the Vietnamese but of fellow Americans who had opposed the war and hampered its prosecution. The antiwar movement was charged with a variety of sins: preventing the military from using all of its potential power; prolonging the war by encouraging the enemy to fight on while also forcing the war to end short of victory; refusing to welcome the returning veterans and even spitting on them. Those who pursued and supported the war could thus think well of themselves by thinking ill of those who opposed it.

With all this, Vietnam continued to disturb the nation's sleep. By the late 1970s, the pervasive popular sense that the war had been immoral, was defined, by government officials and the press, as pathological, a "Vietnam syndrome." Treatment took a variety of forms. The Reagan and Bush administrations tried homeopathy, fighting a series of short healing wars whose victorious conclusions might eliminate the syndrome, or at least ease its symptoms. But nothing really worked. Even the war against Iraq, intended, as President George H. W. Bush said, to "kick the Vietnam syndrome once and for all," failed to do so, and public distaste for military adventures remained and remains profound.

For a long time I was convinced that the ways in which Vietnam disturbed the body politic was a direct product of that particular war and the way it was fought. I have come to see that the aftermath of every war in which the United States has engaged was marked by similar efforts to erase the experience of war itself. The striking difference between Vietnam and earlier conflicts is only (but everything rides on that "only") that the effort has not yet succeeded.

Let me start where the consciousness of war starts in America, with the Civil War. In fact, for its domestic divisiveness, Vietnam has frequently been compared to the Civil War. Although it does speak to the sense of intense internal conflict Americans experienced in the Vietnam war years, this is not really a serious historical comparison. For one thing, the Civil War was literally, rather than figuratively, divisive. Then, the number of American men who died in the Civil War was over ten times as great as the figures for Vietnam, which makes the proportional loss thousands of times greater.[2] Moreover, in contrast to Vietnam, in the Civil War there was little confusion, on either side, as to the virtue of the cause or the necessity to defend it: Northern men fought for unity and the Republic;

Southern men, to defend their land. Later, each side developed additional noble explanations: the North had emancipated the slaves; the South had championed the romance of the cavalier society.

One might have expected, then, that postwar memories of the Civil War would be unproblematic. Indeed, had the war been fought throughout in the manner in which it was projected and begun, perhaps that would have been the case. However, by 1864, the course of the war had plunged those who fought it into situations for which nothing in their civilian lives had prepared them. The young men who went to war in 1861 understood war itself as a testing ground for courage, honor, and the individual manly self. The rules of war were clear. The lines between combatants and civilians were well marked, and no one expected to breach them. On the eve of the invasion of Pennsylvania, General Robert E. Lee ordered his troops to respect the private property of the enemy:

> The duties exacted of us by civilization and Christianity are not less obligatory in the country of the enemy than in our own. . . . It must be remembered that we make war only upon armed men, and that we cannot take vengeance of the wrongs our people have suffered without lowering ourselves in the eyes of all whose abhorrence has been excited by the atrocities of our enemies, and offending against Him to whom vengeance belongeth, without whose favor and support our efforts must all prove in vain.[3]

General George McClellan's effort was to win the war with as little loss of life as possible: "I would be glad to clear [the Confederate troops] out of West Virginia and liberate the country without bloodshed, if possible." When he learned that some of his troops had been burning peoples' houses, he was enraged: "I will issue an order to-day informing them that I will hang or shoot any found guilty of it, as well as any guards who permit it. Such things disgrace us and our cause."[4] But the trajectory of the war soon utterly transformed its conduct and with it the soldiers' sense of themselves. As the Confederacy moved to new forms of partisan warfare, Northern generals adopted a strategy of terror against civilians, and casualties mounted in geometric proportions. Early in the conflict, no one thought of combat as continuous. On the contrary, and to the chagrin of their officers, men on both sides arranged for local, informal truces, and warned each other before picking up their rifles. By 1864, combat was continuous, casualties catastrophic. Cherished notions of individual honor and courage survived intact only on the home front. On the field of battle, by 1864–65, few soldiers thought they fought for anything more than their own survival and that of their comrades.

Oliver Wendell Holmes, swept up by Abolitionist fervor and the romances of Walter Scott, dropped out of Harvard in order to enlist in the Union Army. Wounded at the Battle of Ball's Bluff in October 1861, he comforted himself with the thought that should he die it would be "like a soldier anyhow—I was shot in the breast doing my duty up to the hub—afraid? No, I am proud."[5] But by 1864 he was struggling desperately to hold onto those feelings. One letter thanked a friend who had sent him an essay on Joinville's *Chronicle*, for "we need all the examples of chivalry to help us bind our rebellious desires to steadfastness in the Christian Crusade of the 19th century. If one didn't believe that this was such a crusade, in the cause of the whole civilized world, it would be hard indeed to keep the hand to the sword."[6]

Soon, even that belief was not enough. Holmes went so far as to speculate that perhaps, after all, peaceful evolution would have dealt better with the problem of slavery than war, which was "the brother of slavery—brother—it is slavery's parent, child and sustainer at once."[7] In his letters and diary entries during the terrible battles of the Wilderness in the spring of 1864, he despairs. "Before you get this," he writes to his parents, "you will know how immense the butcher's bill has been. . . . I have felt for some time that I didn't any longer believe in this being a duty & so I mean to leave at the end of the campaign as I said if I'm not killed before."[8] But, returning from the war, the disillusioned men kept silent. "Combat had overthrown their original views," the historian Gerald Linderman observes, "while at home initial conceptions of war, though subjected to stress, had remained the common currency."[9] The war changed those men who fought it, but not those who stayed home. Soldiers, Linderman writes, "yearned for the end of the war, never realizing that it would truly end for them only years later, when they surrendered the war they had fought to the war civilian society insisted they had fought."[10] Such an act of surrender has been, I think, common to all American wars, save one. It is precisely the continued insistence by many Vietnam veterans on *their* understanding of the war, that the war be understood and remembered *their* way, that continues to distinguish Vietnam veterans from those of other American wars, foreign and domestic, and continues, as well, to distinguish the war itself in the national memory.

The silence of Civil War veterans was filled, in the decades following Antietam, by the need of many different groups to honor the memory of war by forgetting its reality. Even those who had fought in the war and despised its glorification, like Ambrose Bierce, wrote, only half ironically, of war as a way of cleansing a society they thought gone mad with greed. "A quarter century of peace," Bierce wrote, "will make a nation of blockheads and scoundrels. Patriotism is a vice, but it is a larger vice, and a nobler, than the million petty ones which it promotes in peace to swallow up in war. . . . I favor war, famine, pestilence—anything that will stop the people from cheating and confine that practice to the contractors and the statesmen."[11]

Bierce revisited battlefields and spoke tenderly of the Confederate dead as "honest and courageous foemen" who had "little in common" with those who had persuaded them to fight or to "the literary bearers of false witness in the aftertime."[12] And he seems not to have felt himself a member of those despised litterateurs when he wrote lyrically of the West Virginia countryside through which he had fought: "If any one of the men who in his golden youth soldiered through its valleys of sleep and its gracious mountains will revisit it in the hazy season when it is all aflame with autumn foliage, I promise him sentiments that he will willingly entertain and emotions that he will care to feel."[13]

Holmes went much further in his celebration of what he had once condemned as sheer butchery. "Through our great good fortune," he told the Harvard graduating class of 1895, "in our youth our hearts were touched by fire." "I do not know what is true," he instructed the young men, themselves leaning with pleasure into the growing fever for war against Spain, "I do not know the meaning of the universe. But in the midst of doubt "there is one thing I do not doubt, that no man who lives in the same world with most of us can doubt, and that is that the faith is true and adorable which leads a soldier to throw away his life in obedience to a blindly accepted duty, in a cause which he little understands, in a plan of campaign of which he has no notion, under tactics of which he does not see the use."[14]

The Civil War revival of the 1880s and 1890s, marked by public ritual and commemoration and a leap in the membership rolls of veterans organizations like the Grand Army of the Republic (from 30,000 in 1878 to 428,000 in 1890), raised the status of veterans everywhere; and they responded, not surprisingly, with delight. In small towns across America the veterans became the "keepers of its patriotic traditions, the living embodiment . . . of what it most deeply believed about the nation's greatness and high destiny."[15] The disturbing domestic changes taking place—actual class warfare born out of deepening economic depression, the violent reassertion of white supremacy in the aftermath of Radical Reconstruction, and nativist reaction to immigration—were subsumed in a pervasive martial enthusiasm.[16] In the Plains wars against the Indians and then in the Spanish-American War, Blue and Gray marched together, become one nation indivisible through the mechanism of conquest and Empire.

It is in this context that Stephen Crane's *Red Badge of Courage* (written between 1892 and 1894 when the author was twenty-two years old) became a best seller. Giorgio Mariani's *Spectacular Narratives* explores the ambiguities of Crane's text, the way it lends itself to pacifist readings and yet "end[s] up . . . reinforcing the martial ideals it meant to criticize."[17] Mariani's argument rests on an analysis of the novel's form and its way of presenting events as spectacles. Henry Fletcher exists, Mariani points out, in a "historical vacuum," and this allows Crane to turn "war itself into a myth." War is presented as a "form of aesthetic entertainment" that recreates "war as pure spectacle."[18]

This spectacular representation worked not only to aestheticize the war but also to vitiate any moral questions a more historical treatment would have raised. The power of *Red Badge* lies in the way it allowed veterans, their families and friends, to remember and forget the war they actually fought without ruining war for the rest of the country. Although Crane mocks Henry Fletcher's Homeric fantasies at the start of the novel, he fulfills them by the end. Fletcher *does* become a man through the crucible of battle, a message few veterans—or prospective veterans—could resist, and one that had obvious resonance in the militarized atmosphere of the 1890s. The rage and brutality of battle, precisely because it is so realistically rendered, attracts as much as it repels. The veterans were not amnesiac, nor the country without fear as it seduced itself into war against Spain. And Crane's novel captures this ambiguity. As Mariani points out, on the last page, hero and reader both understand that "battles, heroes, and war narratives all depend upon death." In the terrible figure of a tattered man who pursues Fletcher, Crane's war spectacle projects "in the form of hallucination, a repressed narrative and political alternative which, if thoroughly embraced, would force us to rewrite the history of all wars, both fictional and real."[19]

Wars, the literary critic Amy Kaplan has pointed out, continue one another. The mounting economic, racial, and social crisis of the 1880s and

1890s, in part a consequence of the changes set in motion by the Civil War, expressed themselves in a gathering storm of domestic and international antiforeign sentiment that preceded, and perhaps made inevitable, the Spanish-American War. The war was not only a major U.S. departure into overseas empire building but simultaneously a unifying force.[20] In a context of violent clashes between labor and capital, of fierce competition between "native" Americans and new immigrants, killing together was proof of unity. In a letter to his wife, Senator Henry Cabot Lodge saw the new war reconciling the nation's past and present divisions. It was with tears in his eyes, he told her, that he watched the Sixth Massachusetts Regiment, which, as it happened, had been attacked by a Baltimore mob thirty-seven years earlier, march through the city again in 1898. "First came the city people, bands and then the drums and fifes of the regiment playing 'Dixie'—the drums and fifes of the 6th Massachusetts—and the crowd cheering wildly. . . . I never felt so moved in my life. The war of 1861 was over at last and this great country for which so many men died was one again."[21]

It was only fitting that Stephen Crane, who had recreated the Civil War from memoirs and photographs, should became one of the premier war correspondents of his day.[22] In his dispatches for Hearst and Pulitzer, Crane offered vivid close-ups of the soldiers' bronzed and blazing faces, the Mauser bullets "sneering in the air a few inches over one's head"; the woods crackling "like burning straw." At the battle of Guantanamo, the "hill resembled . . . those terrible scenes on the stage—scenes of intense gloom, blinding lightening, with a cloaked devil or assassin or other appropriate character muttering deeply amid the awful roll of the thunder-drums. It was theatric beyond words." Indeed, as Mariani puts it, Crane's reports "do not merely call attention to reality as spectacle: they *construct* reality as spectacle."[23]

Beyond spectacle, Crane's reports provide concrete examples, icons for an imperial nationalism that boasted a united American people, confident of their racial superiority and martial power. His account of the Battle of San Juan is a good example: an assault timid foreign observers said couldn't succeed, a "haze of bullets," an infamous enemy firing at the wounded, a contemptible ally and nonstop American courage. In another report from the front, American soldiers stand firm "amid the animal-like babble of the Cubans," and Rough Riders advance "steadily and confidently under the Mauser bullets," forcing the Spanish, who had "never had men fight them in this manner," to flee.[24]

The Spanish-American War was perhaps the first limited war in American history and certainly the only wholly successful one.[25] But ironically, the short war, which had unified the country, yielded to a long, bitter conflict that threatened to redivide it. The brutal history of the war against Filipino nationalists, largely ignored until the 1960s when the war in Vietnam gave it sudden relevance, was more difficult to assimilate than the victory over Spain. General Jacob Smith, a veteran of the Wounded Knee massacre, ordered his troops to kill every Filipino male over the age of ten and turn the island of Samar into a "howling wilderness." By 1901, shocking details of the war against the insurgents forced a congressional investigation. Yet within months, Smith had been forgiven, at least by the mainstream press.[26] American abuses in the Philippines were reimagined as brave and lawful responses to treachery. This is why young men who enthusiastically enlisted in the army in 1917 did so with no sense they were joining a tainted institution. And it wasn't until 1971 that a veteran of the Samar campaign felt moved to tell the press that the massacre at My Lai was hardly unique; his own mission had involved a fishing village. "We snuck through the grass as high as a man's head until both platoons had flanked them. We opened fire and killed all but one. They were unarmed."[27] Returning veterans, when they spoke in public at all, defended army tactics as necessary in a guerrilla war.[28] Indeed, the only sustained protest by veterans was over their loss of benefits, since the conflict in the Philippines was classed as an insurrection rather than a war.

William Vaughn Moody's poem, "On a Soldier Fallen in the Philippines," offers the best explanation of the collective amnesia that followed the suppression of the Filipino movement:

> Toll! Let him never guess What work we sent him to. Laurel, laurel, yes.
> He did what we bade him do.
> Praise, and never a whispered hint but the fight he fought was good;
> Never a word that the blood on his sword was his country's own heart's
>   blood,
> A flag for his soldier's bier
> Who dies that his land may live;
> O banners, banners here,
> That he doubt not nor misgive!
>   . . .

Let him never dream that his bullet's scream went wide of its island mark;
Home to the heart of his darling land where she stumbled and sinned in
the dark.[29]

The public at large, not the dead soldier, was protected by this sympathetic silence; and silence was maintained through two world wars and a "police action" in Korea, until it was finally broken in Vietnam.

Of course, it was not an absolute silence. Paul Fussell has written extensively of the "loquacity" of the Great War.[30] Two American novels by John Dos Passos are indeed eloquent, while at the same time they demonstrate the process by which American wars are incorporated, in their aftermath, into the progressive teleology of the American national narrative.

Three Soldiers, which appeared shortly after the war, is a young man's book, published when Dos Passos was only twenty-five. The tedium and horrors of war it exposed were at the same time redeemed by the romantic image of the novel's hero, John Andrews, who deserts the army—but only after the Armistice—and is subsequently carted off to prison, while the wind blows the pages of his unfinished memoir about "until the floor was littered with them."[31] The novel *1919* is a much darker book, a savage rejection of the society that produced the industrialists, militarists, and politicians responsible not just for World War I but for the imperialist war that had preceded it.

British accounts of the war drew on the literary tradition. By contrast, *1919* is a breathless, breathtaking, nonstop newsreel, composed of flashbacks, dramatic jump cuts, and a virtually audible mocking soundtrack composed of contemporary war songs, patriotic drum rolls, and the sickening hypocrisy of political speeches, peopled indistinguishably by fictional and historical characters. John Doe, the Unknown Soldier, dies meaninglessly. Once dead, he serves the purposes of others:

and the incorruptible skeleton
and the scraps of dried viscera and skin bundled in khaki
they took to Chalons-sur-Marne
and laid it out neat in a pine coffin
and took it home to God's Country ... and draped the Old Glory over it
and Mr. Harding prayed to God and the diplomats and the generals
    and the admirals and the brasshats and the politicians and the
    handsomely dressed ladies out of the society column of the

Washington Post stood up solemn and thought how beautiful sad
Old Glory God's Country.[32]

At the same time, however heartfelt the young Dos Passos's rejection of
the mindless savagery of the battlefield, American readers were as likely to
draw from it, as from the antiwar poems of Pound, Owens, and Sassoon, a
countermessage of the romance of near-death, the compelling attractions of
the Myth of the War Experience. The soldiers in Ezra Pound's "Hugh Selwyn Mauberley" may have "walked eye-deep in hell," only to die for "an old
bitch gone in the teeth, / For a botched civilization." But they were also "dar-
ing as never before. . . . Young blood and high blood, / fair cheeks and fine
bodies; / fortitude as never before, / frankness as never before, / disillusions
as never told in the old days, / hysterias, trench confessions, laughter out of
dead bellies."[33] Who could resist? Literary memories of the First World War
"instead of revulsion produced envy in men too young to have fought."[34]

There is a dreary regularity to this script: youth goes to war with a
song in his heart, experiences war, hates it, with luck survives, maintains
silence, or, if a writer, tries to convey the contradictory experience. In this,
the state and memory conspire: veterans are rewarded with monuments,
memorials, educational funds, the dulling, over time, of individual memories of war, the inflation, over time, of the nobility of the enterprise. On
the home front, the war, while it is taking place, is rendered as spectacle,
for, as Michael Rogin points out, spectacle "is the cultural form of amnesiac representation, for spectacular displays are superficial and sensately
intensified, short lived and repeatable."[35] Just the thing, then, to allow the
possibility of war.

[In a passage repeated in *The Age of Global Power* in this volume, Young
discusses parallels during World War II but also complicates the idea of
spectacle, engaging World War II reporter Ernie Pyle's visceral final column.[36] She then turns to the Cold War era.]

Rogin, among others, has described the rapidity with which the Cold
War served to enshrine World War II as the "good war," a sacred icon of
national virtue, even as World War II served to explain and justify the
Cold War.

The war in Korea was more like the one that followed it in Vietnam than
anti–Vietnam war protestors realized. At first, the 1960s antiwar movement thought the Korean War reflected more morality and logic than the

Vietnam war. In Korea, they argued, there had been a clear violation of an international border, and Munich had taught the world that appeasement of aggression could only lead to a wider war. The ease with which the history of Korea from 1945 to 1950 was simply erased is, in retrospect, surprising, given the active support of the U.S. government for the repressive government of Syngman Rhee. Moreover, the tactics used in Korea were as disproportionately brutal as in Vietnam. In terms of weapons, casualties, and popular doubt about American war aims, Korea was not different from Vietnam. During the first three months of the Korean War, 7.8 million gallons of napalm had been dropped; by November 1950, Bomber Command was grounded because, as its commander testified before Congress, "there were no more targets in Korea." Targets or no, the bombing of North Korea resumed in the summer of 1952 with a ferocity matched only by the Christmas bombing of North Vietnam twenty years later. In July and August 1952, 697 tons of bombs and 10,000 liters of napalm were dropped on Pyongyang, killing 6,000 civilians. In May 1953, North Korean dikes and dams were heavily bombed, destroying the rice crop. Yet there was no public outrage, nor did anyone think to question the national character.[37]

What, then, made the Vietnam war stick? Perhaps one of the most important differences was that the war coincided with the civil rights movement, which had already shaken the nation's confidence in its transcendental morality. The United States was fighting in Vietnam, the public was told, because communism would deny the Vietnamese the most signal privilege of democracy: free elections. Yet on the television screens of the country, night after night, Americans watched as African Americans were set upon by truncheon-wielding police and their attack dogs, swept off their feet by high-power hoses, beaten and killed, in their effort to exercise the most basic rights of citizenship, including the right to vote. The movement for civil rights indicted the past along with the present, went back to query the Founding Fathers along with the history of race relations in America, and made inescapable the "inescapable paradox," as the historian Nathan Huggins put it, of a "free nation, inspired by the Rights of Man, having to rest on slavery."[38]

In that context, the issues of the Vietnam war were now seen to bring into question the founding premise of American history itself. It was an axiom of this history that the United States, from its inception and as an aspect of that inception, stood for self-determination, freedom, and democracy. The longer the Vietnam war lasted, the less tenable that proposition became. The United States was supporting a government that tortured, jailed, and executed those who challenged its rule; along with this dubious ally, the U.S. military, before the eyes of its television-watching citizens, leveled villages, forced their inhabitants into refugee camps, napalmed, carpet bombed, and massacred noncombatants. For an increasing number of Americans, the war seemed to impugn the nation's entire past, recalling, in the language and manner in which it was fought, the extermination of Native Americans and the violence of continental and overseas conquests. Soldiers in the field called Vietnam "Indian country," a phrase whose gloss, historians pointed out, went back to the nation's origins. As the historian Richard Slotkin has analyzed it, starting with the annihilation of the continent's previous inhabitants, America developed a culture that found fundamental, regenerative power in violence. Vietnam was an acid bath in which received myths dissolved. In 1985, Loren Baritz wrote an impassioned polemic against the war, *Backfire: A History of How American Culture Led Us into Vietnam and Made Us Fight the Way We Did*. America, he declared, "must be for freedom, for dignity, for genuine democracy, or it is not America. It was not America in Vietnam."[39] The problem, however, was that many Americans had concluded the reverse: America was never more itself than in Vietnam.

Vietnam was thus the first American conflict since the turn of the century in which the reality of the war that the soldiers fought was acknowledged at home. Soldiers broke the vow of silence that had protected the home front in the past; civilians resisted patriotic blandishments to ignore atrocities and the persistent efforts of all administrations since 1975 to reclaim war as a natural event.

Let me conclude with a brief comparison between Stephen Crane, boy-reporter of the Spanish-American and Greco-Turkish wars, and Michael Herr, boy-reporter in Vietnam. There are many similarities. Herr, anticipating MTV, wrote a rock and roll acid trip prose, but the effect on the reader is very like Crane's close-ups.[40] We watch the reporter watching the war, and it's a terrific show. Both reporters preserve war's glamour, Herr explicitly, quoting at one point his photographer friend Tim Page, who laughs to scorn the idea of "taking the glamour out of war." "Ohhh," Page howls with glee, "war is *good* for you, you can't take the glamour out of that. It's like trying to take the glamour out of sex, trying to take the glamour out of the Rolling Stones."[41] In the tradition of *Red Badge of Courage*,

Herr feels himself "brother to these poor tired grunts, I knew what they knew now, I'd done it and it was really something. Everywhere I'd gone, there had always been Marines or soldiers who would tell me . . . *You're all right, man, you guys are cool, you got balls.*" "If you can't find your courage in a war," he writes elegiacally on the last page of *Dispatches*, "you have to keep looking for it anyway."[42]

Nevertheless, there are places in their narratives where both Crane and Herr project a vision of war at odds with the breathless spectacle that dominates their texts. Giorgio Mariani brings this out in reference to Crane's newspaper column on the Battle of Velestino. After a lyrical description of artillery fire, Crane points out that there is another perspective on all this "beautiful sound," that of "the men who died there. The slaughter of Turks was great." "That uncanny comment," Mariani writes, "casually inserted into the narrative, forces us to acknowledge that both writer and reader are repressing a point of view that would disrupt the entire representational edifice of the text—the point of view of the dead."[43] The repressed point of view Herr introduces, as casually as Crane does that of the Turkish soldiers, is the Vietnamese: "No sounds at all on the road out of Can Tho, twenty of us in a straight line that suddenly ballooned out into a curve, wide berth around a Vietnamese man who stood without a word and held his dead baby out to us. We made tracks and we made dust in our tracks."[44]

If reporters like Herr were the only ones telling the story, however, Vietnam would have joined the list of wars whose memory sets the scene for the next one. One major factor in preventing this and resisting the translation of the war into myth and spectacle is the voluminous writing of the Vietnam veterans themselves. Take this passage from Herr, for example:

> we got out. Because . . . we all knew that if you stayed too long you became one of those poor bastards who had to have a war on all the time. . . . We got out and became like everyone else who has been through a war: changed, enlarged and (some things are expensive to say) incomplete. A few extreme cases felt that the experience there had been a glorious one, while most of us felt that it had been merely wonderful. I think that Vietnam was what we had instead of happy childhoods.[45]

Compare with this from Tim O'Brien:

> A war story is never moral. It does not instruct, nor encourage virtue, nor suggest models of proper human behavior. . . . If a story seems moral do not believe it. If at the end of a war story you feel uplifted, or if you

feel that some small bit of rectitude has been salvaged from the larger waste, then you have been made the victim of a very old and terrible lie. There is no rectitude whatsoever. There is no virtue.[46]

The difficulty President Bush had in mobilizing the country for war in Iraq in 1990, the fact that that war did not cure the Vietnam syndrome, the election as president of a draft evader, these are signs, I would like to think, that many Americans have not been willing, or able, this time, to go back to sleep.

NOTES

1. Quoted in Ward Just, "The American Blues," in *The Other Side of Heaven: Postwar Fiction by Vietnamese and American Writers* (New York: Curbstone Books, 1995), 7.
2. The population at the time of the Civil War was approximately 31,400,000; during the Vietnam war, about 250 million.
3. Quoted in Gerald Linderman, *Embattled Courage: The Experience of Combat in the American Civil War* (New York: Free Press, 1987), 180.
4. Quoted in Linderman, *Embattled Courage*, 203–4.
5. Quoted in Edmund Wilson, *Patriotic Gore: Studies in the Literature of the American Civil War* (New York: W.W. Norton & Company, 1994), 745–46.
6. Wilson, *Patriotic Gore*, 748.
7. Wilson, *Patriotic Gore*, 750.
8. Wilson, *Patriotic Gore*, 751–52.
9. Linderman, *Embattled Courage*, 266.
10. Linderman, *Embattled Courage*, 3.
11. Quoted in Wilson, *Patriotic Gore*, 626.
12. Wilson, *Patriotic Gore*, 625.
13. Wilson, *Patriotic Gore*, 633.
14. Linderman, *Embattled Courage*, 281–2.
15. Bruce Catton, quoted in Linderman, *Embattled Courage*, 280.
16. An exhaustive account of the martial atmosphere of these years can be found in Kristin L. Hoganson, *Fighting for American Manhood: How Gender Politics Provoked the Spanish-American and Philippine-American Wars* (New Haven: Yale University Press, 2000).
17. Giorgio Mariani, *Spectacular Narratives: Representations of Class and War in Stephen Crane and the American 1890s* (New York: Peter Lang, 1992), 143.
18. Mariani, *Spectacular Narratives*, 147, 152, 158.
19. Mariani, *Spectacular Narratives*, 165.
20. Amy Kaplan, "Black and Blue on San Juan Hill," in *Cultures of United States Imperialism*, ed. Amy Kaplan and Donald E. Pease (Durham, N.C.: Duke University Press, 1993), 219.
21. Quoted in Fabian Hilfrich, "History as Argumentative Weapon: Remembering

the Civil War in the American Imperialism Debate at the Turn of the Century," paper delivered at the Organization of American Historians Conference, March 1995.

22. Many readers thought Crane had fought in the Civil War. See letter from Crane to John Northern Hilliard, February 1895, in Stephen Crane, *The Red Badge of Courage*, ed. Donald Pizer, Third Norton Critical Edition (New York: W.W. Norton & Company, 1994), 118.

23. In the same paragraph, rifles rattle, field guns boom, and the "diabolic" Colt automatics clack. Stephen Crane, "Marines Signaling under Fire at Guantanamo," in *The War Dispatches of Stephen Crane*, ed. R. W. Stallman and E. R. Hagemann (New York: NYU Press, 1964), 142, 145, 149, 150; Mariani, *Spectacular Narratives*, 159 (emphasis in original).

24. *The War Dispatches of Stephen Crane*, 108, 172–83, 154, 157. See also Kaplan's reading of this column in Kaplan, "Black and Blue," 220–23.

25. It was not the war against Spain but the one that followed against Filipino insurgents that raised questions about American national identity.

26. Stuart Creighton Miller, *"Benevolent Assimilation": The American Conquest of the Philippines, 1899–1903* (New Haven, Conn.: Yale University Press, 1982), 246.

27. Quoted in Miller, *"Benevolent Assimilation,"* 267.

28. Efforts by the anti-imperialist press to gather antiwar sentiments from returning soldiers had very mixed results. Although an overwhelming majority of officers and men criticized the war, they were equally unanimous in opposing withdrawal short of total victory. Even those opposed to annexation insisted that the United States had first to beat the Filipinos "into submission." Miller finds the sentiments of Corporal Moses Smith typical: "Now I don't believe there is a soldier or American but believes the Filipinos must be whipped thoroughly. After that we can give them independence under an American protectorate." Stuart C. Miller, "The American Soldier and the Conquest of the Philippines," in *Reappraising an Empire: New Perspectives on Philippine-American History*, ed. Peter W. Stanley (Cambridge, Mass.: Harvard University Press), 19.

29. Quoted in Miller, *"Benevolent Assimilation,"* 275–76.

30. Paul Fussell, *Wartime: Understanding and Behavior in the Second World War* (New York: Oxford University Press, 1989), 132.

31. John Dos Passos, *Three Soldiers* (New York: Carroll & Graf, 1988), 433.

32. John Dos Passos, *1919* (New York: Signet Classic, 1969), 466–67.

33. Ezra Pound, "Hugh Selwyn Mauberley: Life and Contacts," in *The Norton Anthology of Modern Poetry*, ed. Richard Ellmann and Robert O'Clair (New York: W.W. Norton & Company, 1988), 346.

34. George L. Mosse, *Fallen Soldiers: Reshaping the Memory of the World Wars* (New York: Oxford University Press, 1990), 193.

35. Michael Rogin, "'Make My Day!': Spectacle as Amnesia in Imperial Politics [and] the Sequel," in *Cultures of United States Imperialism*, 507.

36. See Ernie Pyle, "On Victory in Europe," n.d., found on Pyle's body after his death, April 18, 1945, posted on the Ernie Pyle website, Indiana University School

of Journalism, https://sites.mediaschool.indiana.edu/erniepyle/1945/04/18/on
-victory-in-europe/.

37. Gavan McCormack, Jr., *Cold War, Hot War: An Australian Perspective on the Korean War* (Sydney: Hale and Iremonger, 1983), 126, 124.

38. Nathan Huggins, *Black Odyssey: The African American Ordeal in Slavery* (New York: Vintage Books, 1990), xi.

39. Loren Baritz, *Backfire: A History of How American Culture Led Us into Vietnam and Made Us Fight the Way We Did* (New York: William Morrow, 1985), 341.

40. Michael Herr, *Dispatches* (Knopf: New York, 1977). Indeed, Elizabeth Swados made *Dispatches* into a rock musical, and Herr was one of the screenwriters for the phantasmagoric movie *Apocalypse Now.*

41. Herr, *Dispatches*, 268.

42. Herr, *Dispatches*, 222 (emphasis in original), 279.

43. Mariani, *Spectacular Narratives*, 164.

44. Herr, *Dispatches*, 278.

45. Herr, *Dispatches*, 263.

46. Tim O'Brien, *The Things They Carried* (Boston: Houghton Mifflin Harcourt, 1990), 76.

7

BOMBING CIVILIANS: FROM THE TWENTIETH TO THE TWENTY-FIRST CENTURIES

SENATOR FULBRIGHT: And this [reprisal raids] was interpreted to mean if we showed the will then the North Vietnamese would surrender. I mean, being faced with such overwhelming power, they would stop. Is that really the way they were thinking?

MR. THOMPSON: "Would be brought to their knees" was the phrase that was used.

—Fulbright hearings, 1968

Airpower . . . can profoundly influence the human condition. Through selective engagement, airpower can support a recovering population; encourage one element while discouraging another; monitor, deter, transport, and connect; and assist in establishing the conditions for a safe and secure future.

—Robyn Read, U.S. Air Force Colonel (ret.), 2005

World War II ended with the biggest bang then possible, administered in what was believed to be a righteous cause, the defeat of Japan. A total bombing was the logical conclusion to a total war. Then and since, to many in the armed forces, particularly the air force, anything short of the massive use of available weaponry to attain American ends is immoral. "The memory of World

First published in *Bombing Civilians: A Twentieth-Century History,* ed. Yuki Tanaka and Marilyn B. Young (New York: New Press, 2009), 154–73. Compilation copyright © 2009 by Yuki Tanaka and Marilyn B. Young. Individual essays copyright © 2009 by each author. Reprinted by permission of The New Press. www.thenewpress.com.

War II," Ron Schaffer has written, "seems to have led some air force leaders to feel that all-out annihilation war was the sole tradition of America's armed-forces." The possibility of "obliterating everything in the enemy country, turning everything to ash" gave U.S. Air Force generals like Ira Eaker and Curtis LeMay, wholly secure in the air and able to attack any enemy at will, a sense of irresistible power. Limited war was an oxymoron; worse, it was the world ending in an unseemly whimper.[1] The only problem the advocates of unbridled airpower foresaw was the timorousness of a civilian leadership unwilling to use its weapons.

I shall explore in this essay the ways in which the definition of limited war fought with limited means was, in Korea and in Vietnam, slowly but certainly transformed into total war fought all out—short of nuclear weapons. Starting with Korea and undergoing sophisticated development in Vietnam, airpower was understood as a special language addressed to the enemy, and to all those who might in the future become the enemy. It was, at the same time, a language intended to reassure America's allies. And it was a language that incorporated one very crucial silence: behind all the bombs dropped was the sound of the one that *could* drop but did not . . . yet.

On June 25, 1950, North Korean tanks rolled across the thirty-eighth parallel, an echo of another blitzkrieg eleven years earlier. President Harry S. Truman's first response to the news was to prepare to wipe out all Soviet air bases in East Asia. His logic was impeccable. The North Koreans were acting as Soviet proxies, testing Western resolve as Hitler had tested it in Munich; the history of politics and warfare on the Korean peninsula prior to June 1950 was irrelevant.[2] His second response, upon learning that wiping out the bases would require time and the use of nuclear weapons, was to open all of Korea south of the thirty-eighth parallel to air force bombing. The goal was only in part to halt the North Korean advance. Of equal importance was conveying messages of resolve to Pyongyang and support to Seoul. A few days later, with the same goals in mind, Truman sent the bombers north of the thirty-eighth parallel, opening a campaign of destruction that, in ferocity and total tonnage dropped, rivaled the campaigns so recently concluded in Europe and Japan.

What was it about bombing that made it so attractive to U.S. policy makers as a mode of communication? The answer begins with a fallacy: World War II ended in a blaze of bombing, ergo, bombing ended the war.

According to Earl Tilford, although airpower has never fulfilled the promises of its prophets, after World War II the "doctrine of strategic bombardment, like the doctrine of the resurrection of the body in Christianity, had to be accepted on faith."[3] Those who doubted the efficacy of strategic bombing were committed to tactical bombing.[4] Colonel Raymond Sleeper, contemplating the post–Korean War future, argued that the objective of a limited war was not the total destruction of the enemy but rather a means of waging "peace through air persuasion." His model was the supple use of airpower to punish and coerce ostensibly employed by the British Royal Air Force in various colonial expeditions.[5] Secretary of State Robert McNamara, with the experience of the Cuban missile crisis behind him, developed this idea, convinced, as H. R. McMaster has written, that "the aim of force was not to impose one's will on the enemy but to communicate with him. Gradually intensifying military action would convey American resolve and thereby convince an adversary to alter his behavior."[6]

What and how one bombed could convey different messages to the enemy: a restricted target list held the threat of an unrestricted one, conventional bombing the threat of nuclear possibilities. Moreover, as in Vietnam, bombing could be turned on and off with greater ease and less domestic impact than sending or withdrawing troops. The alert opponent would presumably get the idea and move toward an acceptable settlement. And if he did not? Well, that was the beauty of it: bombing could be intensified, target lists expanded, new airborne ordnance developed, and the lethality of extant weapons improved.

To garner domestic support for war, images of air war also made striking pictures, preferable to those of ground combat—thousands of bombs tumbling to earth, while their effects on impact were never imposed on the viewer.[7] Raining down destruction has been the prerogative of the gods since before Zeus. Combat troops were as awkward as their nickname, *grunts*, suggested. They were burdened by their heavy packs, moving arduously through steaming or frozen landscapes. Pilots were *aces*, carried into the wild blue yonder at unimaginable speed.[8] It is not surprising that President George W. Bush landed a jet on an aircraft carrier to announce the end of combat in Iraq.

Airpower embodies American technology at its most dashing. At regular intervals, the air force and allied technocrats claim that innovations in air technology herald an entirely new age of warfare. Korea and Vietnam were, so to speak, living laboratories for the development of new weapons: the 1,200-pound radio-guided Tarzon bomb (featured in Korean-era Movietone newsreels);[9] white-phosphorous-enhanced napalm; cluster bombs carrying up to 700 bomblets, each bomblet containing 200 to 300 tiny steel balls or fiberglass fléchettes; delayed-fuse cluster bombs; airburst cluster bombs; toxic defoliants; varieties of nerve gas; sets of six B-52s, operating at altitudes too high to be heard on the ground, capable of delivering up to thirty tons of explosives each. A usual mission consisted of six planes in formation, which together could devastate an area one half mile wide by three miles long. Older technologies were retrofitted: slow cargo planes ("Puff the Magic Dragon"[10]) equipped with rapid-fire machine guns capable of firing 6,000 rounds a minute; World War I–era Skyraiders, carrying bomb loads of 7,500 pounds and fitted with four 20-millimeter cannon that together fired over 2,000 rounds per minute.

The statistics stun; they also provide distance. They are impossible to take in, as abstract as the planning responsible for producing them. In Korea over a three-year period, U.S./UN forces flew 1,040,708 sorties and dropped 386,037 tons of bombs and 32,357 tons of napalm. If one counts all types of airborne ordnance, including rockets and machine-gun ammunition, the total tonnage comes to 698,000.[11] Throughout World War Il, in all sectors, the United States dropped 2 million tons of bombs; for Indochina the total figure is 8 million tons, with an explosive power equivalent to 640 Hiroshima-size bombs. Three million tons were dropped on Laos, exceeding the total for Germany and Japan by both the United States and Great Britain.[12] For nine years, an average of one planeload of bombs fell on Laos every eight minutes. In addition, 150,000 acres of forest were destroyed through the chemical warfare known as defoliation. For South Vietnam, the figure is 19 million gallons of defoliant dropped on an area comprising 20 percent of South Vietnam—some 6 million acres.[13] In an even briefer period, between: 1969 and 1973, 539,129 tons of bombs were dropped in Cambodia, largely by B-52s, of which 257,465 tons fell in the last six months of the war (as compared to 160,771 tons on Japan from 1942 to 1945).[14] The estimated toll of the dead, the majority civilian, is equally difficult to absorb: 2–3 million in Korea, 2–4 million in Vietnam.

To the policy makers, air war is abstract. They listen attentively for a response to the messages they send and discuss the possibility that many more may have to be sent. For those who deliver the messages, who actually drop the bombs, air war can be either abstract (in a high-flying B-29 or B-52, for example) or concrete. Often it is a combination. Let me offer an example that combines the abstract with the concrete. During the Korean War, one pilot confided to a reporter that napalm had become the most valued of all the weapons at his disposal. "The first couple of times I went in on a napalm strike," Federic Champlin told E. J. Kahn,

> I had kind of an empty feeling. I thought afterward, Well, maybe I shouldn't have done it. Maybe those people I set afire were innocent civilians. But you get conditioned, especially after you've hit what looks like a civilian and the A-frame on his back lights up like a Roman candle—a sure enough sign that he's been carrying ammunition. Normally speaking. I have no qualms about my job. Besides, we don't generally use napalm on people we can see. We use it on hill positions, or buildings. And one thing about napalm is, that when you've hit a village and have seen it go up in flames, you know that you've accomplished something. Nothing makes a pilot feel worse than to work over an area and not see that he's accomplished anything.[15]

A "hill position," a "building" (in Vietnam, "hooches," sometimes "structures")—not people. For the man with the A-frame on his back, air war can only be concrete. In 1950, in the month of November alone, 3,300 tons of napalm were dropped on North Korean cities and towns, including the city of Kanggye, 65 percent of which was destroyed by incendiary bombs. In Korea, the British correspondent Reginald Thompson believed he was seeing a "new technique of machine warfare. The slightest resistance brought down a deluge of destruction; blotting out the area. Dive bombers, tanks and artillery blasted strong points, large or small, in town and hamlet, while the troops waited at the roadside as spectators until the way was cleared for them."[16]

Years later, another pilot, Major Billings, flying a small spotter plane to call in napalm strikes in South Vietnam, told Jonathan Schell how he identified the enemy: "If they run away." He added: "Sometimes, when you see a field of people, it looks like just a bunch of farmers. Now, you see, the Vietnamese people—they're not interested in the U.S. Air Force, and they don't look at the planes going over them. But down in that field you'll see *one guy* whose conical hat keeps bouncing up and down. He's looking, because he wants to know where you're going." Then, Billings continued, "you make a couple of passes and then, one of them makes a break for it—it's the guy that was looking up at you—and he's your V.C. So you look where he goes, and call in an air strike." Once, he remembered, he "about ran a guy to death," chasing him through the fields for an hour before calling in planes to finish the job. Schell thought this amounted to "sniping with bombs," and the pilot agreed.[17] For Billings, the people themselves were concrete abstractions, ideas all too literally in the flesh.

In addition to the bombs that *were* dropped on Korea, there were those that were constantly contemplated but never used. On June 29, 1950, just four days after the war began, the possibility of using nuclear weapons in the event of Chinese intervention in the war was broached in the National Security Council. In June, as again when the subject came up in July at a State Department policy and planning staff meeting, the question was not so much whether to use nuclear weapons but rather under what conditions they might be used: if there was overt Chinese and Soviet intervention; if their use were essential to victory; "if the bombs could be used without excessive destruction of noncombatants."[18] Talk of using the bomb increased dramatically after the Chinese entered the war in late October 1950, and President Truman's casual reference to the possibility in a press conference brought a nervous Prime Minister Clement Atlee to Washington on the next plane. A joint communique, however, expressed only a sincere hope that "world conditions would never call for the use of the atomic bomb."[19]

General Douglas MacArthur thought the conditions were ripe in December 1950 and requested permission to drop a total of thirty-four bombs on a variety of targets. "I would have dropped 30 or so atomic bombs . . . strung across the neck of Manchuria," he told an interviewer, and "spread behind us—from the Sea of Japan to the Yellow Sea—a belt of radioactive cobalt . . . it has an active life of between 60 and 120 years. For at least 60 years, there could have been no land invasion of Korea from the North." MacArthur's replacement, General Matthew Ridgway, requested thirty-eight atomic bombs.[20] In the event, nuclear weapons were not used; the destruction of northern and central Korea had been accomplished with conventional weapons alone.

The cease-fire that ended the Korean War followed a crescendo of bombing, which was then taken as proof that airpower was as decisive in limited wars as it had been in total war. The cities and towns of central and northern Korea had been leveled; in what Bruce Cumings has called the "final act of this barbaric air war," North Korea's main irrigation dams were destroyed in the spring of 1953, shortly after the rice had been transplanted. "The subsequent floods scooped clean 27 miles of valley below. . . . The Westerner can little conceive the awesome meaning which the loss of [rice] has for the Asian-starvation and slow death."[21] By 1952, according to a UN estimate, one out of nine men, women, and children in North Korea had been killed. In South Korea, five million people had been displaced and one hundred thousand children were described as *unaccompanied*. "The countless ruined villages are the most terrible and universal mark of the war on the Korean landscape. To wipe out cover for North Korean vehicles and personnel, hundreds of thatch-roofed houses were burned by air-dropped jellied gasoline or artillery fire," Walter Sullivan, former *New York Times* Korea correspondent, reported in *The Nation*. J. Donald Kingsley, head of the reconstruction agency, called Korea "the most devastated land and its people the most destitute in the history of modern warfare."[22]

Freda Kirchwey, in an essay for *The Nation*, tried to explain the general indifference of the American public to the destruction:

> We were all hardened by the methods of mass-slaughter practiced first by the Germans and Japanese and then, in self-defense, adopted and developed to the pitch of perfection illustrated at Hiroshima and Nagasaki by the Western allies and, particularly, the Americans. We became accustomed to "area" bombing, "saturation" bombing, all the hideous forms of strategic air war aimed at wiping out not only military and industrial installations but whole populations A deep scar was left on the mind. of Western man, and, again, particularly on the American mind, by the repression of pity and the attempt to off-load all responsibility onto the enemy.

Kirchwey thought that this repression explained the lack of protest "against the orgy of agony and destruction now in progress in Korea." Nothing the North Koreans, Chinese, or Russians had done "excuses the terrible shambles created up and down the Korean peninsula by the American-led forces, by American planes raining down napalm and fire bombs, and by heavy land and naval artillery." And now Korea, "blotted out in the name of collective security, blames the people who drop the fire bombs," which might seem unfair to the military mind but was inevitable: "For a force which subordinates everything to the job of killing the enemy becomes an enemy itself. . . . And after a while plain horror displaces a sense of righteousness even among the defenders of righteousness, and thus the cause itself becomes hateful. This has happened in Korea. Soon, as we learn the facts, it will overtake us here in America."[23]

"The American mind," Kirchwey was certain, "mercurial and impulsive, tough and tender, is going to react against the horrors of mechanized warfare in Korea."[24]

The air force reached different conclusions. In 1957, a collection of essays was published whose title declared its thesis: *Airpower: The Decisive Force in Korea*. The authors of one of the essays in the collection describe an air operation they considered exceptionally successful. Late in 1952, a small group of air commanders set out to demonstrate the extent to which airpower alone could "occupy" territory. Their intention was to show the North Koreans that the United States could "exert an effective form of air pressure at any time or any place, could capture and air control any desired segment of his territory for as long as the military situation warranted." The campaign began in January 1953. For five days, twenty-four hours a day, "a devastating force walked the earth over a 2-by-4 mile target area" and for six days thereafter nothing in the area moved. After 2,292 combat sorties, "Air forces bought a piece of real estate 100 miles behind enemy lines and ruled it for 11 days." But on the fourteenth day, "with typical Communist swiftness," "hordes" of "Red laborers and soldiers" began repair work; six days after the attack, a bypass was in place and rail links had been restored. The bridges attacked had been rebuilt, as had the highways and rail links. Still, the report was certain, "in the gnarled steel and wrenched earth the Communists saw the specter of a new concept in war—air envelopment."[25] One might imagine that the Americans had a lesson to learn here: that bridges could be rebuilt; that a "curtain of fire" created by such raids could cost the enemy a week's time, but not stop them. Instead, against the evidence, many in the air force concluded that had such airpower been applied earlier in the war, it would have ended earlier and on better terms.

In what turned out to be the final phase of the talks, President Eisenhower threatened to use nuclear weapons if the Chinese did not sign a cease-fire agreement. It has become part of the Eisenhower legend that this last threat broke the stalemate and, in Eisenhower's words, gave the United States "an armistice on a single battleground," although not "peace in the world."[26] In the event, as most authorities agree, the Chinese may not have even been aware of the threat, much less responded to it. Chinese acceptance of the concessions demanded at Panmunjom (all of them relating to the issue of repatriation of prisoners of war) was granted for reasons to do with Chinese, North Korean, and Soviet politics, not U.S. atomic flashing.[27] Nevertheless, in addition to the Republican Party, many senior officers in the air force were convinced of the value of such threats and the necessity, if it came to that, of acting on them.[28]

Whatever the air force learned from the Korean War, what the politicians drew from it was more specific and could be boiled down to one dictum: fight the war, but avoid Chinese intervention. Unlike Freda Kirchwey, military and civilian policy makers (and, for that matter, the majority of the American public) never, to my knowledge, questioned the morality of either the ends or the means of fighting in Korea. The difficult question that faced administrations, from Kennedy through Nixon, was tactical: how to use military force in Southeast Asia without unduly upsetting the Chinese. President Kennedy's solution was to concentrate on counterinsurgency, which, as it failed to achieve its end, devolved into a brutal ten-year bombing campaign in South Vietnam.

Although this reverses the actual chronology, I want to deal first with the air war in North Vietnam, keeping in mind that the use of airpower in the south started earlier, lasted longer, and dropped far more tonnage than in the north. The stated goal of the Vietnam war was to create and sustain, south of the seventeenth parallel, a stable anticommunist regime under local leadership friendly to the United States. This is what Eisenhower had accomplished in Korea. The assumption of American policy makers, even those convinced the insurgency had its roots in the south, was that the movement in South Vietnam was dependent on North Vietnam for support and direction. North Vietnamese men and matériel fueled the struggle in the south. Sever that fuel line and the South Vietnamese government would be dealing with an enfeebled guerrilla force, well within its capacity to defeat. Some military men, like General Lawton Collins, argued that "no amount of aerial bombing can prevent completely the forward movement of supplies, particularly in regions where ample manpower is available."[29] President Lyndon B. Johnson also recalled the

Korean experience in conversations with his close friend Senator Richard Russell of Georgia in the late spring and early summer of June 1964. No one, Johnson declared, wanted to send combat troops to Vietnam. Yet *some* sort of military action had to be taken, lest he be considered weak. "America," an old Texas friend had warned him, "wants, by God, prestige and power"; he had no choice but to "stand up for America." Johnson's advisers strongly urged a bombing campaign against North Vietnam, one that would not risk Chinese intervention.

"Bomb the North," Russell asked, "and kill old men, women, and children?" No, no, Johnson reassured him, entering into that abstract world of air warfare in which buildings, highways, and structures are destroyed without killing people, just "selected targets, watch this trail they're coming down."

"We tried it in Korea," Russell protested. "We even got a lot of old B-29s to increase the bomb load and sent 'em over there and just dropped millions and millions of bombs, day and night . . . they would knock the road at night and in the morning, the damn people would be back travelling over it. . . . We never could actually interdict all their lines of communication, although we had absolute control of the seas and the air, and we never did stop them. And you ain't gonna stop these people, either."[30]

Robert McNamara, the secretary of defense Johnson had inherited from Kennedy, was among the most passionate advocates of bombing the north, of "communicating" with bombs,[31] and he now moved to gain approval for this course. On the day of his election victory, Lyndon Baines Johnson convened a working group of the National Security Council to discuss the options in Vietnam. The president was offered three options: to maintain the current level of bombing (including the covert bombing of Laos, which began in May 1964) in which reprisal raids against the north would be flown in response to what the proposal called "VC spectaculars" in the south; to move at once to "fast/full squeeze"—a rapid and powerful increase in bombing of the north; or to begin a program of "progressive squeeze-and-talk," which would involve a "crescendo of additional military moves" against targets in North Vietnam and Laos combined with offers to negotiate with Hanoi. Bombing was a "bargaining chip" to be cashed in for a settlement on U.S. terms.[32] The possibility of using nuclear weapons was raised and rejected, although General Earle Wheeler believed the question remained open and that "in extremis" it should be considered.[33] The choices were structured so that only one made sense, what Raymond Sleeper ten years earlier had named "air persuasion."

On February 13, 1965, McNamara's Operation Rolling Thunder began. It was the "longest sustained strategic air bombardment in history." At lunch each Tuesday, Johnson and his advisers would select the targets, which were then communicated to Admiral U.S. Grant Sharp, the commander in charge of Rolling Thunder. One example of McNamara's effort to hone the messages bombing communicated was reflected in a target list that included attacking "moving targets such as convoys and troops" but not "highways, railroads or bridges with no moving traffic on them." A frustrated officer responsible for carrying out these orders pointed out the "difficulty of recognizing groups of civilians on the ground from troops. "I recognize this as my problem but believe that it can be better defined."[34]

It was especially a problem for the people on the ground. In the first year, 55,000 sorties were flown, and tonnage increased from 200 per week to 1,600 per week. (For a sense of perspective, there were 83,000 sorties in the south in that same year.) Over its course, Operation Rolling Thunder "hammered the north with 304,000 tactical sorties and 2,380 B-52 sorties, which had dropped 643,000 tons of bombs."[35] In an ultimate expression of the abstract nature of the bombing campaign, one presidential adviser, McGeorge Bundy, made it clear that Rolling Thunder did not actually have to work to succeed. Even if the operation failed, Bundy argued, it would "at minimum damp down the charge that we did not do all that we could have done, and this charge will be important in many countries, including our own." Of equal importance, the bombing "set a higher price for the future upon all adventures of guerrilla warfare, and it should therefore somewhat increase our ability to deter such adventures."[36]

In December 1966 and again in 1967, the Pentagon paused and requested that the Jason Division of the Institute for Defense Analysis assess the effect of the bombing on North Vietnam. The report was a "categorical rejection of bombing as a tool of our policy in Southeast Asia." None of the administration's goals had been met: the flow of men and supplies south continued. Indeed, since "the beginning of the Rolling Thunder air strikes on NVN, the flow of men and materiel from NVN to SVN has greatly increased, and present evidence provides no basis for concluding that the damage inflicted on North Vietnam by the bombing program has had any significant effect on the flow." The expectation that bombing would "erode the determination of Hanoi and its people clearly overestimated the persuasive and disruptive effects of the bombing and, correspondingly, underestimated the tenacity and recuperative capabilities of the North Vietnamese." The government had ignored the "well-documented" fact that "a direct, frontal attack on a society tends to strengthen the social fabric of the nation, to increase popular support of the existing government, to improve the determination of both the leadership and the populace to fight back, to induce a variety of protective measures that reduce the society's vulnerability to future attack and to develop an increased capacity for quick repairs."[37]

Despite these reports, the bombing of an ever-expanded list of targets in North Vietnam continued; the bombing halt that Johnson declared in March 1968 did not decrease the tonnage of bombs dropped on Indochina; the area south of the nineteenth parallel in South Vietnam, and Laos and Cambodia, now received the bombs that had been more widely distributed previously. Hanoi got McNamara's message—America's unparalleled military might—but did not listen. By the time it was Richard Nixon's turn to communicate with the Vietnamese, there was only one message left: the United States would continue to bomb until it had broken Hanoi's will.

Richard Nixon's contempt for his predecessors' approach to the war was most clearly expressed in a conversation with Republican delegates to the Miami convention before his election: "How do you bring a war to a conclusion?" he asked his attentive listeners. "I'll tell you how Korea was ended. We got in there and had this messy war on our hands. Eisenhower . . . let the word go out diplomatically to the Chinese and the North [Koreans] that we would not tolerate this continual ground war of attrition. And within a matter of months, they negotiated." The notion that the threat of nuclear bombs had brought the Chinese to heel in Korea was, as Jeffrey Kimball, the historian of Nixon's war, has observed, "part of Republican historical doctrine." Nixon not only believed it, he incorporated its principles into what he called his "madman" approach to negotiations in Vietnam. As he explained to his longtime aide Bob Haldeman during the 1968 presidential campaign: "[The North Vietnamese will] believe any threat of force that Nixon makes because it's Nixon. . . . I call it the Madman Theory, Bob. I want the North Vietnamese to believe I've reached the point where I might do *anything* to stop the war. We'll just slip the word to them that, 'for God's sake, you know Nixon is obsessed about

Communism. We can't restrain him when he's angry—and he has his hand on the nuclear button'—and Ho Chi Minh himself will be in Paris in two days begging for peace."[38] Maddened by Vietnamese resistance, the president of the United States would pretend to be crazy.

Johnson's advisers had been convinced they could, as they put it, "orchestrate the violence" and through the exercise of graduated pressure bring about an acceptable end to the war. Richard Nixon brought to the negotiating table the threat of doing *anything*, which is to say *everything*, to end the war on U.S. terms. One version of the madman approach was Nixon's 1969 full-scale Strategic Air Command alert, intended to frighten the Soviet Union into bringing pressure on Hanoi to make peace on U.S. terms.[39] Other possible threats included a land invasion of North Vietnam, the systematic bombing of dams and dikes, and the saturation bombing of Hanoi and Haiphong. After the war, a North Vietnamese diplomat explained to a reporter the flaw in Nixon's thinking. Both he and Kissinger believed there were good and bad threats: a good threat would be "to make a false threat that the enemy believes is a true threat." A bad threat was one that was true but disbelieved by the enemy. But there was a third category, Nguyen Co Thach observed: "For those who do not care whether the threat is true or not."[40] This possibility, an ongoing refusal to respond to the messages of force, introduces into the militarists' dichotomy an element of uncertainty they have never acknowledged.

The war in Vietnam came to an end, like the war in Korea, with a final act of devastation, one as irrelevant to the outcome of the war as the destruction of Korea's dams had been—an act, then, of pure abstraction. Ignoring the advice of his secretaries of state and defense, Nixon decided to act on one of the plans in his madman scenario: the saturation bombing of Hanoi and Haiphong. "When you bite the bullet," he told Nelson Rockefeller later, "bite it hard—go for the big play." In a reflective mood, he compared his decision with that of Kennedy during the Cuban missile crisis. "Decided," Bob Haldeman noted in his diary, "this [decision] was tougher . . . especially since it didn't have to be made." For twelve days the two cities were carpet-bombed around the clock by a combination of B-52s and fighter bombers that dropped 36,452 tons of bombs.[41] General Curtis LeMay was convinced that had bombing at this level been undertaken from the start, it would have ended in "any given two week period." The Christmas bombing joined Eisenhower's nuclear threats in the sacred canon of Republic Party war-making convictions. But the final agreement signed after the Christmas bombing was virtually identical to the one on the table before the bombing. As John Negroponte, then an aide to Kissinger, put it, "We bombed the North Vietnamese into accepting our concessions."[42] According to Jeffrey Kimball, the bombing was "aimed less at punishing Hanoi into making concessions aimed more at providing Saigon with incentives to cooperate." The decisive potential value of the bombing was that it would convince "hawks that [Nixon] had been tough, compelling the enemy to accept an agreement that was in reality an ambiguous compromise" but could be sold as a "clear-cut victory for his skillful management of war and diplomacy."[43] It is possible, had Watergate not cut his presidency short, that Nixon would have renewed saturation bombing in the face of a Saigon government defeat in 1975. Certainly many politicians and senior military officers, especially in the air force, remain convinced that had he done so the United States would have won the war. In 1978, General Ira Eaker, in whose mind's eye North Vietnam had escaped unscathed, mused, "How much better it would have been, if necessary, to destroy North Vietnam than to lose our first war."[44]

This conviction has had its coda in the doctrine of "shock and awe" embraced by the Bush administration. But what the wars in Korea and Vietnam demonstrate is that immediate massive bombing does not really differ from gradually escalating bombing. It only raises the level at which bombing begins. At the heart of both policies is a genuinely mad conviction: that American power is such that it must prevail in any situation in which it has declared an interest, that the only obstacle to its triumph is the lack of determination to use that power.

In the summer of 1950, Japanese civilians at Yokota Air Base loaded the B-29s that had firebombed Tokyo five years earlier for targets in North and South Korea. Four years later, leftover cluster bombs from the Korean War were shipped from Japanese storage facilities for use by the French against the Vietnamese. For the entire duration of the American war against Vietnam, military facilities in Japan and Okinawa (as well as troops from South Korea) were vital to the U.S. effort. In turn, Japan and Korea shifted from being targets of U.S. bombing to more profitable service as base and supplier. Recently, the United States has made an effort to draw Vietnam into its East Asian "strategic designs, focused primarily on keeping China contained." The current situation in Korea brings us almost full circle (the nuclearization of Japan may complete the circle). Ian Bremer, a senior fellow at the World Policy Institute, recently urged that the only appropriate way for the United States to address North Korea was to "talk tough," using the language of "the real threat of military escalation."[45] This far into the twenty-first century, America's twentieth-century faith in the language of violence has not changed.

CODA: "DOING IT RIGHT"—AIRPOWER FROM GULF TO GULF

The military reforms that followed U.S. defeat in Vietnam are beyond the scope of this epilogue. However, it is important to note that the turning away from counterinsurgency, currently a major charge against the military by prowar pundits, was not an oversight. According to Andrew J. Bacevich, the experience of Vietnam had persuaded senior military officials that the best way to avoid another Vietnam debacle was to avoid a future war that resembled Vietnam in any way. In the wake of the precipitate withdrawal of U.S. troops from Lebanon after the bombing of the Marine barracks in October 1983, Secretary of Defense Caspar Weinberger issued a statement defining, and by defining, hoping to restrict, the terms under which the nation should go to war: forces should be committed to combat only when the vital national interests of the United States or its allies are involved; they should be committed "wholeheartedly and with the clear intention of winning"; and troops should not be sent abroad without a "reasonable assurance" of the support of U.S. public opinion and Congress. Finally, the use of force should be "considered only as a last resort."

In 1990, as the march toward Operation Desert Storm began, Colin Powell, head of the Joint Chiefs of Staff under George H. W. Bush, added to Weinberger's list. As succinctly summarized by Charles Krauthammer, the "idea [of the Powell Doctrine] was not to match Iraqi power but to entirely overwhelm it in planes, tanks, technology, manpower, and will. That would make the war short and make the victory certain." "For decades," Krauthammer went on, enthusiastically but inaccurately, "the United States had followed a policy of proportionality: restraint because of the fear of escalation. It was under this theory that Maj. Powell watched his men bleed and die purposelessly in Vietnam." Under the banner of "never again," instead of the gradual escalation of bombs and troops, both were to be deployed at full strength.

First, however, Iraq was to be "softened up" by airpower. Instead of Vietnam's old, lumbering bombs, new high-tech precision weapons would reduce both U.S. casualties and the damage done to civilians in the course of eliminating legitimate military targets. No one opposed using the new weapons, but tactical disputes remained. The architect of a new strategy, Colonel John Warden, believed the new weapons would allow the air force to target the "central nervous system" of the modern state—electrical power, communications, transportation, and sources of energy.[46] Warden was appalled by those air force officers who seemed to think doing Vietnam very fast was the same as not doing it at all. His opponents called for dropping large payloads ever closer to Baghdad until Saddam Hussein agreed to withdraw from Kuwait. They also insisted on targeting Iraqi ground troops. Like Warden, the officers who advocated such tactics did so in the name of "never again." Warden was adamant: "This is not your Rolling Thunder. This is real war, and one of the things we want to emphasize right from the start is that this is not Vietnam! This is doing it right! This is using airpower!"[47]

The general impression left by the use of high-tech air power in Gulf War I is that it worked very well. TV viewers could virtually merge with precision weapons as, over and over, they looked through the crosshairs in the nose cone of a descending missile. Viewers did not merge with what happened when the missile landed. Indeed, the game-boy TV reporting of the war, as Paul Walker, director of the Institute for Peace and International Security at MIT, wrote, "created an illusion of remote, bloodless, push button battle in which only military targets were assumed destroyed."[48] A Global Security report on airpower in the Gulf War described it with restrained lyricism: "In the final analysis, in its swiftness, decisiveness, and scope, the coalition's victory came from the wise and appropriate application of airpower."[49]

A terrible sense of well-being derived also from the conviction that this, at last, was total war, as opposed to the limited, constrained, one-hand-tied-behind-the-back experience of Vietnam. Publications from the *New York Times* to the *Air Force Journal of Logistics* trumpeted the statistics: Iraq had been pounded, in just a month and a half, more heavily than Germany in World War II, than Southeast Asia in ten years of war. The numbers were wrong, as anyone who did the math at the time could have demonstrated. Edwin E. Moise, a professor at Clemson State, did do the math and questioned the figures at the time. Afterward, when the full statistics were released, it was clear, Moise wrote, "how little had actually been dropped—88,500 tons of aerial ordnance,"[50] less than a month's worth of Vietnam bombing in 1968. Nor were all of the bombs smart. Only 7 percent were at all intelligent, and of those, 40 percent missed their targets. The 60 percent that worked did indeed destroy information networks and Saddam Hussein's command and control system. However, Saddam's system "turned out to be more redundant and more able to reconstitute itself than first thought," and "fiber-optic networks and computerized switching systems proved particularly tough to put out of action."[51]

Less discussed than the high-tech weapons was the reappearance of B-52 carpet-bombing and the ongoing use of cluster bombs and napalm. Some areas of Iraq—the city of Basra, for example—were essentially free-fire zones. The military claimed Basra was entirely a "military town" but failed to explain where the city's eight hundred thousand inhabitants had gone. The *Los Angeles Times* described the city under bombardment as a "hellish night-time of fires and smoke so dense that witnesses say the sun hasn't been clearly visible for several days at a time."[52] Still, smart or dumb, as intense as first claimed or not, the sense that Gulf War I represented a total triumph for the air force remained, As President George H. W. Bush put it in May 1991, "Gulf Lesson One is the value of airpower."

President Bill Clinton and his secretary of state, Madeleine Albright, were fast studies. If airpower was good in a war, it was also good in situations that did not rise to the level of war. Albright put the question to Colin Powell directly: "What's the point in having this superb military that you're always talking about, if we can't use it."[53] And so they used it. For a decade after the war in the Gulf ended, in the Gulf itself, in Bosnia, and again in Kosovo, the Clinton administration used air strikes, Andrew Bacevich noted, the way the Royal Navy used gunboats in the nineteenth century. As in Vietnam, the bombs and missiles were presumed to speak. President Bill Clinton was their interpreter in the fall of 1996, after Saddam Hussein had attacked the Kurdish protected zone in northern Iraq: "Our missiles sent the following message to Saddam Hussein. When you abuse your own people or threaten your neighbors you must pay a price." In December 1998, Saddam Hussein expelled UN weapons inspectors, and the U.S. Air Force, aided by the Royal Air Force, spoke again. The statistics are impressive: for four days, 600 sorties were flown against 97 targets, 330 cruise missiles were fired from aircraft carriers, and, for good measure, B-52s dropped another 90. Saddam Hussein responded by abolishing the no-fly zone and activating his antiaircraft batteries—to which Clinton responded with more bombs.[54]

And so it went for the rest of Clinton's presidency. Bacevich, after listing the names of the multiplying operations and the tonnage they delivered, called it an "inconclusive air war of attrition." There were no U.S. or UK casualties, no lost planes. At the same time, Bacevich concluded, operationally, "the results achieved were negligible." Politically, on the other hand, there were achievements: "In the eyes of American clients in the Persian Gulf . . . the persistent sparring with Saddam affirmed the continuing need for a robust U.S. military presence in the region." In Afghanistan and the Sudan, as in the Balkans, the Clinton administration "made long-range precision air strikes an emblem of American statecraft."[55]

If air strikes were now America's logo, and Lesson One was airpower, the question remained, what sort of air power? Used how? In the years between the Gulf Wars, defense intellectuals applied themselves to this subject. Among these was Harlan Ullman, a senior fellow at the Center for Strategic and International Studies. Ullman and a colleague, James P. Wade, published *Shock and Awe: Achieving Rapid Dominance* in 1996 and seven years later watched as their theories were put into action over Baghdad. Ullman's plan, repeated throughout the "countdown" to the war, looked forward to "showering" Baghdad with more bombs in the first forty-eight or at most seventy-two hours of war than were used for the thirty-nine days of Gulf War I, so as to "take the city down." The idea of shock and awe is to gain "rapid dominance," Ullman wrote. "This ability to impose massive shock and awe . . . will so overload the perception, knowledge and understanding of [the] adversary that there will be no choice except to cease and desist or risk complete and total destruction."

In response to criticism of this frankly barbarous concept, Ullman insisted people had gotten it all wrong. He complained to a British interviewer that the phrase "has created a Doomsday approach," and he much preferred the more technical term: "effects-based operations." He insisted he did not mean "indiscriminate, terror-inducing destructiveness." On the contrary, the idea is to do "minimum damage, minimum casualties, using minimum force—even though," he conceded, "that may be a lot." Context, Ullman told Oliver Burkeman, was all. "The question is: how do you influence the will and perception of the enemy, to get them to behave how you want them to?" The difference between Ullman's theory and a caveman with a very big rock was "the combination of technology and philosophy."[56] His philosophy was explicitly drawn from the use of nuclear weapons in Hiroshima and Nagasaki, which were, in his words, "the maximum case of changing behavior."[57] Baghdad would be hit by eight hundred cruise missiles in the first two days of the war, destroying "everything that makes life in Baghdad livable. . . . You will have this simultaneous effect, rather like the nuclear weapons at Hiroshima, not taking days or weeks but in minutes."[58]

On Thursday, March 20, 2003, at 8:09 p.m., the effects-based operation began. "Wave after wave of explosions rolled down the Tigris valley. . . . The cadence, at once ordered and chaotic, continued as the evening drew towards midnight." Explosions occurred as often as every ten seconds. The bombs hit their targets with greater accuracy than in 1991, but their shrapnel was more generously distributed and their impact blew out windows, shook walls, and collapsed roofs in the surrounding neighborhood. One of the few American reporters who wrote about the bombardment of the city, Anthony Shadid, described what it was like: "Perhaps the most terrifying sensations of life in a city under siege are the sounds of the bombers. In a siege, one's hearing becomes exquisitely sensitive. Much of the time, one waits for the faint sound, the whisper that signals the plane's arrival. The entire body listens. Every muscle tightens, and one stops breathing. Time slows in the interim." Yasmine, one of his Iraqi friends, demanded, "Do those people up there have the faintest idea what is happening down here when they unload?"[59] Harlan Ullman was disappointed. There had not been enough shock, not nearly enough awe. This had been nothing more than the strategic bombing of Baghdad.

It is unnecessary to rehearse here how much of the mission that George W. Bush announced, on May 2, 2003, had been accomplished remains to be accomplished in July 2008. What is necessary, however, is to point out that the air war in Iraq more or less disappeared from sight even as it continued (and continues) to be carried on. I cannot think of another use of airpower—other than spy planes or the openly "secret" bombing of Laos and Cambodia, performed so invisibly. The air war in Iraq sends no messages. Its purpose is to hunt and kill insurgents, and that it does with indifference to the consequences for those who live in or near the precisely targeted buildings. Relatively few reporters pay much attention to it, and, in contrast to Vietnam, the military does not regularly announce the tonnage dropped or the sorties flown.

Some reporters have put isolated figures together that offer some estimation of the extent of bombing. Ellen Knickmeyer, a reporter for the *Washington Post*, estimated that the number of air strikes had increased fivefold from January to November 2005.[60] In an article that ran on January 11, 2006, Drew Brown, reporting for the *Detroit Times*, listed such figures as U.S. Central Command Air Force (CENTAF) had released: there had been 306 close air support strikes in 2005, a 43 percent rise over 2004.[61] Dahr Jamail, an independent journalist, reported that carrier-based navy and marine planes dropped twenty-six tons of ordnance on Fallujah during the battle for that city in November of 2004. Most reports from the CENTAF are vague: "Air Force F-16 Fighting Falcons flew air strikes against anti-Iraqi forces near Balad. The F-16s successfully dropped a precision-guided bomb on a building used by insurgents. F-16s and a Predator also flew air strikes against anti-Iraqi forces in the vicinity of Karabilah. The Predator successfully fired a Hellfire missile against insurgent positions."[62]

After Fallujah, the air war seems to have gone entirely underground. Nick Turse, an investigative journalist, has tried to track it, with marginal success. "A secret air war is being waged in Iraq," he has written. "The U.S. military keeps information on the munitions expended in its air efforts under tight wraps, refusing to offer details on the scale of use and so minimizing the importance of air power in Iraq."[63] There was some irony, therefore, in an op-ed piece by Charles Dunlap Jr., a major general in the air force, who, in the course of insisting that defeating the insurgency in Iraq was not "all about winning hearts and mind," asked how many Americans knew that in 2007 there had been a fivefold increase in air strikes over the preceding year. The answer is, not many. Major General Rick Lynch, in a throwaway reference to airpower, remarked that during a battle on January 10 in Arab Jabour, U.S. bombers had "dropped 40,000 pounds of bombs in 10 minutes to clear an insurgent stronghold."[64]

Robyn Read, a retired air force colonel, has pondered the questions of what airpower can do in counterinsurgency warfare once the period of "'kinetic kill'" is finished: "The answer is about finding and pursuing the path of least resistance to the political end state, caveated with a planner's full understanding that least resistance must successfully contend with collateral effects, unintended consequences, legal and moral restraints, and the well-being of the coalition's aggregate interest in the endeavor. EBO [effects-based operations] provides a functional yet flexible framework for thinking about this problem, or more correctly, this problem set."[65]

The CIA has developed a genuinely new approach to this "problem set": targeted killings. Predator drones originally designed for surveillance have been armed with Hellfire antiarmor missiles and used to assassinate suspected terrorists both in and outside of combat zones. No one knows how many such strikes have taken place, nor how many people they have killed. However, one former official working in the program told a reporter, "We have the plans in place to do them globally." Some problems persist: "In most cases, we need the approval of the host country to do them. However, there are a few countries where the president has decided that we can whack someone without the approval or knowledge of the host government."[66]

We know most about the use of drones outside of combat areas when they go wrong, as they did in the January 2006 in an attack on the village of Damadola, Pakistan, where, it was believed; senior members of al Qaeda were attending a meeting. It remains unclear whether they were or had been in the village; what is known is that eighteen civilians, including, many women and children, were killed. There was bipartisan support for the strike in the United States, although of course the deaths of innocents were regretted. As Senator Evan Bayh (D-Indiana) put it on Wolf Blitzer's show the *Situation Room*, "Now, it's a regrettable situation, but what else are we supposed to do? It's like the Wild, Wild West out there. The Pakistani border [with Afghanistan) is a real problem."[67] Andrew Bacevich, alone among the mainstream commentators I have read, thought the problem lay elsewhere: "For the United States to unleash a salvo of missiles at a Pakistani village thought to house an al-Qaeda chieftain is the equivalent of the Mexican government bombing a southern California condo complex suspected of harboring a drug kingpin."[68] Lee Strickland, who retired from the CIA in 2004, praised the deterrent power of these killings: "You give shelter to Al Qaeda figures, you may well get your village blown up. Conversely, you have to note that this can also create local animosity and instability." This is the venerable wisdom that guided the United States for fifteen years in Vietnam.

NOTES

1. Ronald Schaffer, *Wings of Judgment: American Bombing in World War II* (New York: Oxford University Press, 1985), 215.
2. The single best account is Bruce Cumings, *Origins of the Korean War* (Princeton, N.J.: Princeton University Press, 1990), vol. 2; see also Conrad Crane, *American Airpower Strategy in Korea, 1950-1953* (Lawrence: University Press of Kansas, 1993), 11-22.
3. Earl H. Tilford Jr., *Crosswinds: The Air Force's Setup in Vietnam* (College Station, Tex.: Texas A&M University Press, 1993), 117.
4. Strategic bombing was directed at the "enemy's capability and will to resist"; tactical bombing was "designed to assist ground forces on the battlefield." Mark Clodfelter, *The Limit of Air Power: The American Bombing of North Vietnam* (New York: Free Press, 1989), 2, 3.
5. Col. Raymond Sleeper, "Air Power, the Cold War, and Peace," in *Airpower: The Decisive Force IIn Korea*, ed. James T. Stewart (Princeton, N.J.: Van Nostrand, 1957); see also Schaffer, *Wings of Judgment*, 207.
6. H. R. McMaster, *Dereliction of Duty* (New York: HarperCollins, 1997), 62. The classic analysis of Johnson administration policy remains Wallace J. Thies, *When Governments Collide: Coercion and Diplomacy in the Vietnam Conflict, 1964-1968* (Berkeley: University of California Press, 1980).
7. It was not until quite late in the Vietnam war that Americans (and the rest of the world) saw television and still images of napalm victims. In 1974, Hans Blix, in an effort to ban the use of napalm, reminded his listeners of those images. His colleagues would, he knew, "coldly and rationally analyze the various factors which argue in favour of a ban on use of incendiaries and the factors which, on the contrary, militate against such a ban. But at the same time I confess that I hope and trust we shall be influenced by that picture." Quoted in Eric Prokosch, *Technology of Killing: A Military and Political History of Antipersonnel Weapons* (London: Zed, 1995), 170.
8. During the Korean War, the romance of flight was dimmed by the high toll Soviet MiGs took on U.S. jets. By 1952, the air force had identified "fear of flying" as a major problem in retention and recruitment. The air force took active measures to deal with the problem, and Hollywood helped out; in 1951, dozens of film stars joined in a celebration of the air force held in Hollywood Bowl, and a number of films glorifying the past and present of the air force were produced, including *Twelve O'clock High* and *Strategic Air Command*. See Crane, *American Airpower Strategy*, 97-108.
9. Crane, *American Airpower Strategy*, 132ff, discusses the development of these new bombs—the prototypes of today's "smart" bombs. Of the twenty-eight used in combat, only twelve had been controllable, of which only six hit their intended targets. On cluster bombs, see Prokosch, *Technology of Killing*, and Michael Krepon, "Weapons Potentially Inhumane: The Case of Cluster Bombs," *Foreign Affairs* 52, no. 3 (April 1974): 595-611.
10. The name of a popular children's song, which was number 2 on the charts in

1963. It was performed by Peter, Paul and Mary and used, with conscious irony, by troops in Vietnam to describe the AC-47 gunship.

11. Raphael Littauer and Norman Uphoff, eds., *The Air War in Indochina*, rev. ed. (Boston: Beacon Press, 1972), 209. The U.S. Air Force was responsible for the overwhelming majority of the bombing and strafing, with the U.S. Navy and Marines second and third, respectively. Non-U.S. air forces dropped some twenty thousand tons of the total.

12. Jeffrey Record, *The Wrong War* (Annapolis, Md.: Naval Institute Press, 1998), 75.

13. Cecil B. Currey, "Residual Toxin in Viet Nam: Currey Reports," *Vietnam Generation* 4, no. 3 (1992): 18, *https://digitalcommons.lasalle.edu/vietnamgeneration/vol4/iss3/1*. See also Paul Frederick Cecil, *Herbicidal Warfare* (New York: Praeger, 1986); and J. B. Neilands et al., *Harvest of Death Chemical Warfare in Vietnam and Cambodia* (New York: Free Press, 1972).

14. Michael Clodfelter, *Vietnam in Military Statistics: A History of the Indochina Wars, 1772–1991* (Jefferson, N.C.: McFarland, 1995), 275; on Japan, see Littauer and Uphoff, *Air War in Indochina*, table B-2, p. 204.

15. E. J. Kahn, *The Peculiar War: Impressions of a Reporter in Korea* (New York: Random House, 1951), 105, 132.

16. Reginald Thompson, *Cry Korea* (London: MacDonald, 1952), 94.

17. See Jonathan Schell, *The Real War: The Classic Reporting on the Vietnam War* (New York: Pantheon, 1987), 302–3. At one point in the Korean War, a lack of targets had reduced medium-sized bombers to twenty-five sorties a day. "Finding nothing better to bomb, one 92nd Group crew recorded that it chased an enemy soldier on a motorcycle down the road, dropping bombs until one hit the hapless fellow." Crane, *American Airpower Strategy*, 122–23.

18. See Barton Bernstein, "New Light on the Korean War," in *MacArthur and the American Century: A Reader*, ed. William M. Leary (Lincoln: University of Nebraska Press, 2001), 404. The head of the special weapons project, General Kenneth D. Nichols, on the other hand, thought nuclear weapons should be used to "prevent our being pushed off the peninsula," irrespective of Chinese or Russian intervention.

19. Bernstein, "New Light on the Korean War," 405.

20. The flirtation with use of nuclear weapons ended only with the Korean War itself. For more details, see Cumings, *Origins of the Korean War*. In 1951, this included a simulated atomic run by a single B-29 flying from Okinawa to North Korea. For details on this flight, Operation Hudson Harbor, see Cumings.

21. Cumings, *Origins of the Korean War*, 755. John McNaughton, the assistant Secretary of defense, contemplated attacking North Vietnam's system of dikes and dams in 1966, although the suggestion was never acted upon. If "handled right," he wrote in a memo, it "might offer promise. Such destruction does not kill or drown people. By shallow flooding the rice, it leads after a time to widespread starvation (more than a million?) unless food is provided—which we could offer to do 'at the conference table.'" Cumings, *Origins of the Korean War*, 755. Conrad C. Crane writes that General Mark Clark had expected some

international protest but "the dam attacks received very little notice in the world press. American newspapers were preoccupied with the exploits of the jet aces." Crane, *American Airpower Strategy*, 159–62.

22. Freda Kirchwey, "Liberation by Death," *Nation*, March 10, 1951, 216.

23. Kirchwey, "Liberation by Death," 216.

24. Kirchwey, "Liberation by Death," 215.

25. "The Bridges at Sinanju and Yongmidong," *Quarterly Review* Staff Study, in Stewart, *Airpower*, 141ff.

26. William W. Stueck, *The Korean War: An International History* (Princeton, N.J.: Princeton University Press, 1995), 342.

27. See Stueck, *The Korean War*, 326ff.

28. Stewart, *Airpower*, 290.

29. Crane, *American Airpower Strategy*, 178.

30. Michael Bechloss, *Taking Charge: The Johnson White House Tapes, 1963–1964* (New York: Simon and Schuster, 1998), 368–70.

31. McMaster, *Dereliction of Duty*, 62.

32. *The Pentagon Papers: The Defense Department History of U.S. Decision Making on Vietnam*, vol. 3, ed. Senator Mike Gravel (Boston: Beacon Press, 1971), 593, 599–600, 605; see also 225.

33. *Pentagon Papers*, 3:238. Any ongoing discussion of the possibility of using tactical nuclear weapons came to a head, for the Johnson administration, when four scientists associated with the Jason Division spent the summer of 1966 studying the feasibility of their use in Vietnam. The study was inspired by a remark one of the scientists associated with Jason overheard a high Pentagon official make that it "might be a good idea to toss in a nuke from time to time, just to keep the other side guessing." The result was a fifty-five-page report unequivocally rejecting the notion; it was never raised again in the Johnson administration. See Peter Hayes and Nina Tannewald, "Nixing Nukes in Vietnam," *Bulletin of Atomic Scientists* 59, no. 1 (January–February 2003): 28–37, 72–73.

34. Mark Clodfelter, *The Limits of Air Power: The American Bombing of North Vietnam* (New York: Free Press, 1989), 120–23, on Tuesday lunches and target selection, the quote is on pp. 121–22.

35. Clodfelter, *Vietnam in Military Statistics*, 221.

36. *Pentagon Papers*, 3:687–91.

37. *Pentagon Papers*, 4:222–24. Several years later, in October 1972, the staff report to the Senate Foreign Relations Committee reached a similar conclusion: "There is no indication that any of the major intelligence agencies believed that the bombing of the North could or would reduce the level of support for the war in the South. . . . Rather, the agencies placed their hopes in punishing North Vietnam and in possibly breaking her will."

38. Jeffrey Kimball, *Nixon's Vietnam War* (Lawrence: University Press of Kansas, 1998), 82, 83.

39. William Burr and Jeffrey Kimball, "Nixon's Nuclear Ploy," *Bulletin of Atomic Scientists* 59, no. 1 (January–February 2003); 28–37, 72–73. Nixon called another full-scale alert during the October war in 1973 to demonstrate U.S. readiness to

"to use threats of force to deter Soviet military intervention in regional conflicts (even if the Soviets had no plan to intervene)." The point, Kimball and Burr conclude, was to indicate Nixon and Kissinger's conviction "that a show of force was essential to salvage U.S. Vietnam policy and the credibility of American power."

40. Quoted in Seymour Hersh, *The Price of Power: Kissinger in the White House* (New York: Summit Book, 1983), 125–27, 134.

41. Clodfelter, *Limits of Air Power*, 194.

42. Quoted in Nguyen Tien Hung and Jerrold L. Schecter, *The Palace File* (New York: Harper & Row, 1986), 146.

43. Kimball, *Nixon's Vietnam War*, 209, 211, 363.

44. Schaffer, *Wings of Judgment*, 202.

45. Jim Lobe, "Pentagon Woos Vietnam," *Asia Times*, July 19, 2003. According to Rajan Menon, the invitation is part of a "broader anti-China strategy in which Washington attempts to build up military ties with countries situated along China's periphery." Ian Bremer, "Talk, But Talk Tough," *New York Times*, July 19, 2003, A-27.

46. This would reverse the "traditional equation of air power." In World War II, Korea, and indeed in Vietnam, the issue was "how many planes were needed to take out one target; now it was a question of how many targets *one* plane with precision-guided weapons could take out." David Halberstam, *War in a Time of Peace: Bush, Clinton, and the Generals* (New York: Scribner, 2001), 51. For a general discussion of the new tactics and those who opposed them, see chap. 5.

47. "Sir," Halberstam quotes General Charles Horner saying to General Schwarz-kopf, "the last thing we want is a repeat of Vietnam where Washington picked the targets!" Halberstam, *War in a Time of Peace*, 53. After the war, Warden projected what World War II would have been like had the United States possessed precision weapons; there it took six thousand planes to shut down German military production at the rate of about one thousand planes per target, with high military and civilian casualties. "The circle of error—that is, the circle into which you could realistically expect to put 50% of your bombs stood at 20 miles for night bombing at the start of the war and narrowing to 1000 meters towards the end. The new weapons allowed the circle of error to close to six feet or even smaller." Halberstam, *War in a Time of Peace*, 55; Warden quote on p. 52.

48. Paul Walker, "U.S. Bombing: The Myths of Surgical Bombing in the Gulf War," report to the New York Commission of Inquiry for the International War Crimes Tribunal, May 11, 1991, and the Boston hearing on June 8, 1991, http://balkania.tripod.com/resources/military/wc-myth.htm.

49. "Air Power in the Gulf War," GlobalSecurity.org, n.d., https://www.globalsecurity.org/military/library/report/1999/air-power-v2–5.pdf (no longer available).

50. Edwin E. Moïse, "Limited War: The Stereotypes," https://edmoise.sites.clemson.edu/limit1.html.

51. From official U.S. Air Force history, quoted in Fred Kaplan, "The Flaw in Shock

and Awe," *Slate*, March 26, 2003. The entire episode is reminiscent of Nixon's hunt for the Central Office for South Vietnam during the Vietnam war.

52. Quoted in Walker, "U.S. Bombing."

53. Quoted in Andrew J. Bacevich, *American Empire: The Realties and Consequences of U.S. Diplomacy* (Cambridge, Mass.: Harvard University Press, 2002), 48.

54. Quoted in Bacevich, *American Empire*, 150. As Bacevich points out on p. 155, Clinton's bombing policy was Rolling Thunder redux.

55. Bacevich, *American Empire*, 152, 154.

56. Oliver Burkeman, "Shock Tactics," *Guardian*, March 25, 2003.

57. Ullman makes the case for nuclear bombs as it is usually made: the invasion would have cost a million American casualties and countless Japanese lives. He instructs Burkeman that the Japanese were "suicidal in the extreme. And they could comprehend 1,000 bombers, 100,000 dead Japanese, but they couldn't understand one plane, one bomb, one city gone." He goes further: "We could have de-peopled Japan: no more Japanese. We dropped two nuclear weapons, and they quit. So you focus on things that collapse their ability to resist."

58. Ira Chernus, "Shock & Awe: Is Baghdad the Next Hiroshima?" Common-Dreams.org, January 27, 2003, *https://archive.commondreams.org/views03/0127 -08.htm*.

59. Anthony Shadid, *Night Draws Near: Iraq's People in the Shadow of America's War* (New York: Henry Holt, 2005), 90–91.

60. Ellen Knickmeyer, "U.S. Airstrikes Take Toll on Civilians," *Washington Post*, December 24, 2005, https://www.washingtonpost.com/archive/pol itics/2005/12/24/us-airstrikes-take-toll-on-civilians/fba12f81–45c9-4831-8dc e-8b1b256ffcc0/ (no longer available).

61. Drew Brown, "Air War May Intensify As Ground Forces Leave Iraq," *Detroit Times*, January 11, 2006.

62. Dahr Jamail, "An Increasingly Aerial Occupation," TomDispatch.com, December 13, 2005.

63. Nick Turse, "America's Secret Air War in Iraq: Bombs over Baghdad," TomDispatch.com, February 7, 2007. See also his report on the use of cluster bombs in Iraq, "Did the U.S. Lie about Cluster Bomb Use in Iraq?" TomDispatch.com, May 24, 2007, and Tom Engelhardt, "Looking Up: Normalizing Air War from Guernica to Arab Jabour," TomDispatch.com, January 29, 2008.

64. Associated Press, "Lynch: US 'Surge' Tipped Scales in Iraq," *New York Times*, February 2, 2006.

65. Robyn Read, "Effects-Based Airpower for Small Wars: Iraq after Major Combat," *Air and Space Power Journal* 19, no. 1 (Spring 2005): 104–5.

66. Josh Meyer, "CIA Expands Use of Drones in Terror War," *Los Angeles Times*, January 19, 2006.

67. See "Lawmakers Defend Pakistan Strike," CNN International.com, January 16, 2006, https://www.cnn.com/2006/US/01/15/alqaeda.strike.us/.

68. Andrew J. Bacevich, "War in Error," *American Conservative*, February 27, 2006.

8

PERMANENT WAR

If we have to use force it is because we are America. We are the indispens-
able nation. We stand tall. We see farther into the future.

—MADELINE ALBRIGHT, U.S. Secretary of State, February 19, 1998

I recall all too well the nightmare of Vietnam. . . . I am determined to do
everything in my power to prevent this country from becoming involved
in another Vietnam nightmare.

—SENATOR ROBERT BYRD, June 29, 2002

It is possible that the destruction of September 11 uncovered the
suppressed remains of Vietnam.

—WOLFGANG SCHIVELBUSCH, *The Culture of Defeat*

We're going to get better over time. We've always thought of
post-hostilities as a phase distinct from combat. . . . The future of war
is that these things are going to be much more of a continuum. . . . This
is the future for the world we're in at the moment. We'll get better as
we do it more often.

—LAWRENCE DI RITA, special assistant to Secretary of Defense Donald
Rumsfeld, July 18, 2003

There seem to be only two kinds of war the United States can fight: World
War II or Vietnam. The conviction on the part of some Americans and many
politicians that the United States could (or should or would) have won the

This essay first appeared in *Positions: East Asia Cultures Critique* 13, no. 1 (March 1, 2005): 177–93. Copyright
© 2005 by Duke University Press. All rights reserved. Republished by permission of the copyright holder.
www.dukeupress.edu.

war in Vietnam is a convenient mechanism for getting around a remembered reality of defeat. An alternate strategy is to concentrate the national mind on World War II, skipping not only Vietnam but also Korea. In recent movies and television serials, World War II is depicted as a long, valiant struggle that the United States fought pretty much on its own, winning an exceptionally clean victory that continues to redeem all Americans under arms anywhere, at any point in history.[1] In virtually every military action since 1975, the administration in charge has tried to appropriate the images and language of World War II. Thus, Manuel Noriega, Mohamed Farrah Aidid, Slobodan Milosevic, and Saddam Hussein (twice) were roundly denounced as the Adolph Hitler du jour; September 11, 2001, of course, is the twenty-first-century Pearl Harbor. Nevertheless, in each of these wars or warlike events, some journalist or politician was bound to ask the fearful question: Is this another Vietnam?

What is it that people fear in a repetition of Vietnam? Military and political defeat, of course, but, beyond that, the daily experience of an apparently endless war, one that registered on the home front not in calls for sacrifice and heroism but rather in domestic division, resistance to the draft, high desertion rates, urban riots, popular suspicion of the government, a steadily rising number of U.S. dead and wounded, the shame-inducing images of napalmed Vietnamese children, and the reluctant knowledge of American atrocities like My Lai. In his speech in June 2002, Senator Robert Byrd listed his own nightmare images: "the antiwar protests and demonstrations, the campus riots, and the tragic deaths at Kent State, as well as the resignation of a president. And I remember all too well the gruesome daily body counts."[2]

Because the Vietnam war cannot be assimilated to a triumphal American narrative, presidents must regularly pick their way around it. They have done so mainly by taking its public relations failings to heart rather than by contemplating its history or meaning. Despite calling Vietnam a noble crusade, Ronald Reagan was in no mood to risk repeating other aspects of the conflict. Money and arms substituted for U.S. combat troops in both Nicaragua and El Salvador, and when a suicide bomber killed over two hundred U.S. marines in Lebanon, Reagan quickly withdrew the rest. At the same time, to demonstrate that the world's mightiest military power was not afraid to use its power directly (and to justify a military budget that never responded to the end of any war, including the Cold War), small, predictably winnable miniwars were waged against small, largely defenseless countries. Operation Urgent Fury made it clear to all Grenadians, and most particularly the island nation's left-leaning government, that neither the United States nor those students who went abroad to get medical degrees could be pushed around. Six years later, the first Bush administration taught General Noriega and the people of Panama a similar lesson in Operation Just Cause.

The victories in Operations Urgent Fury and Just Cause were useful, and their titles ambitious enough. Yet they were painted on too small a canvas to take the sting out of defeat in Vietnam. For that, more troops would have to travel longer distances, use greater firepower, and engage a real army. When Saddam Hussein seized more of Kuwait than the administration of the first President Bush thought necessary, the stage was set for a military extravaganza that might indeed mean, as the president so fervently hoped, that "we've kicked the Vietnam syndrome once and for all."[3] Vietnam, by negative example, had taught the civil and military branches of the government how to market a war as well as how to fight one. It was all in the timing: enough time to engage the easily distractable imagination of the public but not so much time that boredom set in, or worse, anxiety. Operation Desert Shield, the period from August 1990 to mid-January 1991, served to create a steadily intensifying crisis atmosphere. Network TV and its cable rival, CNN, used the time to settle on appropriate logos and their musical accompaniment. Operation Desert Storm, first as thirty-nine days of sustained and furious bombing and then in the form of a massive ground invasion, was the longed-for release. The desert theme—modest, descriptive—worked so well that some years later, Clinton, without regard for its World War II invocation of the German enemy, named one of his attacks on Iraq Desert Fox.

Media cooperation was essential if Desert Storm and Desert Shield were to successfully overcome memories of Vietnam. Early in the war, General Norman Schwarzkopf pointed out that inflated body-count figures had led many Americans to distrust military press briefings. Alternatively, when the figures were believed, they had upset people. Therefore there would be no body counts in the Gulf War. Thus, through over a month of bombing and a week of ground fighting, no estimates of Iraqi losses were ever offered, nor did the press demand them. The result was a televised war relatively innocent of dead bodies, a war that, except for images of the bombing of a Baghdad air raid shelter and repeated shots of desperate oil-soaked cormorants, would not spoil one's dinner. Indeed, the wildlife allegedly destroyed by Saddam Hussein's ecological terrorism substituted for images of humans wounded by American bombs. After the war, CBS revealed that one particularly sad cormorant, whose struggle for life was shown over and over again on TV, had actually been the victim of an oil spill caused not by Iraqi sabotage but by Allied bombing.

By the end of the war, it had become possible to take the enemy not as people, but as machines; the tanks, buses, and cars that jammed the highway out of Kuwait City seemed to have fled on their own, their charred hulks containing no human remains. There was thus an apparent, visual purity to the U.S. victory that successfully masked its savagery.

The sense of purity was conveyed by a cooperative press, but the administration took no chances: the press was tightly controlled as well. In Vietnam, reporters learned to treat military press briefings with the respect they deserved, widely mocking what they called the five o'clock follies. Reporters understood that it was the task of the military to report victory and that it was the reporters' task to find out what was going on. This is not to romanticize the role of the press in Vietnam. The overwhelming majority of reporters supported the war, and their criticisms were rarely based on principle but rather on tactics. Even so, the reporters made clear the cavernous abyss between what the U.S. military and State Department wished the public to believe and what seemed to the press to be the case. The abyss was called the credibility gap, and it meant that people began to treat government handouts with an unprecedented degree of skepticism. Since Vietnam, the military has been careful not to allow this process to repeat itself. "Three Pentagon press officers," James LeMoyne reported during the first Gulf War, "said that they spent significant time analyzing reporters' stories in order to make recommendations on how to sway coverage in the Pentagon's favor." Reporters who asked hard questions were warned that their antimilitary attitude would count against them. On-camera TV interviews were halted in the middle if the press officer did not like what was being said, reporters who filed stories on troop doubts about the war found their access to senior military men curtailed, and the soldiers themselves were subjected to close questioning by their officers.[4] The troops were also carefully briefed on how to talk to the press. "Say you are highly trained," Anthony Swofford, a marine sniper in the first Gulf War, was told. "Say you're excited to be here and you believe in the mission and that we'll annihilate the Iraqis." When a marine in the company argues that it is un-American to censor speech, the staff sergeant responds, "You are Marines. There is no such thing as speech that is free. You must pay for everything you say. Especially the unauthorized crap."[5]

Throughout the first Gulf War, generals and retired generals, admirals and retired admirals were given hours of TV time to speculate, point with pointers, describe in sensuous detail the operation of this or that weapon. The Middle East experts of choice, like the military men, supported the president's policy. The peace side received air time, but in proportions that effectively marginalized it. Peace demonstrations in Europe went uncovered, and demonstrations and marches in the United States did not fare much better. Told by Vietnam revisionists that the media had created the peace movement by showing it on TV, the networks exercised due caution.

In the war against terrorism as waged in Afghanistan, there was a similar unanimity of expert opinion but far fewer visuals. No generals instructed the public on the fine points of the map of Afghanistan; no reporters accompanied the troops. When a reporter for the *Washington Post* tried to reach the site of a missile attack on an alleged al Qaeda target, he was stopped at gunpoint.[6] But a press too tightly controlled becomes restive, and the Pentagon has been spurred to invent other means of containing the media. During the first Gulf War, the entire population had the experience of seeing the view from the nose cone of a missile as it descended toward its target, but not the view from the ground looking up. It was difficult to imagine what greater service the news media could offer a warring state. But that was before the television show *Survivor* offered a new model. According to the *New York Times*, the Pentagon planned to "promote its war effort through television's genre of the moment, the reality series." Over the protests of its news division, the ABC entertainment division would produce a thirteen-part series offering, according to the press release, "compelling personal stories" of America's fighting men and women. "There's a lot of other ways to convey information to the American people than through news organizations," Rear Admiral Craig R. Quigley pointed out. "That's the principal means," the admiral went on, "but if there is an opportunity to tell about the courage and professionalism of our men and women in uniform on prime time television for 13 straight weeks, we're going to do it. That's an opportunity not to be missed."[7]

By the second Gulf War, the military had arrived at a more perfect form: the embedded press corps, which has, by and large, fulfilled its punning name. At one point in the war, TV talk show host Charlie Rose conducted a telephone interview with Frederik Balfour, a *Business Week* correspondent who was embedded in the Third Infantry Division. Balfour had opposed the war before it began, but now riding along with the troops, dependent on them for his protection, he found it was impossible not to feel part of their "cause." Rose next asked Colin Soloway, *Newsweek* correspondent with the 101st Airborne Division, if he had been able to go along on any Apache helicopter missions. No, Soloway explained regretfully, Apache helicopters only have seats for the two pilots. Still, he was able to view the videotape when the helicopters returned to base, and the pilots were glad to "walk him through" whatever engagement they had conducted. The TV audience did not get to see the tapes—any more than they had during the first Gulf War.

Looking back on the first Gulf War, it would seem the first President Bush had done everything right. In addition to avoiding that which must not be done—conscription, an uncontrolled press, body counts, gradual escalation—Bush had done that which should be done: sent a massive force immediately; accused the enemy of atrocities before such an accusation could be made against the United States; kept American casualties to an absolute minimum; given the victorious troops a victory parade. Yet the Vietnam syndrome lingered. If the first test of the political success of a war is the reelection of those who made it, then despite all these preparations, the administration had failed. If the second test is how the war is represented in popular culture, the failure proved even greater. The only notable movie to come out of the war, *Three Kings*, depicted the conflict as Vietnam on speed: a war of multiple betrayals and massacres; a war without honor or sense. For all the efforts of the administration to recreate World War II, the first Gulf War never achieved the necessary majesty. It remained a punitive war against an oil ally that had gotten out of hand and had to be punished. The first President Bush chose to retain a presumably chastened Saddam Hussein in power. American troops did not march triumphantly through the streets of Baghdad, as they had in Berlin and Tokyo. The Gulf War planners, many of whom, like Colin Powell, had fought in Vietnam, put great thought and energy into avoiding the dangers of that war, and they succeeded. Still, they could not make war good again.

Clinton's military expeditions, undertaken with a clear memory of what the Vietnam war had been about and why he had opposed it, fared no better. In Somalia, the Clinton administration worked toward the World War II formula by naming one of that country's many warlords as its Hitler and proceeding to hunt him and his lieutenants down. In the course of those unsuccessful efforts, a famine-stricken population, which had initially welcomed U.S. intervention, turned famously ugly. Eighteen dead Americans and one thousand dead Somalis later, Clinton withdrew U.S. forces. For most of the public, the lesson drawn was that if you could not have World War II and did not want Vietnam, it was best to stay home or to participate from thirty thousand feet up. Thus, in Kosovo, safe in the skies, the U.S. Air Force played its part, prevailing over a "pint-sized nation whose entire gross national product amounted to one-sixteenth of the Pentagon's budget."[8] It was a model intervention: no Americans were hurt, and the stock market soared.

Clinton's use of military force was one response to the ghost of Vietnam; George H. W. Bush's more robust resort to arms was another. But neither could meet the contradictory need of the country to see itself as both supremely powerful *and* forever an underdog, as both the only redeemer and the preeminent victim. In Vietnam, its power had not prevailed, it was not the underdog, it had redeemed no one and nothing, and however frequently Vietnam veterans were called upon for surrogate-victim duty, it was difficult to avoid the sense that Vietnam itself remained the main victim. And then came September 11.

For a time, it seemed that terrible event would succeed in burying the ghost of Vietnam. It gave the United States a moral authority it had not had since Franklin Delano Roosevelt was president. In addition, once Bush had declared war on terrorism (a recurring declaration starting with the presidency of Ronald Reagan), the rhetoric of both World War II and the Cold War returned. In the manner of the Cold War, the war against terrorism was perforce endless; in the manner of World War II, it was a struggle against enemies of consummate wickedness, an axis of evil. Best of all, this particular endless war against evil would require little home front effort beyond continuing to consume at normal or preferably exorbitant levels. The first battle in the new war, overthrowing the Taliban, proved to be only a minor challenge to the military. What happened in Afghanistan thereafter—warlord rule, a possible revivification of the Taliban, devastation of the countryside—detained neither the Bush administration nor the general public. The relentless march to war against Iraq, long urged by the second President Bush's close advisers, could now begin.

Yet at a narrative level, the combination of Cold War and World War II stumbled. The most important institutional legacy of World War II, the United Nations, for a time almost brought the march to a complete halt. The grand coalition of the first Gulf War would not reenlist, and the administration was reduced to recruiting international support through highly publicized bribery and threats, only to achieve a "coalition of the willing" made up of, among others, Eritreans and Solomon Islanders. Administration insistence that Saddam Hussein had weapons of mass destruction, up to and including nuclear weapons, joined a collective memory of how World War II ended with the dominant fears of the Cold War era, but convincing proof of the existence of the weapons was never assembled. Not only was the World War II template elusive, but the Vietnam war returned in the form of a mass antiwar movement, global in scope, broadly inclusive, spontaneously organized, clearly and repeatedly saying no to war.

Nothing could have deflected the administration from having its war. Yet the sharp outlines of a victorious war story quickly blurred. Instead of the orderly march into the defeated capital past the cheering thousands, there was looting, arson, anarchy, the shooting and killing of peaceful demonstrators, and shouts of "down with America." Instead of a ceremonial turning over of power to the new rulers, historically the moment that legitimized the new order, senior American officers sat alone on the plush sofas of an empty palace. A historian, Wolfgang Schivelbusch, observed that the "absence of the vanquished from their place at the table of surrender resonated as a sinister silence, like a tragedy ending without a dying hero's last words." The scene of the generals in the palace was a "scene of ersatz surrender, for the simple reason that the defeated regime had vanished without a trace."[9]

The most famous surrender scene in twentieth-century U.S. history took place on the deck of the battleship USS *Missouri* on September 2, 1945. It was a ceremony, John Dower has written, "laden with symbolism." The ship bore the name of President Truman's home state; it flew the flag that had flown from the White House on Pearl Harbor Day, as well as the one that Commodore Perry had flown as he sailed into Tokyo Bay in 1853. Japan's "utter subjugation was reinforced by the dramatic setting of the surrender ceremony itself."[10] During the second Gulf War, George W. Bush, appropriately costumed, copiloted a navy jet onto the deck of the aircraft carrier *Abraham Lincoln*, which had had to put out to sea a bit in order to make the landing feasible. There were no Iraqis there, of course, only cheering American sailors and a largely admiring press corps. But if the surrender was ersatz, so was the victory speech, for to openly declare victory would require the release of Iraqi prisoners of war, and no one wanted to do that. Nor, for that matter, did the president wish to announce the return of peace, as General MacArthur had on board the *Missouri*. Instead, in a great mix of historical references, Bush called upon the spirits of war presidents past (Roosevelt, Truman, Kennedy, and Reagan)[11] in the course of announcing a victory in "one battle" in the ongoing war against terrorism, a victory comparable to the allied landings in Normandy and the battle of Iwo Jima.[12] But what neither Bush nor the press had foreseen was the ongoing resistance to U.S. occupation on the part of various Iraqi groups, a resistance that takes a daily toll in American and Iraqi dead.

Initially, the Vietnam syndrome referred to the reluctance of the public to engage in war. Now, it seems clear, it is the U.S. government that is caught in Vietnam's grip, convinced that the only cure for that long-ago defeat is yet more war. But redeeming Vietnam is only one function of the wars the United States has fought since September 11, 2001. The other, perhaps more significant purpose, is to extend, selectively, the benefits the Cold War had brought to the United States over its forty-five-year life span, benefits that were regrettably lost due to the Soviet Union's withdrawal from the field and its subsequent disappearance.

In the summer of 1950, the majority of Americans (some 57 percent, according to a Gallup poll) believed that with the police action in Korea, World War III had begun.[13] Writing shortly after the fall of the Taliban government in Afghanistan, Eliot Cohen, director of strategic studies at the Johns Hopkins School of Advanced International Studies, made the same calculation in an important op-ed piece for the *Wall Street Journal*.[14] It was crucial, Cohen argued, to call things by their right name. The "less palatable but more accurate name" for the war on terrorism is "World War IV." "The Cold War was World War III," Cohen wrote, and World War IV resembles it in many ways: it is global; it will require "a mixture of violent and nonviolent efforts"; it will last a very long time; and "it has ideological roots." The enemy now is "militant Islam," and Afghanistan was "just one front in World War IV, and the battles there just one campaign." Cohen envisioned at least two others: in Iraq and Iran.

Norman Podhoretz pursued this theme several months later in a long essay titled "How to Win World War IV," and former CIA director James Woolsey embraced the same idea, predicting that World War IV was likely to last longer than World War I or World War II but "hopefully not the full four-plus decades of the Cold War."[15] Notable among all three commentators was their evident zest for war. Podhoretz was explicit: "I fully realize," he wrote, "that we are judged both by others and by ourselves, as lacking the stomach and the skills to play even so limited an imperial role as we did in occupying Germany and Japan after World War II." He sometimes doubted the country's capabilities in this regard and worried about the long history of national inattention and passivity. "Yet," he concluded, "given the transfiguring impact of major wars on the victors no less than on the vanquished, who can tell what we may wind up doing and becoming as we fight our way through World War IV?" The prospect of what the United States (or any other warring state) might become as it fought its way through the twenty-first century did not give Podhoretz pause. He was confident everybody in the world would be better off and that victory in World War IV would mean, as President Bush proclaimed, "an age of liberty here and across the world."[16] In terms of public rhetoric, domestic security policies, militarization of foreign policy and of culture, curtailment of civil liberties, and a pervasive sense of fear and threat, the war on terrorism is the Cold War redux. It takes little historical imagination to see in the permanent war against terrorism a continuation of what was initially imagined as a permanent war against communism. The world that had seemed to crumble with the Berlin wall in 1989 reappeared, a little dusty: good and evil, us and them, enemies everywhere. This view was bipartisan. Senator Joseph Lieberman, who could have been vice president on September 11, described the war on terrorism as "the medieval zealotry and religious fanaticism of a holy war against the universalistic, humanitarian, democratic and tolerant ideals of America." The country's fundamental principles were "as much on the line in this war against terrorism as they were in our battles with Nazism and communism."[17]

Along with the Manichaean language came a revivification of a number of Cold War tactics, such as psychological warfare, embodied in the short-lived Office of Strategic Influence, whose open goal was to spread disinformation abroad. Washington and Hollywood fell into each other's arms. In late October 2001, forty Hollywood executives met with Chris Henick, then deputy assistant to the president, and Adam Goldman, associate director of the Office of Public Liaison. Leslie Moonves, president of CBS, explained their mission: "I think you have a bunch of people here who were just saying, 'Tell us what to do. We don't fly jet planes, but there are skill sets that can be put to use here.'" There was a clear need, both "domestically and internationally to tell the story that is our story."[18]

The government acted quickly to blunt any questioning of administration policy, passing the Uniting and Strengthening America by Providing Appropriate Tools Required to Intercept and Obstruct Terrorism Act. Known as the U.S.A. Patriot Act for short, it provides for an unprecedented peacetime abrogation of civil liberties in a piece of legislation whose name itself discourages dissent.[19] Nine months after its passage, in a move that makes the FBI Cold War informant network look benign, the administration launched Operation TIPS, whose acronym must also have preceded its full naming. Through a pilot project in ten cities, the Terrorism Information and Prevention System would enable one million letter carriers, train conductors, utility employees, and ship captains to report "suspicious activity" by calling a toll-free number that would connect them "directly to a hotline routing calls to the proper law enforcement agency."[20] The post office declined to participate, congressmen protested, and Operation TIPS quietly closed its web site and disappeared. But Operation TIPS was the formalization of a system already in place, the Neighborhood Watch Program, whose original anticrime mandate was now expanded: "With the help of the National Sheriffs' Association, the Neighborhood Watch Program will be taking on a new significance. Community residents will be provided with information which will enable them to recognize signs of potential terrorist activity, and to know how to report that activity, making these residents a critical element in the detection, prevention and disruption of terrorism." One alert citizen in Williamsburg, Virginia, John Chwaszczewski, shot at a helicopter as it landed in his neighborhood to pick up a local businessman. "Maybe I overreacted," Mr. Chwaszczewski said.[21] A Federal Express driver working in a Middle Eastern neighborhood in Brooklyn told a reporter, "Whenever I would go to a place where there was a lot of them [Arab Americans], I would tell the landlord, hey, you got nine people living up there or whatever, and they would call the F.B.I. and get them checked out."[22] Raymond Arnold, a field-service representative for a local gas company, made the Cold War connection explicit, recalling his earlier effort on behalf of patriotic observation: "A long time ago, I saw a Communist flag in someone's basement."[23]

After the demise of Operation TIPS, the Department of Defense Advanced Research Project Agency established the Total Information Awareness program (TIA). Some uneasiness about the Orwellian ring of the title led to a cosmetic change shortly after the program was announced; henceforth it was to be known as Terrorism Information Awareness (TIA). Headed by Ronald Reagan's national security adviser and convicted Iran-Contra felon, Admiral John Poindexter,[24] the TIA planned to gather all available public and private electronic records—financial, media, internet, phone, fax, and so on—into a centralized database in order to discover and then track potential terrorists. Despite the change in name, and also a change in logo,[25] there was growing bipartisan opposition to TIA and a move in Congress to restrict both its scope and its funding. But the greatest blow to Poindexter's plans was self-inflicted. As reported in the press, the admiral had designed an online futures market in terrorism. The Website, www.policyanalysismarket.org, invited investors to join in a process of "group prediction which should prove engaging and may prove profitable." The Pentagon staunchly defended the plan: "Research indicates that markets are extremely efficient, effective and timely aggregators of dispersed and even hidden information. Futures markets have proven themselves to be good at predicting such things as elections results; they are often better than expert opinion."[26] Few were convinced; shortly after the story broke, Poindexter resigned.

The use the Bush administration has made of September 11 echoes the use the Truman administration made of the North Korean attack against South Korea. The stated goal was to drive the North Koreans out of the South in what was at first an unnamed military effort, later a police action, but never a declared war. Having driven the North Koreans back, Truman went on to make war against North Korea, as Bush, who set out to capture Osama bin Laden "dead or alive," went on to make war on the Taliban and then Iraq. After the Chinese joined the North Koreans, Truman denounced them, at an informal lunch with reporters, as "the inheritors of Genghis Khan and Tamerlane, who were the greatest murderers in world history." Truman explained that Western jurisprudence had "originated with Hammurabi in the Mesopotamian Valley, [was] propounded by Moses and elaborated on by Jesus Christ, whose Sermon on the Mount is the best ethical program by which to live." Led by the United States, others could join the battle: "I have been trying to mobilize the moral force of the world—Catholics, Protestants, Jews, the eastern church, the Grand Lama of Tibet, the Indian Sanskrit code—I have been trying to organize all these people to the understanding that their welfare and the existence of decency and honor in the world depends on our working together, and not trying to cut each other's throats."[27] The idiom, even the grammar, has a contemporary ring. Then, as now, working together meant working toward a world order defined by the United States. The enemy then, as now, was a vast, amoebic "ism" that could take up residence in any number of surprising places, instantly deterritorializing them.

Out of the ashes of the Korean War and Ground Zero came analogous convictions about the efficacy of force, the fear that compromise or concession signaled weakness, and the irrelevance of the local causes of conflict. The Korean War enabled the United States to fund the remilitarization of Europe and Japan, create an expanded alliance system, build a chain of military bases that spanned the globe (Japan, South Korea, Taiwan, the Philippines, Thailand, Australia, Diego Garcia, Saudi Arabia, Ethiopia, Turkey, Greece, Italy, Spain, Portugal, Germany, England, and Iceland), and establish an ever-expanding nuclear arsenal. Out of September 11 and the war against Iraq, the United States has dismantled an alliance system it declared overly constricting and expanded its chain of military bases into new areas of the world: Iraq, Afghanistan, Uzbekistan, Djibouti, Pakistan, Georgia, Kazakhstan, Bulgaria, and Yugoslavia (former), in addition to expanding existing base facilities in Kuwait, Saudi Arabia, and Turkey. The combination effectively embraces the richest areas in the world for oil exploration and development.[28]

Ominously, the administration has pressed for and received funding to renew nuclear weapons research and testing, in disregard of the Comprehensive Test Ban and the Nuclear Non-Proliferation treaties. The Pentagon's Nuclear Posture Review argues for a "new triad" approach to nuclear planning: "New capabilities must be developed to defeat emerging threats such as hard and deeply buried targets, to find and attack mobile and relocatable targets, to defeat chemical or biological agents and to improve accuracy and limit collateral damage." The need for these new weapons is based on "classified intelligence" indicating that more than seventy countries have underground facilities of which "at least 1,100" are thought to be "strategic command centers or weapons bases." The administration is committed to useable nuclear weapons as a means of deterring "smaller countries" from developing nuclear weapons systems. "Under this theory," the *New York Times* reports, "those countries may now believe that the stigma of using a large nuclear weapon against them is so great that the United States would never do so." A "less devastating weapon" would thus be a more credible threat.[29]

Inherent in the Cold War was the possibility it could end through the evolution of the Soviet Union into one of "us." Although the Soviet Union never formally surrendered and several communist states remain at large, much of the American public was persuaded that the United States had won the Cold War, and even that peace, with its expected dividends, had arrived. But terrorism is a tactic (not an ideology) that the weak will always have available for use against the strong. In the war on terrorism, the administration of the second President Bush may have discovered the model for permanent war in a unipolar world.

NOTES

1. More daringly, Hollywood revisited the Vietnam war in the 2002 movie *We Were Soldiers* (dir. Randall Wallace), which portrayed a battlefield victory early in the war that obscured the ultimate defeat. For more on this, see Marilyn B. Young, "In the Combat Zone," *Radical History Review*, no. 85 (2003): 253–64.
2. Paul J. Nyden, "Byrd Challenges Bush's Ideas on War; West Virginia Senator Warns of Another Vietnam," *West Virginia Gazette*, June 29, 2002.
3. George H. W. Bush, quoted in Maureen Dowd, "War Introduces a Tougher Bush to the Nation," *New York Times*, March 2, 1991.
4. James LeMoyne, "Pentagon's Strategy for the Press: Good News or No News," *New York Times*, February 17, 1991. The relationship between the press and the military is scathingly caricatured in the movie *Three Kings* (dir. David O. Russell, 1999).
5. Anthony Swofford, *Jarhead: A Marine's Chronicle of the Gulf War and Other Battles* (New York: Scribner, 2003), 14–15.
6. Felicity Barringer, "'Reality TV' about GIs on War Duty," *New York Times*, February 21, 2002.
7. Barringer, "Reality TV."
8. See Andrew J. Bacevich, *The American Empire* (Cambridge, Mass.: Harvard University Press, 2002), 92; see pp. 181–95 for a succinct critique of U.S. policy in Kosovo.

9. Wolfgang Schivelbusch, "The Loneliest Victors," *New York Times*, April 22, 2003. In his book on the culture of defeat, Schivelbusch asks whether "America's post–September 11 war fever is really a response to an earlier and unresolved defeat." His alternative suggestion is not much more comforting: "Could it be that the decades of relative American peacefulness and readiness to cooperate that followed the defeat in Vietnam were merely an interim period, akin to the Weimar Republic?" Wolfgang Schivelbusch, *The Culture of Defeat: On National Trauma, Mourning, and Recovery*, trans. Jefferson Chase (New York: Metropolitan Books, 2003), 294.

10. John Dower, *Embracing Defeat: Japan in the Wake of World War II* (New York: W. W. Norton, 1999), 40–41.

11. See John Prados's analysis of the speech at www.tompaine.com, May 2, 2003 (no longer available).

12. For a transcript of Bush's speech, see https://pix11.com/2013/04/30/transcript-of -president-george-w-bushs-mission-accomplished-speech/.

13. Paul G. Pierpaoli, Jr., *Truman and Korea: The Political Culture of the Early Cold War* (Columbia: University of Missouri Press, 1999), 29.

14. Eliot Cohen, "This Is World War IV," *Wall Street Journal*, November 20, 2001. In an interview Cohen said he used the phrase "World War IV" "tongue-in-cheek" as a way of getting people to think about the current conflict as something bigger than the Afghanistan war." See Stephen Goode, "The Character of Wartime Statesmen," www.insightmag.com, May 27, 2003. (no longer available).

15. Norman Podhoretz, "How to Win World War IV," *Commentary* 11 (2002): 19–29; Charles Feldman, Stan Wilson, CNN, "Ex-CIA Director: U.S. Faces 'World War IV,'" April 3, 2003, https://www.cnn.com/2003/US/04/03/sprj.irq. woolsey.world.war/.

16. George W. Bush, address to Joint Session of Congress, September 20, 2001, https://www.washingtonpost.com/wp-srv/nation/specials/attacked/transcripts /bushaddress_092001.html.

17. David Lightman, "Lieberman's Foreign Policy: Propagate U.S. Values," *Hartford Courant*, January 14, 2002.

18. Jim Rutenberg, "Hollywood Seeks Role in the War," *New York Times*, October 20, 2001.

19. Provisions include indefinite detention of noncitizens for minor visa violations, reduced judicial supervision of telephone and internet communication, and granting to the attorney general and secretary of state the power to label domestic groups terrorist organizations and deport noncitizen members. In general, the act "significantly boosted the government's law enforcement powers while continuing a trend to cut back on the checks and balances that Americans have traditionally relied on to protect individual liberty." See American Civil Liberties Union, "USA Patriot Act Boosts Government Powers" (no longer available).

20. See Andy Newman, "Citizen Snoops Wanted (Call Toll-Free)," *New York Times*, July 21, 2002. See also www.citizencorps.gov (now accessible in different versions through the Wayback Machine: https://web.archive.org/). Protest against Operation TIPS has been vigorous. "Ashcroft's informant corps is a vile idea.

Operation TIPS should be stopped because it is utterly anti-American. It would give Stalin and the KGB a delayed triumph in the Cold War." Editorial, *Boston Globe*, July 17, 2002.

21. Associated Press, "Citing Fear, Man Shoots at Helicopter," *New York Times*, July 21, 2002.

22. Newman, "Citizen Snoops Wanted."

23. Newman, "Citizen Snoops Wanted." In New York, a plane carrying an Indian movie star and her family to the city for a tour was accompanied to La Guardia Airport by fighter jets and the family was detained after passengers reported their "suspicious behavior" to the airline stewards. Apparently, family competition for the window seat frightened their fellow passengers. Lydia Polgreen, "Bollywood Farce: Indian Actress and Family Are Detained," *New York Times*, July 18, 2002.

24. He was later acquitted on a technicality.

25. From an omniscient eye atop a pyramid scanning an illuminated globe to a circle combined with an inverted Nike sneaker swoosh.

26. Carl Hulse, "Pentagon Prepares a Futures Market on Terror Attacks," *New York Times*, July 29, 2003. The focus of trade would be on the "civil and military futures of Egypt, Jordan, Iran, Iraq, Israel, Saudi Arabia, Syria and Turkey." A congressman who had learned about the scheme explained how it worked: "You may think that Prime Minister X is going to be assassinated. So you buy the futures contracts for 5 cents each. As more people begin to think the person's going to be assassinated, the cost of the contract could go up, to 50 cents. The payoff if he's assassinated is $1 per future." In a letter to Poindexter protesting the scheme, two senators pointed out that the scheme would appear "to encourage terrorists to participate, either to profit from their terrorist activities or to bet against them in order to mislead U.S. intelligence authorities."

27. Paul R. Kennedy, "Truman Calls Reds Present-Day Heirs of Mongol Killers," *New York Times*, December 24, 1950. Wordier than President Bush, Truman drew the line of global division as sharply: "Those people who believe in ethics, morals and right associate themselves together to meet those who do not believe in ethics, morals and right, who have no idea of honor or truth."

28. See Paul Rogers, "Permanent Occupation?" *Open Democracy*, April 24, 2003, https://www.opendemocracy.net/en/article_1184jsp/. Rogers writes that the combination of new and old bases marks a "major military investment in . . . the Persian Gulf and Central Asia . . . that are the primary and secondary regions of the world for new oil exploration and development."

29. All quotations in this paragraph are from Carl Hulse and James Dao, "Cold War Long Over, Bush Administration Examines Steps to a Revamped Arsenal," *New York Times*, May 29, 2003. The House of Representatives removed bans on research into "smaller" nuclear weapons, provided funding for the development of "turning existing nuclear warheads into weapons capable of piercing underground bunkers," paved the way for renewed underground testing, and provided funds for research into "'advanced' concepts."

9

U.S. IN ASIA, U.S. IN IRAQ: LESSONS NOT LEARNED

In 2008 conference remarks, Marilyn Young reflected on "lessons not learned" five years after the beginning of the 2003 U.S. war in Iraq.

Of course, lessons were learned: indeed, since Vietnam, a veritable primer has been developed on the dos and don'ts of war fighting so as to maintain public support for an enterprise until long past its sell-by date. I've made a list of ten lessons I think the Bush administrations (the father's and the son's) learned from the Vietnam war. And then one very important lesson they did not learn.

First, controlling the press is a good idea, although not always easy to achieve. The common wisdom, post-Vietnam, was that the press—in particular television—was responsible for the erosion of public support for the war and thus its loss. Harping on this theme had the effect of making reporters wary, and it made successive administrations determined to limit press access to the action. In Grenada, Panama, and Gulf War I, the press operated under stringent rules and through a pool of reporters. The current war perfected the technique, offering the press the opportunity to be "embedded" with the troops.

Second, controlling the historical narrative is no easier than controlling the press, but it's also important. For a time, when opponents of the war in Iraq used the example of the Vietnam war to denounce it, the Bush administration and its supporters protested. But then—and I do not suggest a conspiracy here—a more effective approach emerged: the administration itself

Remarks by Marilyn B. Young, panel on "The United States in Asia, the United States in Iraq: Historical Lessons Not Learned," American Historical Association, January 4, 2008. Thanks to Neil S. Oatsvall for this copy of Young's remarks, which he received from her after hearing her speak on the American Historical Association panel.

remembered Vietnam, only differently than most, though not all, historians. The United States in this version really won the Vietnam war, or would have if not for Congress and/or the press and/or the peace movement.

Third, perhaps the most important rule responds to the widely accepted view that Americans let the soldiers down in the Vietnam war. Preemptively, even those who oppose the war in Iraq explain that they nonetheless support the troops. But this is not an easy distinction. To attack the war necessarily impugns the morality of the troops' actions and the righteousness of their sacrifices. A Doonesbury cartoon of a presidential press conference captures the difficulty brilliantly. "Mr. President, you've been arguing that we must remain in Iraq to ensure that those who've given their lives didn't die in vain. What if our troops are still dying at the current rate a year from now? Will we withdraw then?" "No," the president answers. "Because if we do all of next year's deaths will have been in vain." "What about two years from now? Or five years?" And Bush answers: "Again, we'll stay the course. We cannot dishonor the upcoming sacrifice of those who have yet to die. Remember, some of them haven't even enlisted yet. If we cut and run, what kind of message would that be sending them and their families?" "That they might live?" "Dishonoring their own future deaths? I don't think so."[1]

Fourth, at all costs avoid a draft; do not call upon the public to do more for the war effort than tolerate it except when called upon to support the troops.

Fifth, also avoid body counts.

Sixth, when atrocities are uncovered, direct attention firmly down the ranks to the inevitable bad apples. This worked in My Lai; it can be made to work in Iraq.

Seventh, try to avoid language that evokes bad memories: an increase in the number of troops is a "surge" not an "escalation." The withdrawal of that increase counts as a drawdown of troops. When counting, don't include the forty-eight thousand mercenaries under contract.

Eighth, when in trouble, up the ante—Iran is this war's Cambodia.

Ninth, a war needs heroes. The only heroes in Vietnam were the returning POWs—ambiguous figures at best and in any case unavailable to serve in Operation Iraqi Freedom. It took a while, but on the model of the NYPD and NYFD heroes of 9/11, General David Petraeus, PhD, and his circle of warrior intellectuals have emerged as reasonable facsimiles.

Tenth, criticism of tactics is acceptable and can possibly even be useful. Some military analysts believe that had counterinsurgency tactics and strategies been consistently applied in Vietnam, that war would have been won. Now, at last, under General Petraeus, those tactics are in place and have had a telling effect. To withdraw when things are going so well would be to repeat the tragedy of Vietnam, snatching defeat from the jaws of victory.

What, in my view, should have been learned from Vietnam? That a bad war can't be fixed except by ending it; that failing to have dealt with old bad wars means repeating them.

Let me say a little more about this last point. Journalists and historians have written about the "defeat" of the United States in Vietnam. However, although the United States acknowledges having lost the Vietnam war, it has never acknowledged that the war it fought and lost was, in many respects, criminal. Defeat in a war in which criminal acts have taken place or because it was a war of aggression or constituted a violation of international law as such has resulted in international trials, an acknowledgement of the crimes of war and crimes against humanity committed, even the payment of reparations to victims. Germany, Japan, and Serbia come to mind. Other countries that have lost colonial or neocolonial wars, France in Indochina and Algeria, the Soviet Union in Afghanistan, for example, have gone through extended periods of national soul-searching.

Moreover, this process of dealing with the past is ongoing, for Japan, Germany, France (with respect to Vichy), to name a few. As Patrick Hagopian put it in a symposium on the Vietnam war published in the *Journal of American History*, about U.S.-perpetrated crimes in Vietnam, "there is still an embarrassed silence."[2] It is indeed impossible to imagine an international trial or an official national self-examination with respect to widely recognized criminal behavior of the United States in Vietnam or Iraq, although the town of Brattleboro, Vermont, may soon get to vote on whether to declare Bush and Cheney war criminals who can be arrested and prosecuted should they ever step foot in the neighborhood.[3] The closest the United States ever came to a formal acknowledgement of what it had done in Vietnam was when President Jimmy Carter deemed the destruction caused by the war to both the United States and Vietnam to have been "mutual."

The United States believes itself to be, by definition, incapable of waging an aggressive war, or committing war crimes or crimes against humanity that would require an international trial. When the evidence that these things have occurred is overwhelming, understanding has nowhere to go but the exceptional: this low-level guard, that misunderstood order, these soldiers grieving for comrades and under great stress. Surprisingly, even open debate about the abrogation of the Geneva Convention on the treatment of prisoners does not move the discussion beyond the particular. Yet torture as an instrument of "counterterror" has a known history in the United States. Those complaining that the military in Iraq has failed to learn the lessons of counterinsurgency note that some lessons had been fully learned: techniques of torture, assassination, and the use of indigenous death squads developed by the CIA in Vietnam and widely disseminated since. Rob Corddry has explained this phenomenon best when he reported on Abu Ghraib to *The Daily Show*: "Jon, there's no question what took place in that prison was horrible, but the Arab world has to realize that the U.S. shouldn't be judged on the actions of a . . . well, that we shouldn't be judged on actions. It's our principles that matter; our inspiring, abstract notions. Remember, Jon, just because torturing prisoners is something we did doesn't mean it's something we would do."[4]

Most Americans now know that, in Vietnam, the United States fought a war of great violence in a small country whose national choices could not have affected the safety and security of the United States. Most Americans now know that terrible crimes were committed in the course of that war: specific crimes of rape, torture, massacre and more general crimes of unparalleled bombing of civilians. But this knowledge has had few consequences.

Because these lessons of the Vietnam war have not been learned, the central issues it raised over four decades ago about the United States in the world remain the central issues today. Unresolved, they come back not as ghosts but as the living: the Phoenix Program of targeted assassinations, torture, and wholesale detentions; bombing of densely populated areas; the credibility of the United States as an explanation for an indefinite commitment to a chosen war gone sour; the unchecked expansion of presidential power; the demoralization of the military; illegal domestic spying; dissent defined as treason; the insistence that fighting "them" over there protects "us" over here—all continue in daily practice.

The refusal to force the country to deal directly with the crimes of war and the crime of war in Vietnam means that one day when the war in Iraq ends, or simply stops, the United States will once again fail to come to terms with the damage done by this unprovoked war of aggression, laying the ground for the next war.

NOTES

1. G. B. Trudeau's Doonsbury, October 9, 2005, *Washington Post* Archive, *https://www.washingtonpost.com/doonesbury/strip/archive/2005/10/9*.

2. "Interchange: Legacies of the Vietnam War," *Journal of American History* 93, no. 2 (2006): 457.

3. As Young anticipated, Brattleboro and Marlboro, Vermont, voted on such a measure in March 2008, approving the arrest of President George W. Bush and Vice President Dick Cheney for "crimes against our Constitution." "Vermont towns vote to arrest Bush and Cheney," *Reuters*, March 4, 2008, https://www.reuters.com/article/us-usa-politics-vermont/vermont-towns-vote-to-arrest-bush-and-cheney-idUSN0454699420080305.

4. "Prison Abuse Scandal," *The Daily Show with Jon Stewart*, May 6, 2004, http://www.cc.com/video-clips/2rrxzn/the-daily-show-with-jon-stewart-prison-abuse-scandal.

10

"I WAS THINKING, AS I OFTEN DO THESE DAYS, OF WAR": THE UNITED STATES IN THE TWENTY-FIRST CENTURY

The postwar period quickly assumed the appearance and
generated the atmosphere of a new pre-war period.

—DELMORE SCHWARTZ, *Partisan Review*, 1951[1]

A soldier pleading to be allowed to stay in Afghanistan:
"You can't send me home. This is my home."
"Kandahar is your home?" "No—war. War's my home.
War is simple, I know what to do. War makes complete sense to me."

—*Doonesbury*, May 14, 2011[2]

I take the title of my talk from a poem by C. K. Williams, "The Hearth," written after listening to the news on a cold winter evening in February 2003. He writes that he has been thinking "as I often do these days, of war" and "wondering how those who have power over us / can effect such things and by what / cynical reasoning pardon themselves." The poem spells it out: war is "radar, rockets, shrapnel / cities razed, soil poisoned / for thousands of generations; . . . suffering so vast / it nullifies everything else."[3]

First published as the 2011 Presidential Lecture for the Society for Historians of American Foreign Relations, in *Diplomatic History* 36, no. 1 (January 2012): 1–15, doi:10.1111/j.1467-7709.2011.01004.x. By permission of Oxford University Press on behalf of The Society for Historians of American Foreign Relations (SHAFR).

I find that I have spent most of my life as a teacher and scholar thinking and writing about war. I moved from war to war, from the War of 1898 and U.S. participation in the Boxer Expedition and the Chinese civil war, to the Vietnam war, back to the Korean War, then further back to World War II and forward to the wars of the twentieth and early twenty-first centuries. Initially, I wrote about all these as if war and peace were discrete: prewar, war, peace, or postwar. Over time, this progression of wars has looked to me less like a progression than a continuation: as if between one war and the next, the country was on hold. The shadow of war, as Michael Sherry called it fifteen years ago, seems not to be a shadow but entirely substantial: the substance of American history.[4]

The subject of American wars is not new, and in recent years it has become a constant subject. But I think it is a good thing in a historian of American foreign policy to be preoccupied with war. I think our continuous task must be to make war visible, vivid, an inescapable part of the country's self-consciousness, as inescapable a subject of study as it is a reality.

The constancy of war and its constant erasure is linked intimately to the pursuit and maintenance of an American empire similarly erased. Like Tolstoy's unhappy families, nations are each imperial in their own way, and each way has its own euphemism. The euphemisms change over time, as does the nature of the empire: in the nineteenth century, expansion was the preferred description, up to and including expanding across the Pacific.[5] In the mid to late twentieth century, it was the establishment of a liberal capitalist world order that, Dean Acheson explained, would "help people who believe the way we do, to continue to live the way they want to live."[6] In both the twentieth century and this one, the projection of American power was equated, by all administrations, many pundits, and some historians, with the fundamental and universal values of freedom and democracy. This is to say that in all three centuries the pursuit of empire was usually accompanied by a denial that the United States was or could be an empire, its policies imperialist. Or, if recognized, then, as John Lewis Gaddis put it, the empire Americans built was "a new kind of empire—a democratic empire—for the simple reason that they were, by habit and history, democratic in their politics."[7]

Walter Lippmann complained of an American propensity to deny the existence of its empire in a 1927 essay entitled "Empire: The Days of Our Nonage Are Over." He observed that "all the world thinks of the United

States as an empire, except the people of the United States." He believed the "reluctance [was] genuine," that there was no hypocrisy "in the pained protest which rises whenever a Latin American or a European speaks of us as imperialistic." But other countries paid attention to what the United States said and did. "We on the other hand think of what we feel. And the result is that we go on creating what mankind calls an empire while we continue to believe quite sincerely that it is not an empire because it does not feel to us the way we imagine an empire ought to feel."[8]

Not feeling like an empire, the United States fought imperial wars nonetheless. The War of 1898, as it became a war of occupation and colonization, was at first vigorously opposed and then remembered as an aberration—as not the beginning of an American overseas empire, but a one-off. This misremembering attained one impressive peak when George W. Bush spoke to the Filipino Congress in October 2003 and declared America "proud of its part in the great story of the Filipino people. Together our soldiers liberated the Philippines from colonial rule," erasing the years of counterinsurgency warfare.[9] Never feeling like an empire, the United States could fight a series of wars in Central America and the Caribbean that led Major General Smedley Butler to declare himself a "racketeer, a gangster for capitalism" and to call war itself a "racket" conducted "for the benefit of the very few at the expense of the masses" and understood by only a "small inside group."[10]

The wars of the American empire did not end in Manila on July 4, 1902, but have continued to the present. This afternoon I want to speak about some of these wars: the hot wars of the Cold War, Korea, and Vietnam, the homeopathic small wars that followed Vietnam, and the current state of permanent war. I will speak mainly of the process through which public opinion has been persuaded to take war rather than peace as the normal state of affairs.

The disproportional American use of force was also taken as natural. In Korea, 635,000 tons of bombs and 32,557 tons of napalm were dropped, and some two to three million Koreans died. The United States was not bombed; there were 33,000 plus combat dead. Some commentators in the liberal press did take note of the discrepancy, but the general public was indifferent.

Vietnam was different, and protests against the ferocity of the air war grew over the years. But after Vietnam, massive bombing returned, without undue public comment, and today, though the bombers are often drones rather than B-52s, the air war is barely visible.[11]

World War II, the war politicians and patriots have enshrined as ideal, a war fought for unimpugnable reasons by the "greatest generation," ended not just decisively but triumphantly in public euphoria. "To resume one's own life!" William Barrett, philosopher and *Partisan Review* editor, recalled. "It seemed a small and humdrum thing to be asking for, and yet most of us believed it would not be the same old life again. Hitler and the Nazis were gone, the whole face of the world seemed changed, and a long period of peace and promise must surely lie ahead."[12] George C. Marshall remembered it the same way and some years later complained about the way people had "rush[ed] back to their civilian jobs and [left] the tanks to rot in the Pacific and military strength that was built up fade away."[13]

He need not have worried. Within months of V-J Day, America's Soviet ally was being portrayed as America's rival. At Washington, D.C., dinner parties, observers as different as Secretary of Commerce Henry Wallace and the British novelist E. M. Forster were taken aback by the bloody-minded comments of their companions. After a Washington dinner party early in 1946 during which the high-powered guests had alternately called for "kick[ing] the Russians in the balls" and encircling the Soviet Union with military bases, Wallace worried in his diary that "only one logical action" could follow such a worldview "and that is to provoke a war with Russia as soon as possible."[14] Forster remembered a similar event a year later: "I shall never forget a dinner party . . . at which one of the guests, a journalist, urged that atomic bombs should be dropped upon the Soviet Union without notice. . . . They were cultivated men, but as soon as the idea of Russia occurred to them, their faces became blood red; they ceased to be human. No one seemed appalled by the display but myself, no one was surprised and our hostess congratulated herself afterwards on the success of her party."[15]

Readers of this journal are familiar with the drumbeat of the next few years, the alarums and excursions of the early Cold War from Greece to Berlin to the Communist victory in China, all culminating unexpectedly in a hot war in Korea. Accompanying these distant conflicts was the danger awaiting us at home, the possibility of nuclear annihilation, and the warnings that America was at risk: the struggle between freedom and democracy had not ended in 1945 but transformed itself. Only the opponents were different: Russians instead of Germans, Chinese rather than Japanese.

The headlines warned that nuclear war was entirely possible; magazine articles described how quick and deadly it could be. Educational films circulated to high schools, and community groups worked to accustom their audience to the immanence of an annihilating war they were nevertheless virtually certain to survive.

Other films were dedicated to changing what their producers saw as an American "cultural pattern" that led "boys and girls" to "abhor violence and value peace and 'getting along with others'" above all else. Coronet films, with the support of the National Education Association, the U.S. Office of Education, and the Department of Defense, produced fourteen short films entitled "Are You Ready for Service?" which were intended to persuade the young to join in the "great struggle of our times. The struggle between freedom and tyranny." Every high school boy "should be starting to form himself into the mold of the soldier, adjusting himself both physically and emotionally to conform to the demands of military service."[16]

Hollywood did its share by preparing moviegoers of the early postwar period for wars to come. The 1943 movie, *The North Star*, an epic in praise of Soviet resistance to the German invasion (script by Lillian Hellman, score by Aaron Copland, starring Anne Baxter, Dana Andrews, Walter Huston, and Erich von Stroheim) played in my local Brooklyn movie theater in the late 1940s as *Armored Attack*. In its postwar incarnation it had been recut and was now introduced by clips of a May Day military parade in Moscow with a voice-over warning the audience that the Russian partisans of the past had been replaced by goose-stepping Soviet troops. A stream of movies were produced that could double as advertisements for the various branches of the military in their competition for congressional appropriations: frogmen, submarines, aircraft carriers, close air support units, the service academies (*West Point Story* in 1950, *Air Cadet* in 1951), the Coast Guard, the Marines (several times). In 1949, eight World War II movies were released, and all did well at the box office. The appeal of World War II, the film historian Thomas Doherty has written, "wasn't merely the attraction of adventure romance or high melodrama, but the consolation of closure and serenity of moral certainty. For Hollywood and American culture the Second World War would always be a safe berth."[17]

At the same time, and it is important to stress this, a number of post-war movies (*Best Years of Our Lives* in 1946, *Crossfire* in 1947, *All My Sons* in 1948 among them) were somber, even angry meditations on the willful ignorance, indifference, inequality, prejudice, and greed of the home front during the war and the difficulties facing returning veterans. Americans learning to acquiesce in the domestication of war could not be asked to deny their still fresh knowledge of war. When he was called to serve his country in 1950, the journalist Mike Royko recalled thinking, "What is this? I didn't know anyone who was in Korea who understood what the hell we were doing there. . . . We were over there fighting the Chinese, you know? Christ, I'd been raised to think the Chinese were among the world's most heroic people and our great friends. . . . I was still mad at the Japs."[18]

It was one thing to continue to fight World War II on the big screen virtually; it was another thing to mobilize the population for an actual war in Korea, a war no one seemed able even to name. Richard Rovere's "Letter from Washington" column in the *New Yorker* called it a "perplexing and diplomatically important question." "All week long here," he wrote in the July 27, 1950, issue, "in Congressional hearings on legislation growing out of our involvement in Korea, administration witnesses and congressmen have been arguing over whether the present state of affairs should be officially described as a war, a national emergency, or a limited emergency, or by some new title." Rovere reported that congressmen felt the question mattered because "unless we get an accurate designation for whatever it is that is happening, we shall never be able to tell when it has come to an end, if it ever does." Most newspapers referred to it as a "police action," probably unaware of the imperial ring. But the Marines were not so unaware. On the retreat from the Chosin reservoir in November 1950, they sang a parody of the British Indian Army song, "Bless 'em All": "Fuck 'em all, fuck 'em all / The Commies, the UN and all / . . . we're saying goodbye to them all / We're Harry's police force on call / So put back your pack on / The next stop is Saigon / Cheer up my lads, fuck 'em all!"[19]

To mobilize the population, Truman had to convince people that the use of force was vital to the national interest, as vital as World War II had been. He could hardly explain the Korean War in Acheson's terms as Bruce Cumings has recently summed them up: the establishment of a "'great crescent' from Tokyo to Alexandria, linking Japan with Korea, Taiwan, Southeast Asia, and ultimately the oil of the Persian Gulf."[20] At the

same time, people had to be deflected from demanding the sort of satisfying total victory achieved in 1945, as that way lay the danger of a war that
would indeed end all wars. But the Korean War was a hard sell, and the
public never bought it wholeheartedly.

However, insofar as the Korean War could be assimilated to the template of World War II it was briefly acceptable. The Korean civil war under
way since 1946 and the role of the United States in that civil war were
either ignored or randomly reported as instances of Communist subversion. More familiar, as North Korean tanks rolled over the thirty-eighth
parallel on June 25, 1950—sixty-one years ago almost to the day—was
blitzkrieg, the dangers of appeasement, the advance of totalitarianism.
The North Korean army even goose-stepped. As long as the war remained
in rapid movement—with arrows sweeping first one way, then the other
across the peninsula—the public paid anxious attention. But as the fighting settled into a war of attrition with the opening of peace talks in July
1951, the Korean War became background noise in America, never wholly
silent but only occasionally audible. By October 1951, *U.S. News & World
Report* had already given the Korean War the name it has borne ever since:
"The 'Forgotten War." The journal reported that that week alone claimed
2,200 American casualties; yet it was "almost forgotten at home, with no
end in sight."[21] In 1952, Samuel Lubell concluded that the first preference of
popular opinion was "a peaceful settlement" but that if peace was impossible "then all-out war was their next best choice."[22]

The Korean War did not so much end as stop. An editorial in the *Wall
Street Journal* observed that "it ha[d] been a strange war. It came with sudden stealth in an unsuspected place. Now it seems to end in a whimper.
In the strange quiet that follows the silenced guns, none of us feel great
transport; we have too often been brought to hope only to meet disillusion. Rather, we feel a numbness. Tomorrow we may have to pick up our
arms again—if not in Korea, then elsewhere." The one thing that had been
gained was that "neither we nor our enemies can any longer doubt our
resolution. That is the victory of the truce of Panmunjon."[23] (A sentiment
echoed with some irony in Lewis Milestone's 1959 film *Pork Chop Hill*:
the desperate fight to wrest a hill devoid of strategic meaning from the
enemy who, it is noted, "aren't just Orientals—they're Communists!" has
only one purpose: to answer the question—"are we as willing to spend our
lives for nothing" as they are?)[24]

So the Korean War, after three furious years of fighting, ended in stale-mate and a sense of futility. The cease-fire terms agreed to in 1953 could probably have been secured four months after the fighting started, when U.S./UN forces drove North Korean forces across the thirty-eighth parallel. In the aftermath, there was no investigation of how the war had been fought, nor why. Attention focused briefly on the number of prisoners accused of collaborating with the enemy and in particular on the twenty-one who chose to remain among the Communists rather than return home. Public dissatisfaction with the war was clear and clearly expressed in the definitive defeat of the Democratic Party in 1952. Succeeding administrations would remember this political price, and the admonition against fighting the Chi-nese in a land war in Asia, but otherwise Korea seemed to hold few other lessons for the future.[25] There was no Korea Syndrome.

Yet in retrospect, the Korean War was a sort of primer for the condition of permanent war I am trying to anatomize today. In its brief span, Korea had demonstrated the multiple forms of war the United States would fight for the rest of the twentieth century and into the twenty-first: the arming and training of a foreign military; the internationalization of civil war; bombing on a massive scale; conventional "big unit" warfare; resolution short of vic-tory; and even, in its early days, counterinsurgency, to which I will return.[26]

During the Eisenhower administration, warfare was confined to the occasional war scare (the Taiwan Straits), sabotage (China, Cuba), the precautionary dispatch of Marines (14,000 to Lebanon for a peaceful five-month stay) and full-scale covert operations (Guatemala, Iran), but none involved the dispatch of American troops. The basso continuo of potential nuclear annihilation was sustained by a policy of massive retali-ation, maintaining the nation as a whole in a state of near war. On leaving office, Eisenhower warned against the military-industrial complex that his two administrations had helped build; his successor's inaugural address invited the country to a new era of endless struggle.

The preferred form of the struggle introduced by the Kennedy admin-istration was counterinsurgency. The phoenix-like rise, fall, and again ris-ing of counterinsurgency is the profile of permanent war, bringing the "suffering so vast / it nullifies everything else" that troubles C. K. Williams' nighttime thoughts.[27]

Counterinsurgency is the logic of any struggle between a central authority—legitimately or illegitimately constituted—and an armed resistance movement, between formally organized armies and guerrillas. In short, counterinsurgency is standard colonial policing, with larger wars breaking out when the policing fails.

Less than two months after his inauguration, in his special message to Congress on the defense budget, Kennedy announced a new clear and present danger, and matched it with a new approach to national security. The free world was threatened "not only by nuclear attack, but also by being slowly nibbled away at the periphery, regardless of our strategic power, by forces of subversion, infiltration, indirect or non-overt aggression, internal revolution, diplomatic blackmail, guerrilla warfare or a series of limited wars." The new approach was a logical response. The United States must now be ready "to deal with any size force, including small externally supported bands of men; and we must help train local forces to be equally effective."[28] In the words of Deputy Special Assistant to the President Walt W. Rostow, guerrilla warfare "was a systematic attempt by the communists to impose a serious disease on those societies attempting the transition to modernization."[29] The threat this posed to national security was posited, not argued.

To figure out how best to develop a counterinsurgency/unconventional war capacity (he did not always discriminate between the two), Kennedy created a task force—the "Special Group (Counterinsurgency)," whose job was to coordinate an integrated program. It was, in Maxwell Taylor's words, "a son of Joint Chiefs of Staff for the control of all agencies involved in counterinsurgency" and included Robert Kennedy, who reported directly to the White House after each weekly meeting. The mission of the Special Group (CI) was to "recommend actions to obtain recognition . . . that subversive insurgency ('wars of liberation') is a new and dangerous form of politico-military conflict for which the US must prepare with the same seriousness of purpose as for the conventional warfare of the past."[30]

Since "new and dangerous" forms of "politico-military conflict" were unlikely to stop appearing, this was a prescription for perpetual military engagement abroad. In effect, the policy set the United States against any movement for social change that involved the use of force: not on the wrong side of history but, astonishingly, against history itself. Six years later, Thomas Hughes, director of Intelligence and Research at the State Department observed wryly of this first year of the Kennedy administration: "We were . . . all younger then—armed with the zeal of adventure, the discovery of a new doctrine, and ready opportunities for testing it.

Not unlike the 24-year old Winston Churchill writing to his mother in 1898, we thought, 'It is a pushing age, and we must shove with the best.'" Since 1961, Hughes said, there had been "dozens of books, hundreds of contracts, thousands of lectures," and if you wished "to participate in an effective dialogue inside either the university or the government," you had to speak the language of counterinsurgency. He described "Watch Committee radars" scanning the globe, "hoping to discern early warning data on pre-insurgency. Let an actual insurgency start to stir and Counter-insurgency committees will compete to claim it, task forces will move smartly to take possession of it." He warned that counterinsurgency "comes close to proclaiming the desirability of drying up all politically significant violent protest" except for right-wing coups.[31]

Kennedy's romance with unconventional and counterinsurgency warfare has been well described, including his personal supervision of the outfitting of the expanded Special Forces units at Fort Bragg's Special Warfare Center. Simultaneously, the Navy created the SEALS, the Air Force an Air Commando Group, and a Marine general, Victor Krulak, was named the Joint Chiefs' Special Assistant for Counterinsurgency and Special Activities.

By August 1962 counterinsurgency had moved from tactic to doctrine. The "purpose and scope" of Overseas Internal Defense Policy, NSAM 182, were capacious. The opening paragraph declared that the "most pressing U.S. national security problem now, and for the foreseeable future, is the continuing threat presented by communist inspired, supported, or directed insurgency" as well as "other types of subversion and insurgency in all countries of the free world, primarily those that are underdeveloped, whether they are pro-Western, or basically neutral."[32] This was a global brief in which even a pro-Western or neutral movement for change could invite the attention of U.S. counterinsurgency efforts. A staff member, Charles Maechling, remarked years later that this was "the most interventionist statement of American policy ever promulgated." U.S. counterinsurgency doctrine was not restricted to the United States but was exported to a number of allies, especially in Latin America. Colombia, the only Latin American country to have joined the U.S. effort in Korea, was a major recipient of U.S. funds and training, and its subsequent history of counterinsurgency and paramilitary violence owes much to the United States, as has also been the case in Nicaragua, Argentina, Guatemala, and El Salvador, as well as Indonesia.[33]

When counterinsurgency failed in Vietnam, the war became one of attrition, applying the Maoist aphorism that counterinsurgency had also embraced: the guerrillas ate fish swimming in the ocean of the people; therefore, dry up the ocean. When this war of attrition failed to win the war, counterinsurgency returned in the form of the "accelerated pacification" that characterized the final days of the Vietnam war: a determined effort to destroy the National Liberation Front "infrastructure" in the villages and small unit operations using massive fire power. When the combination of counterinsurgency and the "hard hand of war" were no more successful, the Nixon administration brought U.S. involvement there to a close.

I have gone into some detail on Kennedy-era counterinsurgency because it has remained a powerful model. However, at the time, its failure in Vietnam inspired resistance to counterinsurgency as a model of war, not least at the highest level of the military. Congress passed the War Powers Act in an attempt to constrain the war-making power of the executive, and the general repudiation of the use of armed force abroad was so fierce it was given a name: the "Vietnam Syndrome," suggesting that the county had developed an allergic reaction to war.

Senior American military officials were determined to avoid any repetition of their experience in Vietnam. (General David Petraeus, in a 1987 article for the journal *Parameters*, dubbed these officials the Never Again Club, on the model of those officers who insisted after the Korean War that the United States should never again fight a limited land war in Asia.[34] Secretary of Defense Robert Gates voiced a similar sentiment recently, adding to the list of places to be avoided the Middle East and Africa.[35]) This group, which included Colin Powell, moved to fashion an army whose capacity for counterinsurgency operations would be severely limited and whose war-fighting capacity would be directed where they felt it belonged: against major military powers such as the Soviet Union. Their approach to war, ultimately known as the Powell/Weinberger Doctrine (after Reagan's Secretary of Defense) was composed of several simple premises: the United States would never again go to war unless the military had the enthusiastic backing of the American people, a clear and explicit goal, an equally clear exit strategy, and the ability to apply massive force to the problem. The self-limiting conditions imposed by the doctrine presumably made counterinsurgency warfare, as in Vietnam, impossible. It also imposed strict limits on the use of the military.

Counterinsurgency was dropped from the service academies' curriculum and replaced by courses that imagined war more on the model of World War II. Eventually, Desert Storm fulfilled the new requirements. It was fought against a tyrant who had invaded a peaceful neighboring country, at the head of an international coalition, and in support of a UN resolution. Desert Storm was in every particular *not* Vietnam: this was a war that ended before the public could either lose interest or oppose it, as clean as press control could make it (no pictures of Iraqi dead buried in sand trenches, but only of oil-soaked birds, said to be the victims of Saddam Hussein's irresponsible tactics), few American casualties, and a victory parade.

Perhaps most important, Desert Storm was fought by a volunteer, professional army. Policy makers could not be indifferent to public opinion, but they need no longer run the risk of the widespread protest a conscript army threatened. This army, combined with increasing numbers of mercenaries, offered the possibility of politically cost-free warfare.

However, counterinsurgency did not disappear entirely. Renamed "low intensity conflict," it was pursued, though without U.S. combat troops, in El Salvador and Nicaragua, among other countries in the hemisphere. Still, despite its reputed successes in these countries, it never came to dominate military doctrine as its advocates had hoped. David Fitzgerald in his history of U.S. counterinsurgency concluded that "the Army at the close of the Cold War still overwhelmingly focused on its conventional role, and the counterinsurgency mission remained sidelined, its brief resurgence in the guise of Low Intensity Conflict notwithstanding."[36]

After September 11, 2001, the first long war, the Cold War, mutated without pause into a second long war, the War against Terror. There is a distinction between the two wars that is important to my argument: the first long war, the Cold War, *could* come to an end since it was said to be against an ideology embodied in a geopolitical pole of power, the Soviet Union. The second long war, the War against Terror, since its objective is the elimination of a tactic, can never come to an end. The Cold War as it was conducted required a major arsenal whose deployment was visible on the ground and in the air and a system of conscription engaging the whole population. The second, the War against Terror, relies on a professional army enhanced by mercenaries, high-tech weaponry, counterinsurgency tactics, and an invisible air war. This combination makes war an abstraction: "armed social work," as one counterinsurgency expert put it, on the one hand, "hunter-killer" teams, on the other.[37]

Counterinsurgency is a war for all seasons. Its principles have no time limit, no clear goal, no exit strategy. They are all tactical: clear, hold, and build; use less rather than more force; be sensitive to the local culture; support only legitimate governments; be population-centric; employ nonkinetic means whenever possible. These means are said to have worked in Iraq. It is believed that they will work in Afghanistan. Judging by the past, if counterinsurgency does not work in Afghanistan, it will be interpreted as *having* worked, or it will be said not to have been pursued long or hard enough.

This is how it worked in Iraq: according to Wikileaks, some fifteen thousand more civilians were killed by U.S. and allied forces than were reported at the time; suspected insurgents were often killed after they surrendered (a lawyer reassured a helicopter pilot that "you cannot surrender to an aircraft"); the United States knew and refused to investigate the large number of the suspects turned over to Iraqi authorities who were raped, tortured, and sometimes murdered. The public was relatively well informed on the sectarian warfare that turned Iraqi cities into killing fields. But few people knew the extent to which U.S.-trained death squads, modeled on operations in El Salvador, participated in this sectarian violence.[38] It was perhaps because so much of the violence of the war in Iraq was hidden that the revelations about Abu Ghraib had such force.

The press, the military, and the president all credited the return of counterinsurgency, guided by a new field manual and implemented by General Petraeus with the help of additional troops (constituting not an escalation but a surge), with bringing the level of violence in Iraq down to manageable levels. A status of forces agreement with an elected Iraqi government was negotiated, and the United States was said to have finally achieved success, if not victory, in Iraq. The next test for counterinsurgency was in Afghanistan.

General Petraeus and Secretary of Defense Gates now report steady progress. As they did in Vietnam, reporters and junior officers tell a different story. In February 2011, C. J. Chivers wrote an angry column about the withdrawal of U.S. forces from the Pech Valley. It opens on a contradiction: "After years of fighting for control of a prominent valley in the rugged mountains of eastern Afghanistan, the US military has begun to pull back most of its forces from ground it once insisted was central to the campaign against the Taliban and Al Qaeda." The major in charge of this area of Afghanistan insists that the move was not an abandonment of the area (in which over one hundred American soldiers and uncounted others have died), but rather a "realigning to provide better security for the Afghan people." A less senior officer put this differently: "What we figured out is that people in the Pech really aren't anti-US or anti-anything; they just want to be left alone. Our presence is what's destabilizing this area." Neither the reporter nor the officer went on to generalize from this observation. In theory, the Afghan National Army will remain in the Pech to protect those who cooperated with the Americans and are thus now at risk of Taliban retaliation. No one believes the Afghan Army capable of protecting them.[39]

In southern Afghanistan this spring, villages were destroyed to save them, a tactic whose likelihood of success was questioned by a headline in the *New York Times*: "Winning Hearts While Flattening Vineyards Is Rather Tricky."[40] At the same time, the number of drone attacks and Special Forces hunter-killer teams has steadily increased. According to David Ignatius in the *Washington Post*, Petraeus was experimenting with a new mix of counterterrorism and counterinsurgency, or in Petraeus's own enhanced term, "comprehensive counterinsurgency."[41]

Over the past two years, the war has become less and less visible. The number of hunter-killer teams operating in Afghanistan has increased exponentially along with drone attacks. The *Wall Street Journal* reported in May 2011 that these hunter-killer teams, operating with maximum secrecy, had conducted thousands of raids over the past year, killing 3,200 insurgents and capturing well over twice that number.[42] Worldwide, Special Operations forces operate in seventy-five countries, a deployment the Obama administration justifies on the basis of the 2001 congressional mandate to "use all necessary and appropriate force against those nations, organizations, or persons [the President] determines planned, authorized, committed or aided" the attacks. A senior legal adviser to the Bush administration observed that "many of those targeted . . . had nothing to do with the 2001 attacks."[43]

The fate of Greg Mortenson's *Three Cups of Tea* may be a counterinsurgency parable.[44] The book, a lyrical account of Mortenson's winning hearts and minds in remote and violent areas of Afghanistan by drinking tea with tribal elders and building schools, was widely distributed to

U.S. troops. General Petraeus, Admiral Mike Mullen, and General Stanley McChrystal all embraced Mortenson, and he made the rounds of bases in Afghanistan lecturing on "the nuances of tribal warfare." Two enthusiasts, Lieutenant Colonel Gaydon and Captain Pan, wrote that their excellent relations with one district governor was, "like Greg Mortenson's best seller . . . forged over chai." But then Mortenson's description of his success turned out to be fraudulent, and the local governor with whom Gaydon and Pan bonded was killed in a "mob hit" by rivals who resented his failure to share funds skimmed from U.S. reconstruction projects. Michael Miklaucic, an official with U.S. AID, drew the moral: "No amount of tea with Afghans will persuade them that we are like them, that our war is their war or that our interests are their interests. The war in Afghanistan isn't about persuasion or tea. It is about power."[45]

A secret war of high-tech intelligence gathering, enhanced Special Forces operations, heavily armed drones, and the training of local forces may well become the new form of America's wars, probably combined with some form of counterinsurgency operations. The involvement of the CIA in military operations, indeed the appointment of General Petraeus to head the agency, blurs the distinction between civilian and military functions. A militarized CIA now oversees the drone bombings in Yemen, Pakistan, and Afghanistan; the mandated secrecy of CIA activities makes war as invisible, as slight a burden on the conscience of the country as it could conceivably get. I began with a C. K. Williams' poem and I should like to end with one. Its subject is Lieutenant Remy Shrapnel's invention of the shell that has immortalized his name.[46] After describing the effect of shrapnel on the human body, Williams goes on,

> Shrapnel's device was superseded by higher-powered, more efficient projectiles, obsolete now in their turn.
> One war passes into the next. One wound is the next and the next.
> Something howls. Something cries.

It probably will not do for historians to howl or cry, but it is certainly our work to speak and write so that a time of war not be mistaken for peacetime, nor waging war for making peace.

NOTES

1. Delmore Schwartz, "Comment," *Partisan Review* 18, no. 1 (January–February 1951): 13.

2. Garry Trudeau, *Doonesbury*, May 14, 2011, http://www.gocomics.com/doonesbury/2011/05/14.

3. C. K. Williams, "The Hearth," *Collected Poems* (New York: Farrar, Straus and Giroux, 2006), 614.

4. Michael Sherry, *In the Shadow of War: The United States since the 1930s* (New Haven, Conn.: Yale University Press, 1995).

5. See Marilyn Young, *Rhetoric of Empire* (Cambridge, Mass.: Harvard University Press, 1968).

6. Quoted in William Appleman Williams, *The Tragedy of American Diplomacy* (New York: W.W. Norton, 1972), 14.

7. John Lewis Gaddis, *We Now Know: Rethinking Cold War History* (Oxford: Clarendon, 1998), 289.

8. Walter Lippmann, "Empire: The Days of Our Nonage Are Over," in *Men of Destiny*, quoted in "By Way of Introduction: The United States, Decolonization and the World System," in *The United States and Decolonization: Power and Freedom* ed. David Ryan and Victory Pungong (Basingstoke, UK: MacMillan Press, 2000), 18–19.

9. The full text of the speech can be found at *https://www.presidency.ucsb.edu/documents/remarks-joint-session-the-philippine-congress-quezon-city-philippines*. There is an acidic account of Bush's eight-hour visit to Manila by David Sanger: "Bush cites Philippines as Model in Rebuilding Iraq," *New York Times*, October 19, 2003, 1.

10. Smedley Butler, *War Is a Racket: The Profit Motive behind Warfare* (1935; repr., Los Angeles: Feral House, 2003), 27.

11. The drone program is divided between the military and the CIA, and it is difficult to get cumulative statistics on the amount of tonnage dropped. Unlike Harrison Salisbury during the Vietnam war, reporters are rarely in a position to witness their impact.

12. William Barrett, *The Truants* (New York: Anchor Press 1982), 20.

13. Oral history interview of Frank Pace, Jr., by Jerry N. Hess, February 26, 1972, http://www.trumanlibrary.org/oralhist/pacefj4.htm.

14. Quoted in John C. Culver and John Hyde, *American Dreamer: The Life and Times of Henry A. Wallace* (New York: W.W. Norton, 2000), 410.

15. E. M. Forster, *Two Cheers for Democracy* (New York: Mariner Books, 1951), 335.

16. The films were directly connected to current congressional debates over Universal Military Training and Selective Service and aroused considerable protest from a variety of peace groups. The vice president of Coronet Films assured Secretary of Defense Robert Lovett that the protesters were small and powerless, but the Defense Department answered every letter, insisting they had offered only "technical support" to the filmmakers. By 1952, with Selective Service in place, the controversy had died down. Larry Suid, *Film*

and Propaganda in America: A Documentary History (New York: Greenwood, 1990), vol. 4. See documents 43–68, which include announcements about the series; correspondence between J. M. Abraham, vice president of Coronet and Lt. Col. Clair E. Towne, head of the Department of Defense Motion Picture Section Pictorial Branch; letters of protest from various quarters, etc. The fourth film in the series, *Are You Ready for Service*, number 4, can be viewed online at Prelinger Archives, http://www.archive.org/details/prelinger. For more on war films in general, see his *Sailing on the Silver Screen: Hollywood and the U.S. Navy* (Annapolis, Md.: Naval Institute Press, 1996) and *Guts and Glory: Great American War Movies* (Reading, Mass.: Addison-Wesley Publishing, 1978).

17. Thomas Doherty, *Projections of War: Hollywood, American Culture and World War II* (New York: Columbia University Press, 1993), 271.

18. Studs Terkel, "The Good War," in *An Oral History of World War Two* (New York: Pantheon Books, 1984), 137.

19. Richard Rovere, "Letter from Washington," *New Yorker*, August 5, 1950, 48, quoted in James R. Kerin, "The Korean War and American Memory" (Ph.D. diss., University of Pennsylvania, January 1, 1994), https://repository.upenn. edu/dissertations/AAI9503784/. Allan Millett, in his history of the Marine Corps, *Semper Fidelis*, has a slightly different version. Millet's rhymes, so I am fairly sure he has the refrain right; but he uses "bless them all" rather than "fuck 'em all," and I am equally sure the latter is correct.

20. Quoted in Bruce Cumings, *The Korean War: A History* (New York: Modern Library, 2010), 209.

21. Cited in Marilyn B. Young, "Hard Sell: The Korean War," in *Selling War in a Media Age: The Presidency and Public Opinion in the American Century*, ed. Kenneth Osgood and Andrew K. Frank (Gainesville: University Press of Florida, 2010), 130–31.

22. Cited in Marilyn B. Young, "Hard Sell," 131–32. Lubell's account of public opinion appeared first in the *Saturday Evening Post*, June 7, 1952, 19–21, 48–54. It was recapitulated in his 1956 book, *Revolt of the Moderates* (New York: Harper, 1956).

23. "The Truce," *Wall Street Journal*, July 27, 1953, 6.

24. *Pork Chop Hill*, directed by Lewis Milestone (1959; Century City, Calif.: MGM), DVD. Milestone, also director of the aforementioned *The North Star*, is perhaps best known for directing *All Quiet on the Western Front* (1930).

25. There were many specific lessons: a new Uniform Military Code of Conduct, designed to stiffen the spine of future prisoners of war, was issued, and everyone agreed that China should never be provoked into participating in a new war in Asia. And there was one very misguided notion: that Eisenhower's threat to use nuclear weapons is what had brought China to yield at the negotiating table.

26. See Cumings, *The Korean War*, chaps. 1 and 6 in particular.

27. Williams, "The Hearth," 614.

28. Quoted in Michael McClintock, *Instruments of Statecraft: U.S. Guerrilla Warfare, Counter-Insurgency, and Counter-Terrorism, 1940–1990* (New York:

Pantheon Books, 1992), 164. For the full text, see http://www.presidency.ucsb.edu/ws/index.php?pid=8554.

29. W. W. Rostow, "Guerrilla Warfare in the Underdeveloped Areas," *Department of State Bulletin* 45, no. 1154 (August 7, 1961): 233–38.

30. McClintock, *Instruments of Statecraft*, 166.

31. Thomas L. Hughes, "The Odyssey of Counter-Insurgency," Remarks at the Foreign Service Institute, July 3, 1967 (unpublished).

32. McClintock, *Instruments of Statecraft*, 170–73. The full text is available online at https://www.statecraft.org/.

33. Charles Maechling, Jr., "Camelot, Robert Kennedy, and Counter-Insurgency—a Memoir," *Virginia Quarterly Review* 75, no. 3 (1999): 438–58. (Maechling put it this way: "We reoriented the [Latin American] military away from continental defense to a counterinsurgency mission backed by a river of American equipment with no human rights strings attached" creating "more efficient instruments of repression than existed before.")

34. David H. Petraeus, "Korea, the Never-Again Club, and Indochina," *Parameters* 17, no. 4 (1987): 59–70.

35. Thom Shanker, "Warning against Wars Like Iraq and Afghanistan," *New York Times*, February 25, 2011.

36. David Fitzgerald, *Learning to Forget? The US Army and Counterinsurgency Doctrine and Practice from Vietnam to Iraq* (Ph.D. diss., National University of Ireland, Cork, Ireland, June 2010), 149. (Fitzgerald's dissertation was published under the same title by Stanford University Press in 2013.)

37. David Kilcullen, "Twenty-Eight Articles: Fundamentals of Company-Level Counter-insurgency," *Military Review* 86, no. 3 (2006): 106.

38. See Marilyn B. Young, "Counterinsurgency Now and Forever," in *Iraq and the Lessons of Vietnam: Or How Not to Learn from History*, ed. Marilyn B. Young and Lloyd Gardner (New York: New Press, 2007). For Wikileaks, see Nick Davies, Jonathan Steele, and David Leigh, "Iraq War Logs: Secret Files Show Who US Ignored Torture," *Guardian*, October 22, 2010.

39. C. J. Chivers et al., "U.S. Pulling Back in Afghan Valley It Called Vital to War," *New York Times*, February 24, 2011.

40. Carlotta Gall and Ruhullah Khapal Wak, "Winning Hearts While Flattening Vineyards Is Rather Tricky," *New York Times*, March 11, 2011.

41. David Ignatius, "Petraeus Rewrites the Playbook in Afghanistan," *Washington Post*, October 19, 2010.

42. Julian Barnes, "US Secretly Adds Strike Teams—As 'Hunter-Killer' Squads Gain Favor in Afghan Effort, White House Has Bolstered Their Raids," *Wall Street Journal*, May 6, 2011, A6. At the moment there are no fewer than thirteen thousand special operations forces deployed in seventy-five countries. See Tom Engelhardt, "A World Made by War," *Nation*, October 17, 2010, https://www.thenation.com/article/archive/world-made-war/.

43. Quoted in Karen DeYoung and Greg Jaffe, "U.S. 'Secret War' Expands Globally as Special Operations Forces Take Larger Role," *Washington Post*, June 4, 2010, A01.

44. Greg Mortenson and David Oliver Relin, *Three Cups of Tea: One Man's Mission*

to Fight Terrorism and Build Nations—One School at a Time (New York: Penguin Books, 2006).

45. Greg Jaffe, "How the US Military Fell in Love with 'Three Cups of Tea'" *Washington Post*, April 21, 2011. Jaffe adds that "not everything about the military's embrace of Mortenson's tea philosophy has been counterproductive." Joshua Foust, an Afghanistan analyst working for the military said that it "would be a shame to abandon the idea of trying to respect the people you're trying to reform with guns and money just because one of the people promoting the concept is shown to be a fraud." Jaffe, "Three Cups of Tea."

46. Williams, "Shrapnel," *Collected Poems*, 661.

AFTERWORD

Andrew Bacevich

The hallmarks of Marilyn Young's career as a historian of the United States were these: courage, tenacity, single-mindedness, and implacable honesty, combined with immense personal generosity. I myself was a beneficiary of that generosity, which I had not earned and did not deserve. So I make no pretense of writing this appreciation from a detached point of view.

An appropriately respectful obituary published in the *New York Times* described Marilyn as "a leftist, feminist, antiwar historian who challenged conventional interpretations of American foreign policy."[1] While accurate as far as it went, this summary fell well short of being adequate. Above all else, as scholar, activist, and citizen, Marilyn devoted herself to deciphering the relationship between war and the political project known as the United States of America.

Marilyn arrived early on at the conviction that embedded in the nation's various wars are abiding truths about America's past and present, even if few Americans and even fewer members of the American political elite are willing to reckon with those truths. In effect, she devoted herself to establishing war as an essential explanatory theme—perhaps, a master key—of American history.

The more traditional themes of that history—the ones that Marilyn sought to displace—are nothing if not familiar. Differing in emphasis from one generation to the next, they recount a narrative of aspiration and ascent. Together, they comprise the common knowledge of the American past. This endlessly reiterated story, as Marilyn writes in these pages, provides the source material for "what politicians tell the country about itself, what high school teachers teach, what students believe."[2] Together, they describe America as it wishes to see itself.

Key elements of that narrative include responding to God's call to embark upon an Errand in the Wilderness; winning Independence and creating a Land of Liberty; enlarging the restless American Republic so that it stretched from Sea to Shining Sea; destroying the Original Sin of slavery in order to preserve the Union; welcoming the world's "huddled masses yearning to breathe free"; taming the frontier while amassing unprecedented riches; instituting reforms to mute the brutalizing effects of industrialization; and coming out on the winning side of successive world wars labeled First, Second, and Cold.

At the conclusion of this sequence, the United States had emerged as far and away the richest and most powerful nation on the planet, the accumulation of wealth and power serving, in effect, to validate all that had gone before. Yet emphasizing wealth and power as the ends of human existence has this additional effect: it imposes blinders and marginalizes dissenting perspectives that prize other values, whether offered by contrarians of the right or of the left.

Is the United States today a better place than it was in 1976 or 1876 or 1776? Are Americans today freer than were their forebearers in the twentieth or nineteenth or eighteenth centuries? The consensus answer to those questions is emphatically in the affirmative. So whatever missteps and setbacks occurred along the way, the history of the United States taken as a whole qualifies as a good news story. Through booms and busts, triumphs and failures, the vast majority of ordinary Americans have clung to that proposition with all their might.

There are, to put it mildly, problems with this good news story. One of those problems pertains to race, which in our own time has gained recognition as an issue of transcendent historical (and contemporary) importance. Not long ago, this growing appreciation of the significance of race prompted the *New York Times* to undertake a massive journalistic project intended to "reframe the country's history by placing the consequences of slavery and the contributions of black Americans at the very center of our national narrative."[3] The ultimate impact of this 1619 Project, which is less journalism than propaganda in a worthy cause, remains to be seen. Indeed, several prominent historians have already weighed in to question its very premise.[4] Yet if nothing else, as an exercise in "reframing," the *Times* initiative suggests that ours may be an opportune moment for recasting American history in other ways, moving to the forefront themes that have been present all along but were classified as subordinate or peripheral.

One such theme is war. As Marilyn Young understood from the very outset of her career as a scholar-activist, war complicates and subverts every aspect of American history rendered as a good news story. No less than race, war calls into question the logic of employing the accumulation of wealth and power as criteria for judging the merit of any collective enterprise, be it a business, a church, a university, a newspaper like the *New York Times*, or indeed a nation.

To place war "at the very center of our national narrative" is to challenge our understanding of the American past in ways that might discomfit even the architects of the 1619 Project. Yet that is precisely the cause to which Marilyn devoted herself.

For her 2011 presidential address to the Society for Historians of American Foreign Relations, Marilyn chose a title that was simultaneously unusual and perfectly apt: "I was thinking, as I often do these days, of war." In fact, she was always thinking about war, its causes, conduct, and consequences, especially as they pertained to the United States.

Few of her fellow citizens have shared her preoccupation with war. To consider just the period since 9/11, the failures, frustrations, and unwelcome consequences resulting from U.S. interventions in Afghanistan, Iraq, Libya, and Syria among other places have had little noticeable impact on Washington's propensity to employ force, much less American attitudes toward war. All in all, therefore, Marilyn's efforts to dissuade the public from acquiescing in this normalization of war came up short.

Why have her exertions, along with those of other like-minded scholars and activists, proven to be of so little avail? How is it that Americans can move, however haltingly, toward an honest accounting about race, while remaining willfully ignorant about war? Why, to state the matter bluntly, does American militarism persist—flourish, even—despite its gargantuan failures? I submit that Marilyn herself would be in the forefront of those insisting on the need to confront these questions head-on.

Drawing on insights contained in Marilyn's own writings, herewith is one very provisional attempt to provide an answer.

PERPETUALLY SEARCHING FOR ANOTHER "GOOD WAR"

Allow me to propose the following as a working hypothesis: a penchant for politically motivated violence was from the outset inherent in the nature of the enterprise.

Relatively few Americans and far fewer American politicians will admit to an intimate connection between war and their collective aspirations, typically advertised under the banner of freedom. All peoples wish to think of themselves as wishing to live in peace. Americans are no exception. Yet Marilyn understood that the truth is more complicated.

In the summer preceding her birth in 1937, for example, President Franklin Roosevelt delivered a famous address at Chautauqua, New York. In the course of that speech, FDR declared unequivocally that, "I hate war," going on to assure his listeners that "I have passed unnumbered hours, I shall pass unnumbered hours thinking and planning how war shall be kept from this nation." The president vowed to "make certain that no act of the United States helps to produce or to promote war."

Roosevelt delivered his Chautauqua address at a moment when his countrymen were notably receptive to antiwar sentiments. Memories of the Great War were then still fresh. By the middle of the 1930s, the vast majority of Americans had concluded that U.S. intervention in that conflict had been a disastrous mistake, over one hundred thousand American soldiers dying in a foreign war for no purpose. When he insisted that "the conscience of America revolts against war," the politically adept Roosevelt was tapping into this sentiment.[5] The United States was irrevocably committed to peace.

Within a few short years, FDR would revise his views and lead the United States into another and even more destructive war. Even so, the conviction that the conscience of America revolts against war persisted, no more questioned than the claim that the United States from the moment of its birth had been a land committed to "liberty and justice for all." Also persisting was an inclination to give Roosevelt's successors the benefit of the doubt when they too proclaimed their devotion to peace.

Crucial to propping up these notions was the sacralization of World War II itself. Recount the Anglo-American war as a heroic crusade against fascism and you'll likely end up succumbing to manufactured triumphalism, with stirring speeches by George S. Patton and a sweeping soundtrack by Richard Rogers (and Stalin's Red Army airbrushed out of the picture).[6] Study what Marilyn called the nation's "small dirty wars" and you just might learn something.[7] This is where she made her mark.

In no small measure, the chronicle of U.S. military history since 1945, beginning with Douglas MacArthur's northward thrust across Korea's thirty-eighth parallel in 1950, encompassing the debacle of Vietnam, and extending to George W. Bush's initiation of Operation Iraqi Freedom in

2003, expresses a deep desire to replicate the saga that Americans have chosen to remember as the "Good War." That quest has yet to find meaningful success, albeit not for want of trying by U.S. forces.

In the introduction to her best-known book, *The Vietnam Wars*, completed in August 1990, just as the United States was formulating its response to Saddam Hussein's invasion of Kuwait that very month, Marilyn wrote, "We have been at war since the end of World War II."[8] Thirty years on, the statement stands, requiring neither amendment nor caveat, with the preferred American interpretation of World War II—the United States as redeemer nation—still justifying all that followed.

If anything, the passing of the Cold War relieved Americans of having to maintain any further pretense of abhorring war. With the chief ostensible threat to global peace and security having now been removed, Washington's propensity for armed intervention increased appreciably. Over the following decades, a sustained bout of military activism ensued, with the *New York Times* not least among prominent institutions treating this behavior as unremarkable, more or less akin to changes in the weather or fluctuations in the stock market.

To review Marilyn's scholarly legacy is to appreciate that post–Cold War American militarism represented not a departure from past practice, but its fulfillment. While the conflict with Nazi Germany and Imperial Japan still today forms the point of origin of our remembered past (with the Civil War serving as a nineteenth-century precursor), Marilyn herself attended to conflicts that found U.S. troops sent to fight in faraway places, typically pursuant to highly suspect motives, with the American people either indifferent or deceived or pressed into service as accomplices. These, after all, tend to be more resistant to mythmaking.

Marilyn's work focused primarily on wars that occurred after 1900, a span of decades during which the rationale for American expansionism became both overtly ideological and increasingly detached from tangible U.S. interests. She rarely attended to the period of territorial acquisition and consolidation that occurred during the interval between the winning of independence in 1783 and the "closing" of the frontier announced by the census of 1890. This is surely our loss for had she chosen to do so she would have assuredly had important things to say.

It is certainly true that the Civil War, enshrined in popular memory as an "American Iliad," overshadows all other military episodes during this century-long period. In comparison with the bloody struggle of 1861–65, everything else becomes a footnote. So while novels about the Civil War sell, novels about the War of 1812 essentially don't exist. Write a screenplay about General Winfield Scott Hancock at Gettysburg and you'll have a decent chance of attracting financing. A script about General Winfield Scott's assault on Chapultepec bringing the Mexican War to a victorious conclusion is guaranteed to sit in your desk drawer forever.

Yet fence off the Civil War from events that preceded and followed it and you end up with a breathtakingly successful chronicle of violence-fueled expansion. To obscure the reality of what actually occurred, Americans opted to employ terms such as Manifest Destiny or descriptive phrases such as "winning the West." Both of these were euphemisms for raw conquest, supplemented by actions that in modern parlance we know as ethnic cleansing. Put the Civil War back into the frame, however, and the through line of nineteenth-century U.S. military history shifts from conquest and imperial policing to liberation (or for proponents of the Lost Cause, justified defense), with most Americans happy to play along. Actions that Americans would have unhesitatingly condemned if perpetrated by Tsars or Kaisers became tolerable when orchestrated by the likes of Andrew Jackson and James Polk.

Of course, it's with the radically misremembered Spanish-American War of 1898 that things really got interesting. The United States went to war to liberate Cuba and ended up annexing the Philippines and various other overseas properties, a change of course that was both astonishing and revelatory. Just as George W. Bush's decision to invade and occupy Iraq after 9/11 made it apparent that Washington's strategic aim was something other than preventing further terrorist attacks, so too with President William McKinley's decision to keep the Philippines: the advertised purpose for going to war did not describe the actual purpose.

To insist that God had all along intended residents of Texas and California to grow up speaking English instead of Spanish is one thing. It's quite another to contend that He also wanted the Stars and Stripes to fly over an archipelago consisting of more than 7,600 islands located roughly 7,000 miles west of San Francisco. This is also where Marilyn weighs in on the conversation.

While she never strayed from her conviction that Vietnam defined the emblematic event of *her* generation, Marilyn correctly sensed that the misnamed Philippine Insurrection of 1899–1902 signified a crucial turning point in the evolution of American imperialism. From this point going forward, when it came to using force, the United States admitted fewer constraints and demanded greater latitude.

The war to "pacify" the Philippines (and its immediate sequel, the even longer campaign to pacify the Moros) stands as the most instructive overseas American war that virtually no American today has ever heard of. My own first encounter with the Philippines War as a graduate student in the mid-1970s was a consciousness-altering experience, radically at odds with all that I had learned about the "American way of war," whether as a boy or as a cadet at West Point.

It was Vietnam before Vietnam. In due course, it became Iraq before Iraq: ugly, protracted, replete with actions that today would qualify as war crimes and many deaths of both combatants and noncombatants, albeit with vastly more Filipinos killed than U.S. troops. And once the conflict ended, it was, in Marilyn's words, promptly "absorbed, dismissed, and erased."[9]

Erasing these nasty memories was essential, Marilyn observed, to sustaining the illusion that "the United States was not and, by definition, could not be an imperialistic nation," even when using force to annex remote territories and classifying their inhabitants not as citizens but as subjects.[10] "To help their countrymen sleep better," Marilyn wrote, "historians and politicians have often transformed past unpleasantness into something palatable," thereby accurately describing how the Philippines War was incorporated into the American past.[11]

Much the same fate befell Korea and Vietnam, other conflicts to which she devoted recurring attention. Marilyn understood that to define them as episodes in the Cold War was to conceal their actual significance, both moral and political. Situating Korea and Vietnam in the context of a larger struggle depicted as defensive, necessary, and morally justified offered, she wrote, a way of sustaining the self-aggrandizing claim that the United States is "incapable of waging an aggressive war, or committing war crimes or crimes against humanity."[12] To do otherwise—to incorporate Korea and Vietnam where they belong in a larger narrative of American imperialism— was, in Marilyn's words, "to impugn the nation's entire past" and thereby "bring into question the founding premise of American history itself."[13]

Marilyn believed passionately in the need to confront and, if necessary, to impugn that founding premise, not least because of the harm that the

American penchant for war does to those that the nation sends to fight on its behalf. She opposed war; she did not hold American soldiers responsible for war.

Taken as a whole, her scholarship and activism point inescapably to this conclusion: the political experiment tracing its origins to the founding of the Anglo-American colonies in the first decades of the seventeenth century was from the outset an expansionist enterprise drenched in violence.

For Americans, stasis has always meant decline. Averting decline entails a willingness to amass and employ armed force. In the twenty-first century this proposition is taken for granted, so much so that it almost entirely escapes notice. Invited to Chautauqua today to reflect on war, an honest president would be obliged to say, "Given our existing circumstances, war has become necessary and unavoidable; and so it will remain, with peace indefinitely postponed."

We honor Marilyn's memory by refusing to sanitize and falsify war. We honor her legacy by refusing to join those who accept war as inevitable.

NOTES

1. Sam Roberts, "Marilyn Young, Historian Who Challenged U.S. Foreign Policy, Dies at 79," *New York Times*, March 9, 2017.
2. Marilyn B. Young, "The Age of Global Power," this volume, 21.
3. "The 1619 Project," *New York Times Magazine*, August 14, 2019.
4. "Letter to the Editor: Historians Critique the 1619 Project, and We Respond," *New York Times*, December 20, 2019.
5. "Address at Chautauqua, N.Y., August 14, 1936," in *The Public Papers and Addresses of Franklin D. Roosevelt, 1936* (New York: Random House, 1938), 289.
6. *Patton*, dir. Franklin J. Schaffner (20th Century Fox, 1970); *Victory at Sea*, soundtrack by Richard Rodgers and Robert Russell Bennett (NBC Television Network, 1952–53).
7. Marilyn Young, "Counterinsurgency Now and Forever," in *Iraq and the Lessons of Vietnam*, ed. Lloyd C. Gardner and Marilyn B. Young (New York: New Press, 2007), 216.
8. Marilyn Young, *The Vietnam Wars* (New York: HarperCollins, 1991), x.
9. Marilyn B. Young, "The Big Sleep," this volume, 123.
10. Marilyn B. Young, "'The Same Struggle for Liberty': Korea and Vietnam," this volume, 84.
11. Young, "Age of Global Power," 34.
12. Marilyn B. Young, "U.S. in Asia, U.S. in Iraq: Lessons Not Learned . . . ," this volume, 183.
13. Young, "Big Sleep," 133.

SELECTED ADDITIONAL WORKS OF MARILYN B. YOUNG

BOOKS

The Routledge Handbook of the Global Sixties: Between Protest and Nation-Building. New York: Routledge, 2018 (coedited with Chen Jian, Martin Klimke, Masha Kirasirova, Mary Nolan, and Joanna Waley-Cohen).

Bombing Civilians: A Twentieth-Century History. New York: New Press, 2009 (coedited with Yuki Tanaka).

Making Sense of the Vietnam Wars: Local, National, and Transnational Perspectives. New York: Oxford University Press, 2008 (coedited with Mark Philip Bradley).

The New American Empire: A 21st Century Teach-In on US Foreign Policy. New York: New Press, 2005 (coedited with Lloyd C. Gardner).

A Companion to the Vietnam War. Malden, Mass.: Blackwell Publishing, 2002 (coedited with Robert Buzzanco).

Human Rights and Revolutions. Lanham, Md.: Rowman & Littlefield Publishers, 2000 (coedited with Jeffrey Wasserstrom and Lynn Hunt).

The Vietnam Wars, 1945–1990. New York: Harper Collins, 1991.

Promissory Notes: Women in the Transition to Socialism. New York: Monthly Review Press, 1989 (coedited with Sonia Kruks and Rayna Rapp).

Transforming Russia and China: Revolutionary Struggle in the Twentieth Century. New York: Oxford University Press, 1982 (coauthored with William G. Rosenberg).

American Expansionism: The Critical Issues. Boston: Little, Brown, 1973.

Women in China: Studies in Social Change and Feminism. Ann Arbor: Center for Chinese Studies, University of Michigan, 1973.

The Rhetoric of Empire: American China Policy, 1895–1901. Cambridge: Harvard University Press, 1968.

ARTICLES & ESSAYS

"How the United States Ends Wars." In *Not Even Past: How the United States Ends Wars*, edited by David Fitzgerald, David Ryan, and John M. Thompson, 252–66. New York: Berghahn Books, 2020.

"The Vietnam War as a World Event." Co-authored with Sophie Quinn-Judge. In *The Cambridge History of Communism: Volume 3, Endgames? Late Communism in Global Perspective, 1968 to the Present*, edited by Juliane Fürst, Silvio Pons, and Mark Selden, 50–71. New York: Cambridge University Press, 2017.

"Lost in the Desert. Lawrence and the Theory and Practice of Counterinsurgency." In *America and Iraq: Policy-Making, Intervention and Regional Politics*, edited by David Ryan and Patrick Kiely, 76–91. London & New York: Routledge, 2009.

"Introduction: Why Vietnam Still Matters." In *The War That Never Ends*, edited by David L. Anderson and John Ernst, 1–11. Lexington: University Press of Kentucky, 2007.

"The Vietnam Laugh Track." In *Vietnam in Iraq: Tactics, Lessons, Legacies and Ghosts*, edited by John Dumbrell and David Ryan, 31–47. London & New York: Routledge, 2007.

"Two, Three, Many Vietnams." *Cold War History* 6, no. 4 (November 2006): 413–24.

"Still Stuck in the Big Muddy." In *Cold War Triumphalism: The Misuse of History after the Fall of Communism*, edited by Ellen Schrecker, 262–73. New York: New Press, 2004.

"Resisting State Terror: The Anti-Vietnam War Movement." In *War and State Terrorism: The United States, Japan, and the Asia-Pacific in the Long Twentieth Century*, edited by Mark Selden and Alvin Y. So, 235–49. Lanham, Md. & Oxford, England: Rowman and Littlefield, 2004.

"One Empire under God." *European Contributions to American Studies* 55 (2004): 8–18.

"In the Combat Zone." *Radical History Review* 85 (Winter 2003): 253–64.

"Ground Zero: Enduring War." In *September 11 in History: A Watershed Moment?*, edited by Mary L. Dudziak, 10–34. Durham, N.C.: Duke University Press, 2003.

"Remembering to Forget." In *Truth Claims: Representation and Human Rights*, edited by Mark Bradley and Patrice Petro, 11–21. New Brunswick, N.J., Rutgers University Press, 2002.

"An Incident at No Gun Ri." In *Crimes of War: Guilt and Denial in the Twentieth Century*, edited by Omer Bartov and Mary Nolan, 242–58. New York: New Press, 2002.

"Korea: The Post-War War." *History Workshop Journal* 51, no. 1 (Spring 2001): 112–26.

"The Forever War." *Itinerario* 22, no. 3 (November 1998): 79–89.

"The Vietnam War in American Memory." In *The Vietnam War: Vietnamese and American Perspectives*, edited by Jayne S. Werner and Luu Doan Huynh, 248–57. Armonk, N.Y.: London: M.E. Sharpe, 1993.

"Ne Plus Ultra Imperialism." *Radical History Review* 1993, no. 57 (Fall 1993): 33–37.

"Chicken Little in China: Women after the Cultural Revolution." In *Promissory Notes: Women in the Transition to Socialism*, edited by Sonia Kruks, Rayna Rapp, and Marilyn B. Young, 233–47. New York: Monthly Review Press, 1989.

"Virtuous Wives and Good Mothers—Women in Chinese Society." In *Tradition and Creativity: Essays on East Asian Civilization*, edited by Ching-I Tu, 20–40. New Brunswick, N.J.: East Asian Studies, University Publications, Rutgers, the State University of New Jersey, 1987.

"Revisionists Revised: The Case of Vietnam." *Newsletter of the Society for Historians of American Foreign Relations* 10, no. 2 (Summer 1979): 1–10.

"American Expansion, 1870–1900: The Far East." In *Toward a New Past: Dissenting Essays in American History*, edited by Barton J. Bernstein, 176–201. New York: Pantheon Books, 1968.

ARCHIVES

Marilyn Young Papers, The Tamiment Library & Robert F. Wagner Labor Archives, Elmer Holmes Bobst Library, New York University.

ACKNOWLEDGMENTS

Working together on this book has reminded us just how many lives Marilyn Young touched in very deep ways over the course of her life, and of the enduring goodwill toward her that continues even after she passed. Like us, so many colleagues saw the urgency of bringing together Marilyn's writing for a new generation of readers, and we are grateful to them for helping to bring this book into the world. Marilyn's colleagues at New York University have been generous with their time, their knowledge of her life and work, and in helping us locate materials, among them Barbara Weinstein, Linda Gordon, Allen Hunter, Molly Nolan, Rebecca Karl, Monica Kim, Edward Berenson, and Karin Burrell. We thank Michael Koncewicz, Danielle Nista, and other archivists and staff at the Tamiment Library at NYU for enabling our research in Marilyn's papers. We are also grateful to Marilyn's longtime collaborator and friend Andrew Bacevich for contributing the afterword. Ed Martini and Scott Laderman have been enthusiastic from the beginning about including this book in their series *Cultural and Politics in the Cold War and Beyond*. It is an ideal home. We are grateful to the two anonymous readers for their feedback on our approach to the volume and for Matt Becker's careful editorial guidance. Our thanks to Syrus Jin, a doctoral student in history at the University of Chicago, for his excellent work with the manuscript and its production. We also greatly benefitted from Emory University School of Law staff member Marianne D'Souza's careful work in preparing the manuscript, and we thank Emory Law Librarians, particularly Amy Flick, and law students Joe Pinto and Catherine Smith for their assistance. We thank photographer Sara Krulwich for allowing us to use her beautiful photograph. Marilyn's children Michael and Lauren Young enthusiastically blessed this enterprise at the outset, including the plan to send the royalties from the book to the Marilyn B. Young Memorial Fund at New York University, and her sister Leah Glasser was immensely helpful throughout. We know how close Marilyn was to her grandchildren Oliver, Jacob, and Claudia, and we hope that as they grow up this volume will introduce them to another dimension of their grandmother just as we hope it will inspire a new generation of scholars as they take their own work forward. For the two of us, this project has been a welcome opportunity to work together to honor a person who has played a central role in both of our lives. It has been a labor of love.

INDEX

9/11 attacks, 171, 176–77, 197, 207

Abu Ghraib, 184, 198
Acheson, Dean, 15, 19, 98, 187
Afghanistan, 171
Afghanistan War, 116, 169, 198–200;
    press coverage of, 169, 199
African Americans, 23, 69, 76, 80, 133;
    soldiers, 47, 76–77
airpower, 139–42, 144–47, 154–56,
    163n46, 197. *See also* bombing; U.S.
    Air Force; *names of individual wars*
Albright, Madeleine, 19, 155
al Qaeda, 199
American exceptionalism, 15, 16, 27
American Indians, 23, 36n24; U.S. wars
    against, 24, 36n24, 128, 134
Americans for Democratic Action
    (ADA), 67–68
anticommunism, 18, 32, 67–70, 77–81,
    99, 100, 102, 174
antiwar movements, 66, 70–73, 77–78,
    81, 133, 172; Iraq War, 172, 181–82;
    Korean War, 39, 42–45, 51, 60n15, 66,
    70–71, 76–77; Spanish-Philippine-
    American War, 137n28; Vietnam
    War, 4–5, 29, 66, 71, 73, 77–78, 80, 81,
    124, 133, 166, 182, 188
Arbenz, Jacobo, 20
Atlee, Clement, 144
atomic bombing of Hiroshima and

Nagasaki, 28, 123, 139, 145, 157,
    164n57

Balkans: U.S. bombing campaign,
    155–56
Bao Dai, 86, 103n6
Beat Generation, 79
Berlin, 174; Soviet blockade of, 69
body count, 108–13, 116–17, 118n12, 167,
    182. *See also names of individual
    wars*
bombing, 58, 97, 101, 139–47, 153–55;
    atomic bombing of Hiroshima
    and Nagasaki, 28, 123, 139, 145, 157,
    164n57; as communication, 141–43,
    146, 148–50, 152, 155–56, 202n25;
    drone, 159, 201n11; napalm, 53, 97,
    133, 142–43, 155; strategic bombard-
    ment doctrine, 141, 145, 149. *See also
    names of individual nations; names
    of individual wars*
Burnham, Forbes, 17, 36n16
Bush, George H. W., 153, 171, 181; dirty
    wars, 167, 197
Bush, George W., 171, 176, 181, 188, 199,
    210; mission accomplished press
    conference, 141, 157, 173

Cambodia, 182; U.S. bombing
    campaign, 142, 150, 157
Caribbean, 22